AF291686

RUSSIAN CRIMINAL TATTOO
POLICE FILES

VOLUME I

TEXT AND PHOTOGRAPHS Arkady Bronnikov collection

EDIT AND DESIGN Murray & Sorrell FUEL
TRANSLATOR Lisa Wasserman
CO-ORDINATOR Julia Goumen

Russian Criminal Tattoo POLICE FILES

Volume I

FUEL

Contents

Arkady Bronnikov
Perm, 1993

No one has ever counted the number of tattooed prisoners in the Commonwealth of Independent States, as the loose association of eleven of the former Soviet Republics is known. The Corrective Labour Administration remains silent on this issue: to admit that between seventy and ninety-eight per cent of the prison population flout the prohibitions against tattoos would be an acknowledgement of how badly the system is functioning.

However, since the introduction of *glasnost*, our less-censored press has published some stunning figures, revealing that from the mid-1960s to the late 1980s, thirty-five million people were incarcerated – few other nations have had such a large prison population. According to the most conservative estimates, twenty-eight to thirty million of the Russian inmates were tattooed.

Who are these people? What motivates them to bear the acute pain of getting their bodies covered in tattoos? A criminologist by training, I first started studying tattoos in the mid-1960s as a means of identifying the corpses of criminals. Immediately, I began to suspect that the tattoos directly matched the crimes in some way.

During my time at the Ministry of Internal Affairs, I interviewed and photographed tattooed prisoners, visiting correctional facilities and labour camps across the USSR. In the regions of Perm, Yekaterinburg, Chelyabinsk, Kirov and Sakhalin, and in the autonomous republics of Udmurt, Mari El, Tatarstan, and Komi, they posed willingly for the camera and spoke with pride about their tattoos.

Tattooing methods in prisons are primitive and painful. The convict often makes the tattoo himself, and the process can take several years to complete. A single small figure, for example, can be created in four to six hours of uninterrupted work. The instrument of choice is an adapted electric shaver to which prisoners add needles and an ampule with liquid dye. Scorched rubber mixed with urine is used for pigment. Dubious sanitation creates serious health complications, including gangrene and tetanus, but the most common problem is lymphadenitis,

an inflammation of the lymph nodes accompanied by fever and chills.

In most cases, the inmates I interviewed claimed they started wearing tattoos only after they had committed a crime. As convictions increase and the terms of incarceration become more severe, the tattoos multiply. In minimum-security prisons, for example, sixty-five to seventy per cent of the convicts wear tattoos; that figure increases to eighty per cent in medium-security prisons, and to between ninety-five and ninety-eight per cent in maximum-security facilities. In the female corrective facility near the Perm region – about 700 miles northeast of Moscow – I found only 201 out of 962 were tattooed, but as many as forty per cent were tattooed in the high-security prison. As a rule, criminal leaders do not wear large numbers of tattoos, only a pair of seven- or eight-pointed stars on the collarbones. In any prison tattoos are reserved for the criminal element, so they are not found among prisoners serving sentences for political crimes.

According to an unwritten law among criminals, a convict without tattoos is looked down on. Such individuals appear as white sheep in a black herd. The immediate reaction of newcomers to a camp when they first see the tattooed prisoners is respect and a certain fear, as well as an understanding of the tattooed prisoners' seniority. The tattoos that a convict wears endow him with both material and psychological advantages inside prison.

At the top of the pyramid are the *pakhaniie*, or 'ringleaders'. Below them are the ones who carry out the leaders' orders, variously known as authorities, enforcers, overseers or soldiers. Next come the 'men', the hard labourers who are capable of standing up for themselves. Finally, in the lowest category, are the outcasts, or untouchables, the ones who have been broken in prison, beaten, and whipped.

A prisoner's place in the hierarchy of the criminal world depends on his experience as a criminal, his professionalism, and his knowledge of the customs, traditions and unwritten laws of the criminal world. He must be adept at communicating in code, at speaking *fenya* (criminal argot), at using cryptography, tapping gestures, signs and other secret methods of communication. Tattoos are another category of secret language, understandable only to the initiated.

The *pakhaniie* and the authorities usually come from the most common and widespread type of crime network, the *vory v zakone* (thieves-in-law). This term describes professional criminals of a superior rank in the hierarchy of criminal law, both inside the prison and in the criminal culture on the outside as well. Matching eight-pointed stars tattooed on an inmate's chest, just below the collarbone, would indicate to other prisoners that he is a professional criminal. When a convict has the same symbol tattooed on his kneecaps, it means that he has an anarchical world view: 'I do not bow to other powers. No one can make me fall to my knees.'

A cross tattooed on the chest is a symbol used by thieves. Often the person wearing such a tattoo goes by the nickname 'Cross'. A cross symbolises subordination, bondage or slavery. Sometimes it is accompanied by text such as: 'A heavy cross is my lot; prison ruined my life.' The eight-pointed star is found tattooed most commonly on authorities, while the cross usually indicates a rank-and-file criminal, a commonplace thief.

Ring tattoos are the most common type of tattoos found on criminals. Being always visible, they are a kind of coat of arms, continuing to display the criminal's status when tattoos on other parts of the body are covered by clothing. Each ring tattoo stands for a conviction (in slang, a trip through the 'zone' – the penal colonies). One repeat offender had two tattoos on each finger (but none on the thumbs), indicating a total of sixteen convictions. The pictures and symbols are supposed to correspond to the criminal's deeds. Punishment for a person wearing incorrect symbols is extremely severe, sometimes even death.

A prisoner can learn a lot about his cellmates by looking at their fingers. A black-and-white diamond means the convict pleaded not guilty and is a bitter prisoner and a dangerous neighbour. A domino with six dots indicates a *shestyorka*, a broken man who need not be feared. A gambler wears the symbol of a suit of cards (a spade, diamond, club or heart). A skull or a pirate between the fingers means a murderer, sadist or robber. The dollar sign indicates a 'bear hunter', a thief who can open safes.

A person wearing a tattoo of a tree branch is a so-called Polish thief, one who has left his gang and now works in isolation. A sailboat tattooed on the chest can mean simply that the criminal loves the sea, although such a tattoo can also indicate that the convict is a travelling thief, with no home base, or that the person yearns for freedom and plans to escape from prison. 'I am a free man! Iron bars cannot keep me here against my will.' Indeed, tattoos may convey intentionally mixed messages.

Traditionally, in accordance with their code, professional thieves are not supposed to engage in any useful activity that could benefit society. Instead they must live off their 'professional' earnings, that is, only on income gained through criminal activity. Furthermore, they are not supposed to commit any other type of crime except robbery.

A four-time offender gave the following explanation of the tattoos on his body:

> My first three convictions were for robbery. When I was sitting out those sentences I had tattoos made that symbolised my trade – an eight-pointed star on the shoulders. But my last sentence was for beating up a woman. Once this crime became known in the 'zone' [penal colony], I was told that I no longer had the right to be a thief. In other words, my life as a thief was over. Now my trademark tattoo indicates that 'I am alone on an iceberg' [a fallen tree branch].

Often, words tattooed on prisoners' bodies mean one thing, but the words' individual letters form acronyms with different meanings. For example, the letters in the Russian word for cat, *kot*, stand for 'Native prison resident'. However, a cat's head tattooed across the chest means that the person could easily double-cross, lie or rip someone off. The letters in *Berlin* stand for 'I will be jealous of her, I will love her and hate her.' *Vino*, the Russian word for wine, stands for 'Return and stay for a century.' A picture of a beetle (*zhuk*) indicates a pickpocket, but when the word *zhuk* is spelled out, it means 'Good luck with your robbery'. The Russian word for snow leopard, *bars*, stands for 'Beat up the Party Activists, knife the bitches'.

Facial tattoos fall into a special category. Typical facial tattoos include swastikas, prison bars, the words 'Slave of the zone', 'Junta' or 'Communist Party slave'. Facial tattoos are usually the result of a 'card game of chance', a particularly popular pastime among convicts. When a loser runs out of money and valuables, he agrees to fulfil any demand of the winner, even murder. The winner can make the loser his slave, sodomise him, or force him to get a facial tattoo of his choice. The loser will often willingly agree to the facial tattoo, since he knows it could be removed in a surgical procedure performed in the prison hospital. Once in the hospital, he has a good chance of being transferred to another penal colony, where he can escape his former debts and bondage.

The trademark tattoo of murderers is a skull with a dagger through it (sometimes the dagger is below the skull) or a skull with bolts of lightning zigzagging through it. Bird wings on both sides of the skull indicate that a life has left this world. Murderers also wear tattoos of pirates, a tombstone cross, a spade from a deck of cards (the winning suit in a game of chance for money), a severed head or a human skeleton. Heads of predatory animals such as wolves, rats, tigers, lions and snow leopards are also favoured.

Drug addicts, as well as drug pushers and manufacturers, wear a variety of symbols: needles for shooting up; gin pouring out of a bottle; a beetle or a fly caught in a spider's web (a symbol that means 'I'm mixed up in drugs like a beetle in manure and I'll never get out'). Addicts are marked by the flower-head of a poppy, a deformed skull or the devil on a rocket flying in circles towards the moon with the text: 'I'm headed to the moon for marijuana.' A twisted snake, usually tattooed on the forearm and accompanied by the words 'No blood flows through my veins, only morphine', gives a clear message of inescapable addiction. Addicts often cover their arms and legs with dark tattoos in an attempt to hide needle marks. Such tattoos generally do not have any special meaning.

The lowest of the low in the prison pyramid are men who have been raped. They account for up to a quarter of the population of the zone. According to an unwritten law in camp life, anyone convicted of a sexual

crime deserves to be raped. Convicted law-enforcement agents are usually incarcerated in a special penal colony for police, but if they end up in an ordinary prison, they will also be fair game for rape.

The pederast – variously called 'Washed-out', 'Dirty', 'Scab', 'Insulted', 'Violated' and 'Armenian king' – is a complete outcast. His bed is underneath the bunk or next to the latrine. He is forced to do all the dirty work, from cleaning the toilet to washing the bed sheets. Made to eat from a specially marked bowl and given feminine nicknames, he is tormented, frequently raped, and forcibly tattooed. Among the symbols that are used are the black eyes of a fly, commonly tattooed around the nostrils, on the cheeks, upper lip, ear lobe, near the eyes or on the neck, and a round sun with rays radiating from it, a black spot in the centre, and then white and black circles (the symbol is ironic – if tattooed on a thief it would mean 'I am in a circle of friends').

The corrective labour system in Russia is ineffective, giving priority only to work production plans. Instead of rehabilitation, convicts in prisons and penal colonies receive advanced training in their criminal fields, and this is reflected in tattoo art. Body tattoos are often statements such as 'The Crown Prosecution is not a teacher and prison is not a school' or 'For a convict, prison is a crime college'.

Criminals have many motives for marking themselves in this way. Some do it for reasons of vanity, to show off in front of one another, while others are intimidated into it by more seasoned criminals. Still others want to prove themselves, to show their bravery and strength, to demonstrate that they are unaffected by pain. The importance of these signs cannot be underestimated. These words and symbols state profession, association, the number of convictions, the bearer's place in the 'table of ranks', the hierarchy of the criminal world.

Tattoos are a passport and biography; they reflect the convict's interests, his outlook on life, his world view. There are certain 'distinguished' tattoos that a convict earns the right to wear – visible signs of his authority and prestige. A prisoner has nothing of his own, no decent clothes, only the changeless prison garb. The only thing that belongs to him is his body and because of this it can be violated, bartered or turned into a picture gallery.

i 'Gop-stop' (a slang expression for a street robbery or stick-up), the ring tattoo of a person who has been sentenced under article 145 of the Criminal Code of Russian Soviet Federative Socialist Republic.

ii A ring tattoo which signifies the bearer has had a 'ruined youth'.

iii 'Eternal prisoner', a tattoo applied to a prisoner who has had at least three convictions.

iv A ring tattoo originating from the Baltic States, meaning faithfulness, happiness, love and freedom.

v The ring tattoo of a juvenile delinquent who has authority among inmates with a negative attitude. This type of tattoo is made when the juvenile prisoner 'graduates' (when he is moved into a camp for adults).

vi The ring tattoo of a *patsan* (boy) or *baklan* (lad).

vii In memory of convicted parents. Also known as 'UTRO' (literally 'morning') *Ushel Tropoy Rodimogo Ottsa*, meaning '[I] followed in my father's footsteps'. A symbol of criminal family ties or dynasty.

viii 'Alone, among friends... I was the only underage detainee in my circle of friends.'

ix 'Muzhik', an inmate who does not belong to any criminal group. The person disguises the fear for his life behind a mask of neutrality, indifference and non-interference.

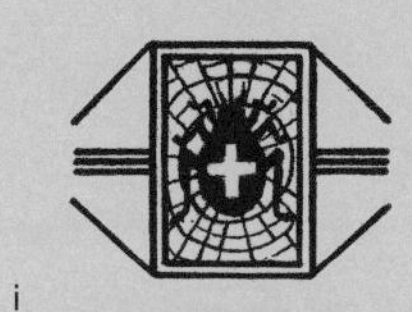

i

ii

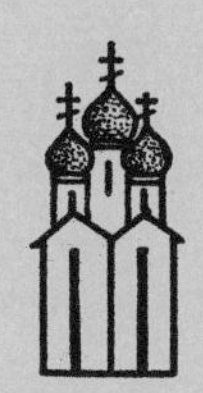

iii

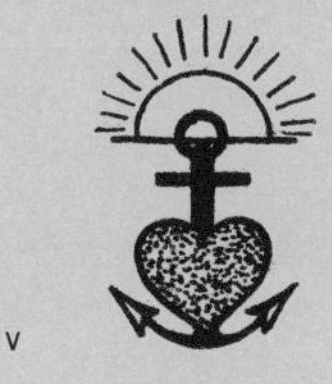

iv

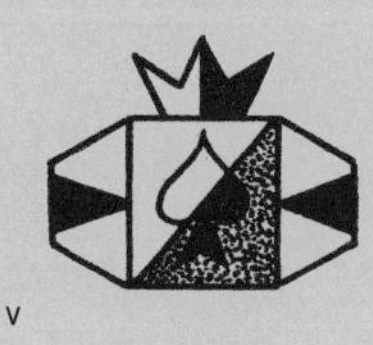

v

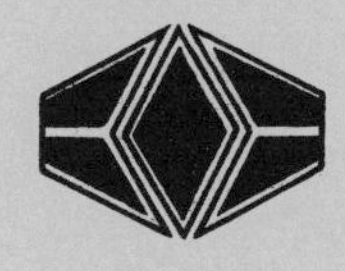

vi

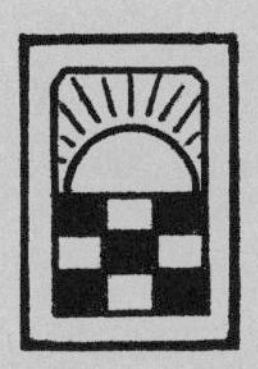

vii

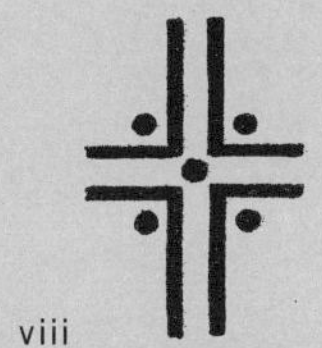

viii

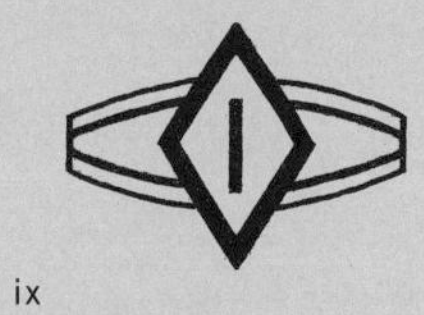

ix

x   The tattoo of a Muslim who served his sentence in the IUT strict regime.

xi   The sign of a thief. Tattooed on the thumb.

xii   A tattoo denoting that the bearer is serving his third prison sentence.

xiii   Denotes drug abuse. Worn by an inmate who is serving a sentence for the sale and possession of drugs.

xiv   The sign of an authoritative thief. It is tattooed on the thumb of the right hand.

xv   A symbol that is believed to bring luck to the bearer.

xvi   I was convicted for robbery.

xvii   Sentenced for rape. A rare tattoo.

xviii The symbol of a gambler or fraudster.

x

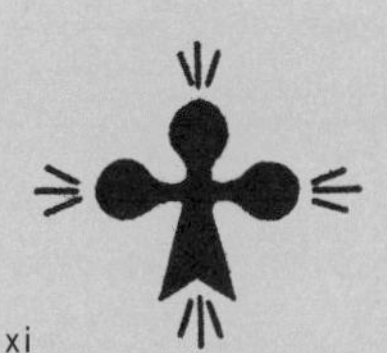

xi

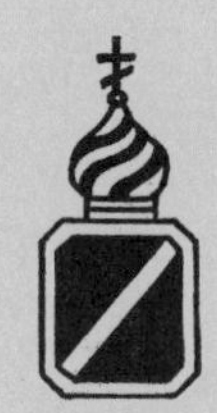

xii

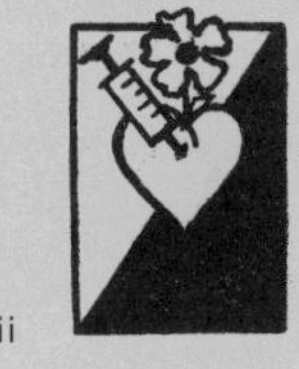

xiii

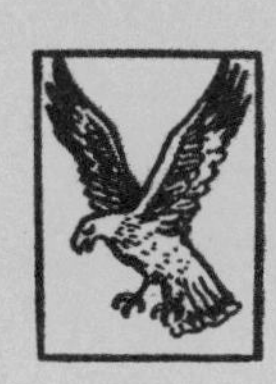

xiv

xv

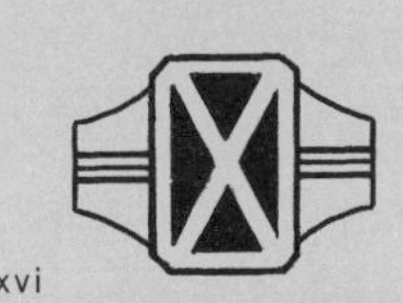

xvi

xvii

xviii

Prisoners generally start tattooing rings from the index finger of the left hand and move on towards the little finger, they then start on the right hand. Once this is filled, a second row may be started on the left hand. All ring tattoos have to accurately reflect the real criminal record of the bearer; any deviation will result in punishment.

A spider in a web is a tattoo of a drug addict, positioned between the thumb and index finger.
Index finger: A *baklan* (a prisoner sentenced for a misdemeanour).
Middle finger: A 'thieves' suit. A crown of any kind over a ring is a sign of an authoritative thief.
Third finger: A *patsan*, young authoritative thief, the most privileged inmate of the VTK [Educational Labour Colony].
Little finger: 'Six' or *shesterka* – sometimes shown as three dots on either side like a dice. This is the lowest card in the Russian thirty-six card deck denoting the low position of the bearer. He runs for a criminal 'authority' (who may have as many as ten or twelve 'sixers'), protecting them from the claims and assertions of other criminals and acting as a 'footman' or servant, see also pages 145 and 221.
'1954' – date of birth.

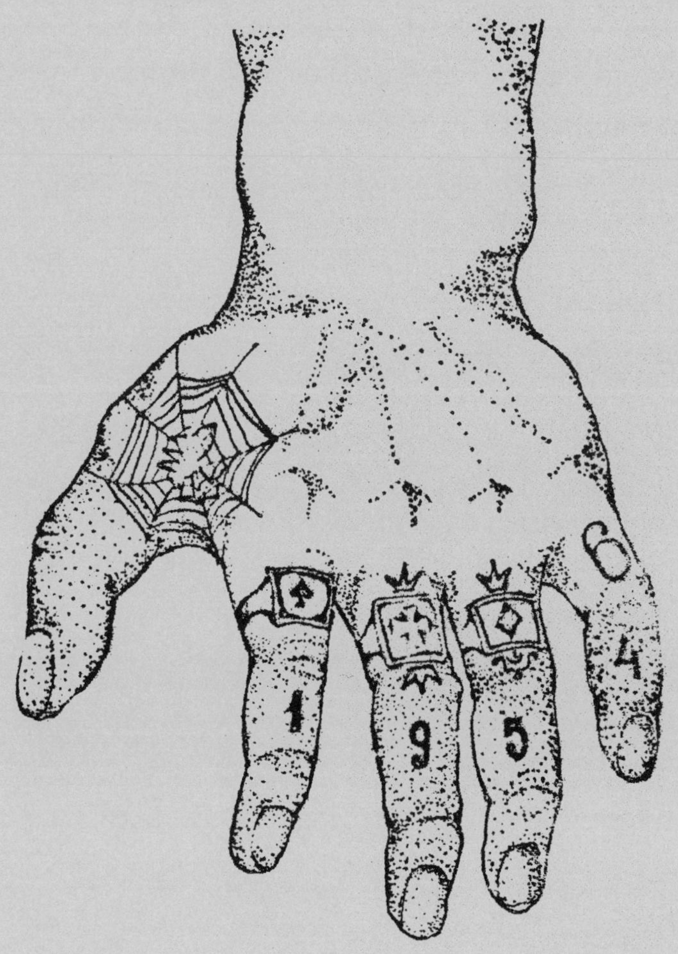

Single dot between thumb and forefinger: 'I escaped.'
A butterfly tattoo is a symbol of an inmate who is inclined to escape.
Index finger: A convicts' symbol – the 'cross of clubs'.
Middle finger: Spade
Third finger: Diamond
Little finger: Heart
When the card suits are tattooed across the hand in this order, the first letters form the phrase *Kogda Vyidu Budu Chelovekom* (I'll be a man when I get out). The slang term *chelovek* (man or person) means an 'honourable' criminal (it can also be tattooed as a bracelet on the wrist).
'BARS' – an acronym for the phrase *Bey aktiv, rezh suk* (Beat up activists, kill the bitches).

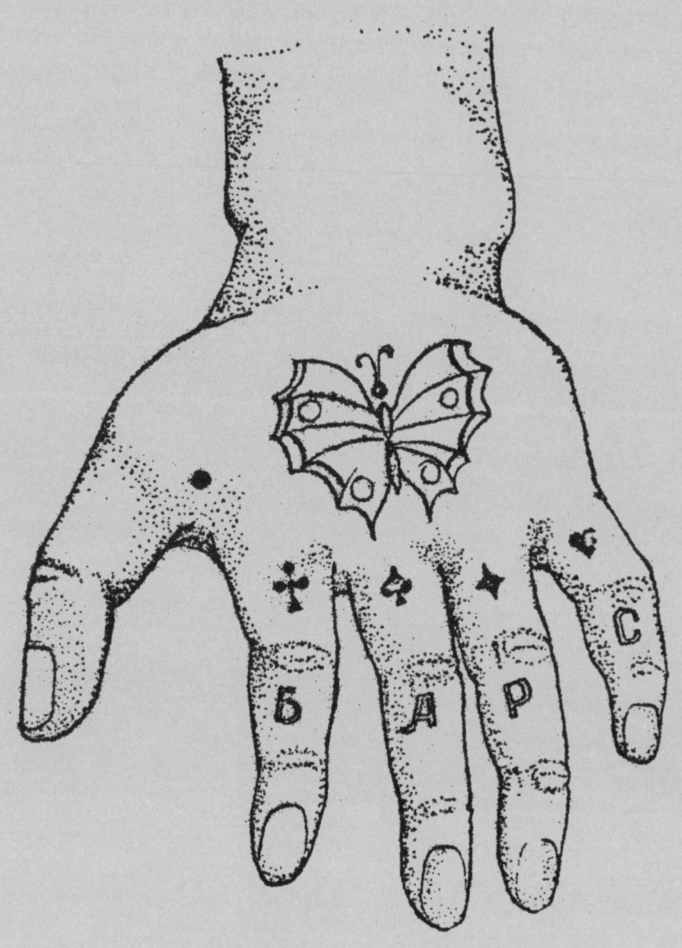

A tattoo can offer vital clues for successful detection and for identification of missing people and unknown bodies, as well as in the search and identification of suspects who have fled the crime scene.

Case Study 1: The court was hearing the case of citizen 'Y', who had been charged under Article 117, Section 4 (rape of an underage girl). He had previously been convicted of similar crimes. In his final statement the defendant declared his innocence, claiming that he had been forced to incriminate himself under the threat of bodily harm by police officers. In his address to the judges he stated that, 'During the investigation the victim said she didn't see the general appearance of the rapist, only his penis with the word "XAM" (*ham*) tattooed on it [the Russian word for *cad*, tattooed on this part of the body it also stands for *ham dlya dam*, 'Ham for the Ladies']. She accused me of poking it in her face, mouth and eyes. But I've got a different word tattooed on my penis, you can see for yourselves!' The judge announced a break and asked the head of the guard to take the defendant to the toilet and read what was tattooed on his genitalia. The tattoo turned out to read 'НАХАЛ' [the Russian word for *snot*] instead of 'XAM'. An expert was called and addressed with two questions: what was the original text tattooed on the member and what method was used to add to it or change it? The expert concluded that the initial tattoo was indeed 'XAM', and that it had later been adapted to read 'НАХАЛ'. The expert's evidence was proved by means of chemical and biological tests.

Case Study 2: In the Kama river near the village of Nizhnyaya Kurya a male body was found between some log piles. The corpse was clothed only in underwear and had a rope around its neck. Decomposition made fingerprint identification impossible. However, the number and type of tattoos on the body suggested that this individual had been previously convicted. Using these tattoos detectives were able to trace and identify the person as V. D. Ogorodin, born in 1929, with numerous convictions for theft in the cities of Izhevsk, Donetsk, Taganrog and Perm.

Case Study 3: A retired woman stated that she had been attacked by a young man in the Sverdlovsky District of Perm. He had snatched her grocery bag and escaped. During her fight for the bag, the victim noticed that the man had the name 'Robert' tattooed on his right hand. Using this information detectives searched through prison photographic records, identified the perpetrator and arrested him.

Case Study 4: A member of the armed forces 'N' was on leave in the city of Leningrad and failed to return to his quarters at the appointed time. Two months after his disappearance, an unidentified body was found in a water reservoir in the district of Petrodvorets. The surface of the skin was badly damaged by putrefaction, which made the corpse barely recognisable. However, following a careful examination of the body a tattoo was discovered on the back of the left hand. The tattoo depicted a symbol of aviation with the date 1929 underneath. This was assumed to be the year of birth of the deceased person. There were a number of persons born in 1929 in the card-file catalogue of missing people, one of which was identified as 'N'. A photograph of him contained in his file showed a clearly visible tattoo on his left hand, identical to the one on the dead body.

Anatomical Regions of the Body

The standard anatomical regions of the body for the purpose of locating and identifying the position of criminal tattoos.

1	Parietal region		33	Dorsal aspect of the foot
2	Forehead		34	Medial region of the leg
3	Eye		35	Anterior aspect of the leg
4	Nose		36	Lateral aspect of the leg
5	Cheek		37	Kneecap
6	Mouth		38	Medial region of the thigh
7	Anterior of the neck		39	Lateral aspect of the thigh
8	Side of the neck		40	Anterior surface of the thigh
9	Supraclavicular fossa		41	Scrotum
10	Deltopectoral region		42	Penis
11	Sternal region		43	Pubic region
12	Anterior surface of the rib cage		44	Inguinal fold
			45	Lateral side of the abdomen
13	Upper third of the arm		46	Navel
14	Middle third of the arm		47	Anterior surface of the abdomen
15	Lower third of the arm		48	Hypochondrium
16	Hypochondrium		49	Nipple
17	Volar aspect of the elbow		50	Axillary cavity
18	Lateral side of the abdomen		51	Dorsal aspect of the arm
19	Upper third of the forearm		52	Medial aspect of the arm
20	Middle third of the forearm		53	Elbow joint area
21	Lower third of the forearm		54	Ulnar region of the forearm
22	Upper third of the thigh		55	Volar aspect of the forearm
23	Hand dorsum		56	Volar aspect of the fingers
24	Middle third of the thigh		57	Palm
25	Lower third of the thigh		58	Anterior aspect of the arm
26	Knee joint area		59	Deltoid region of the shoulder
27	Upper third of the leg		60	Clavicular region
28	Middle third of the leg		61	Infraclavicular fossa
29	Lower third of the leg		62	Ear
30	Foot			
31	Dorsal aspect of the toes		A	Thigh
32	Medial ankle-bone region		B	Leg

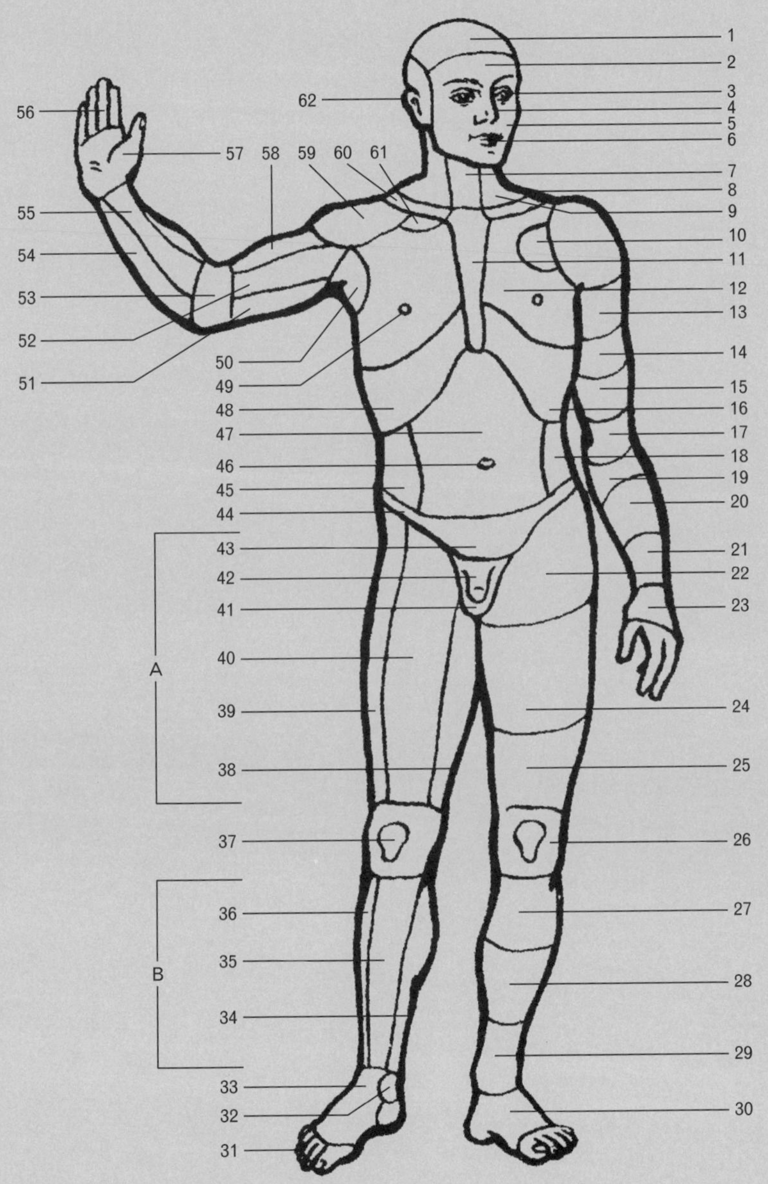

1
2
3
4
5
6
7
8
9
10
11
12
13
14
15
16
17
18
19
20
21
22
23
24
25
26
27
28
29
30
31
32
33
34
35
36
37
38
39
40
41
42
43
44
45
46
47
48
49
50
51
52
53
54
55
56
57
58
59
60
61
62
A
B

1	Parietal region	27	Lateral ankle-bone region
2	Temporal region	28	Sole of the foot
3	Nape of the neck	29	Heel of the foot
4	Suprascapular region	30	Dorsal aspect of the foot
5	Radial region of the forearm	31	External malleolus
6	Dorsal aspect of the fingers	32	Lower third of the leg
7	Dorsal aspect of the hand	33	Middle third of the leg
8	Ulnar region of the forearm	34	Upper third of the leg
9	Dorsal aspect of the forearm	35	Lower third of the thigh
10	Dorsal aspect of the elbow	36	Middle third of the thigh
11	Flexor aspect of the arm	37	Upper third of the thigh
12	Lateral aspect of the arm	38	Lower third of the forearm
13	Posterior aspect of the arm	39	Middle third of the forearm
14	Scapular region	40	Upper third of the forearm
15	Infrascapular region	41	Lower third of the arm
16	Vertebral column region	42	Middle third of the arm
17	Lumbar region	43	Upper third of the arm
18	Sacral region	44	Deltoid region of the shoulder
19	Buttock	45	Interscapular region
20	Perineum	46	Ear
21	Lateral aspect of the thigh	47	Occipital region
22	Posterior aspect of the thigh		
23	Medial region of the thigh	A	Arm
24	Posterior aspect of the knee	B	Forearm
25	Posterior aspect of the leg	C	Thigh
26	Lateral aspect of the leg	D	Leg

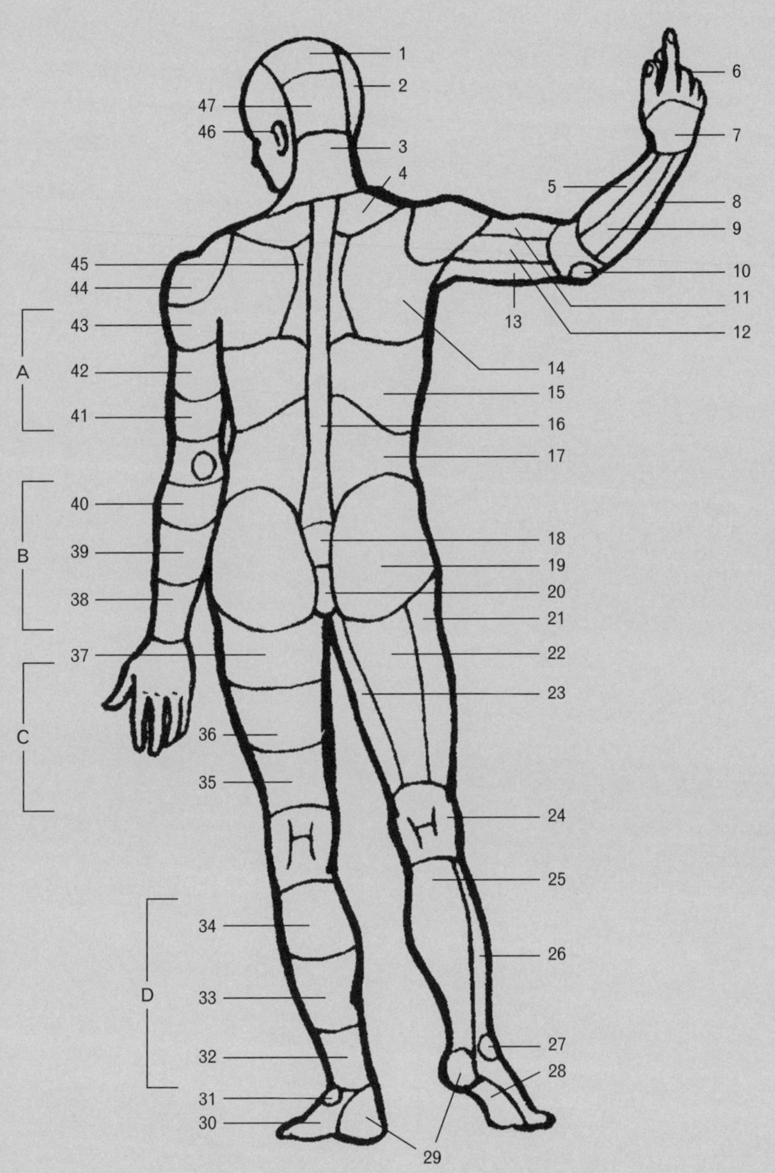

Distinguishing facial features and personal characteristics to assist in the identification of the perpetrators of crimes.

HAIR COLOUR

1. Light blond
2. Dark blond
3. Auburn
4. Chestnut
5. Black
6. Red
7. Grey
Bald (crown / whole head)

EYE COLOUR

1. Blue, grey
2. Yellow
3. Amber
4. Light brown
5. Hazel
6. Dark brown
7. Black

HEIGHT

Very short - VS
Short - S
Shorter than average - /S/
Average - A
Above average - /T/
Tall - T
Very tall - VT

FOREHEAD

Inclination	Height	Width

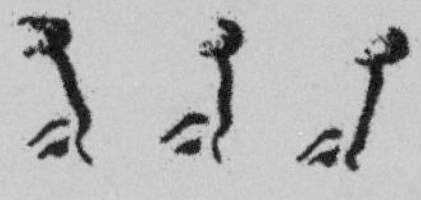
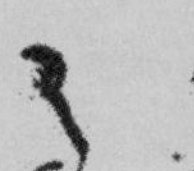
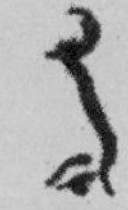
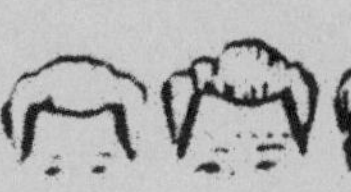
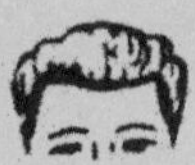

skewed   vertical   inclined   low   medium   high   narrow   medium   wide

NOSE

Nasal dorsum shape   Nasal base inclination   Width

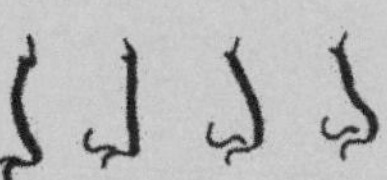
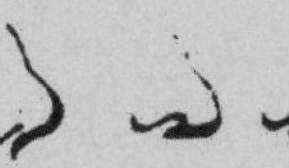
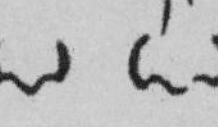
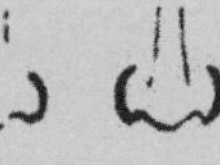

concave   straight   convex   curved   elevated   horizontal   dropped   narrow   medium   wide

LIPS

Protrusion   Height   Width

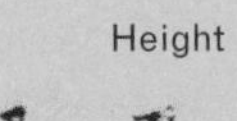

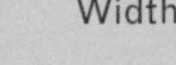
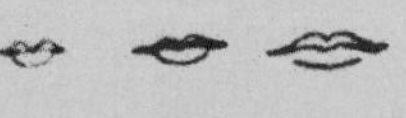

upper   both   lower   low   medium   high   narrow   medium   wide

CHIN

Inclination   Height   Width

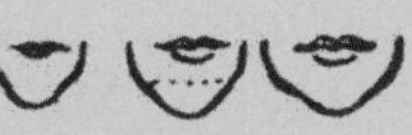

skewed   vertical   protruding   small   medium   big   narrow   medium   wide

EAR LOBE

Shape   Attachment   Protrusion

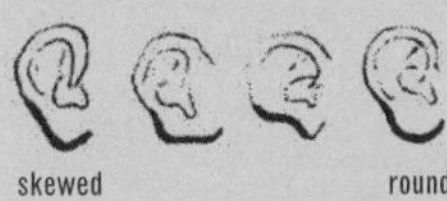
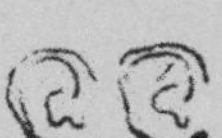
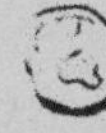
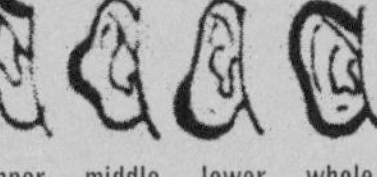

skewed   round   joint   separate   sulcal   upper   middle   lower   whole

rectangular   rectangular-skewed

ANTITRAGUS

Shape   Inclination   Shape

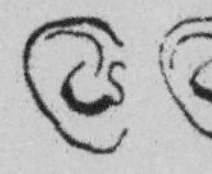
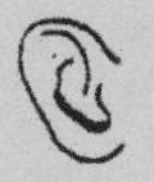

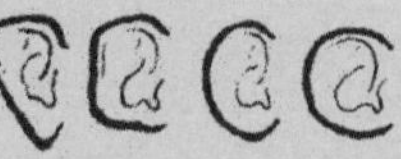

concave   straight   convex   skewed   horizontal   triangular   rectangular   oval   round

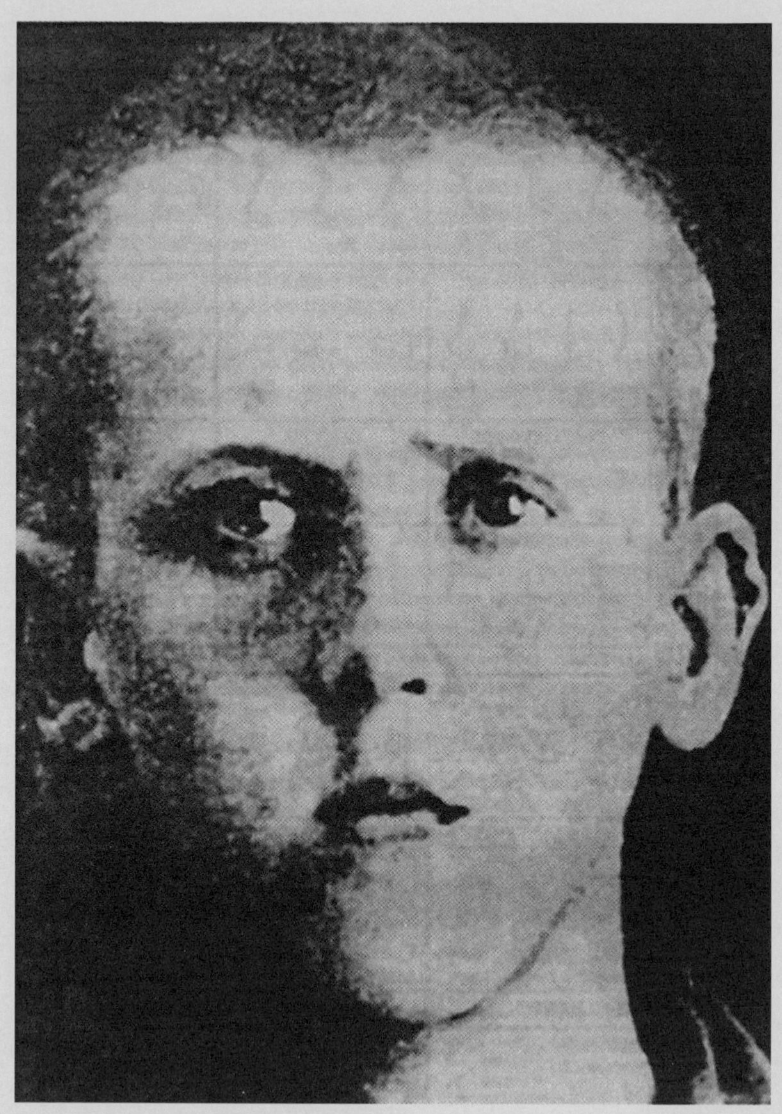

Small mouth

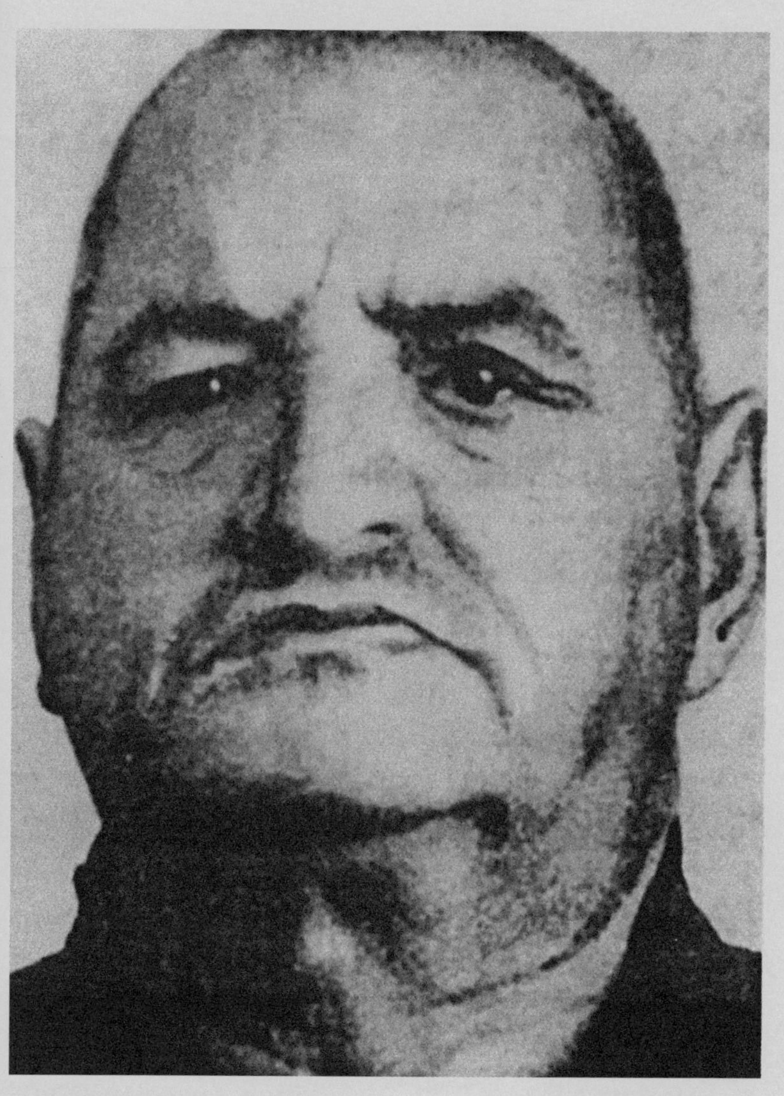

Large mouth

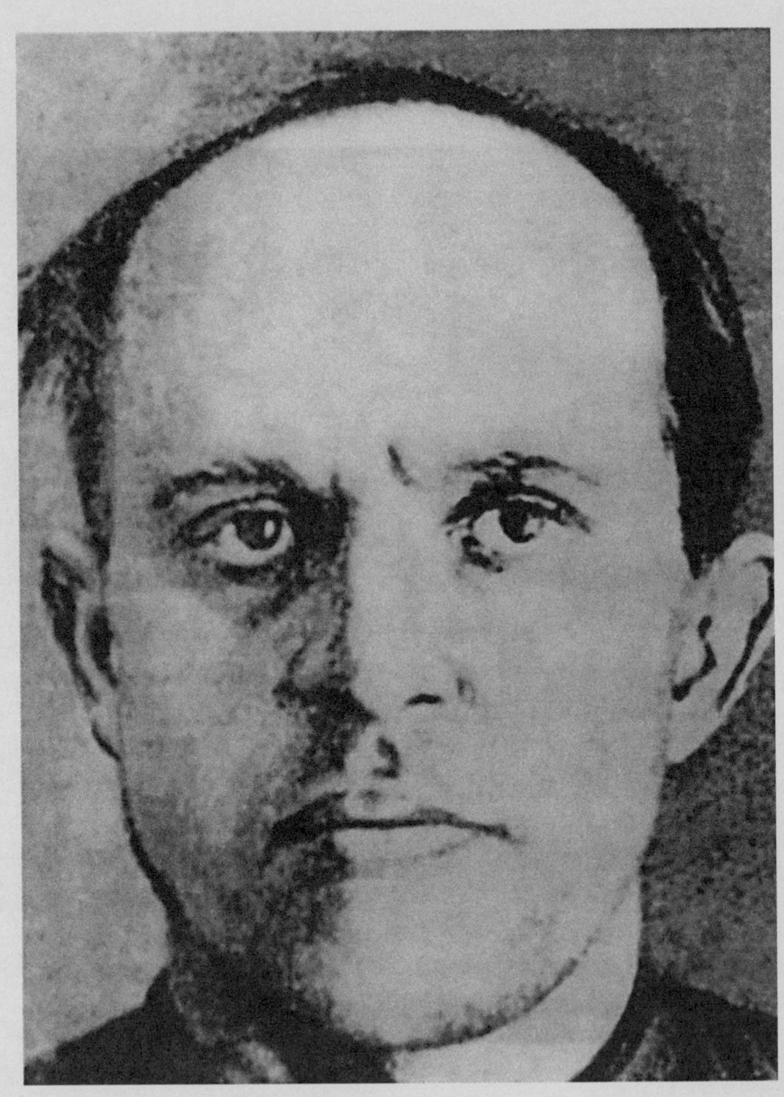

Balding forehead

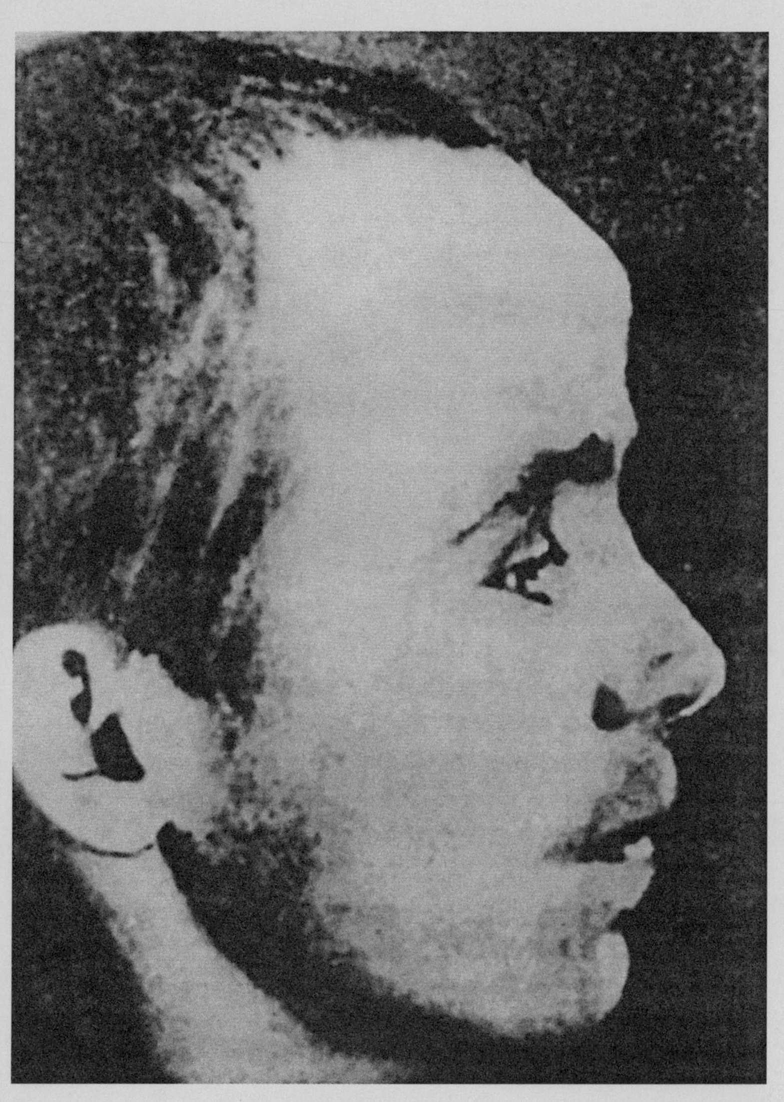

Frontal eminence

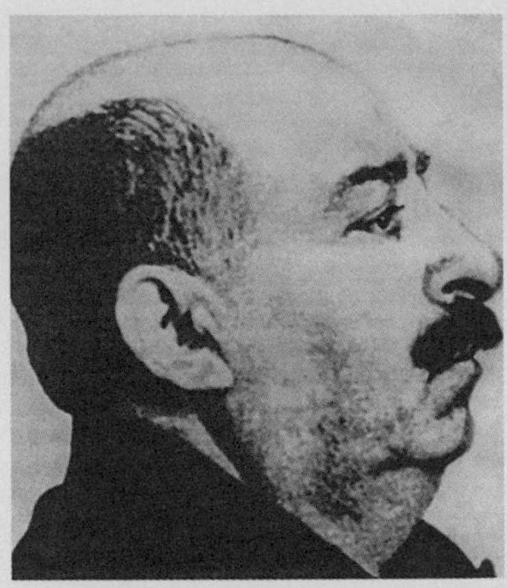

Frontoparietal baldness

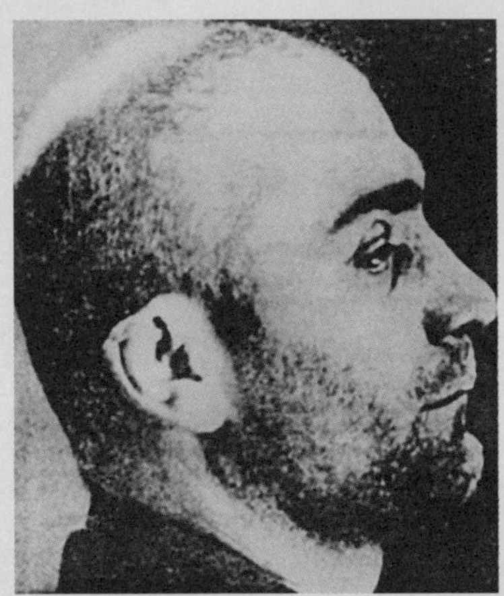

Bald patch on the crown

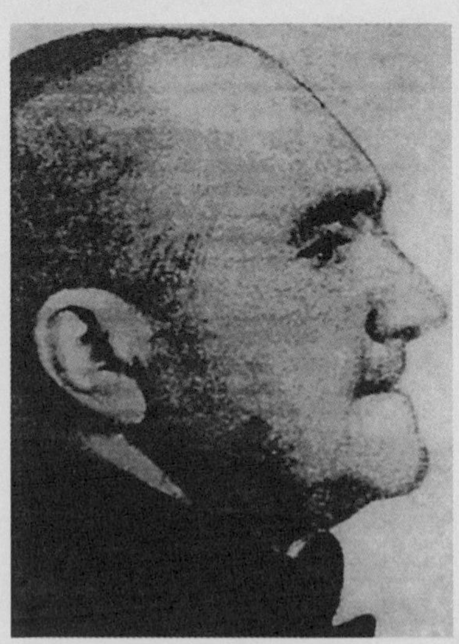

Senile lip retraction

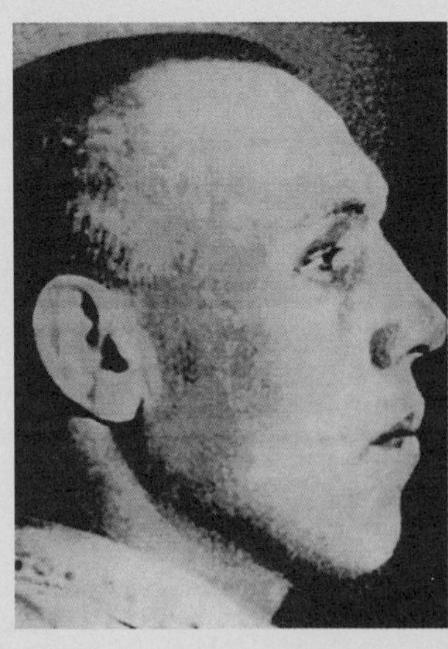

Skewed ear position

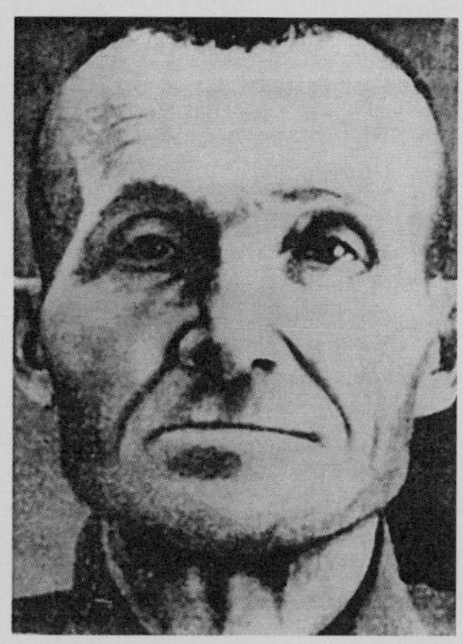

Balding temples

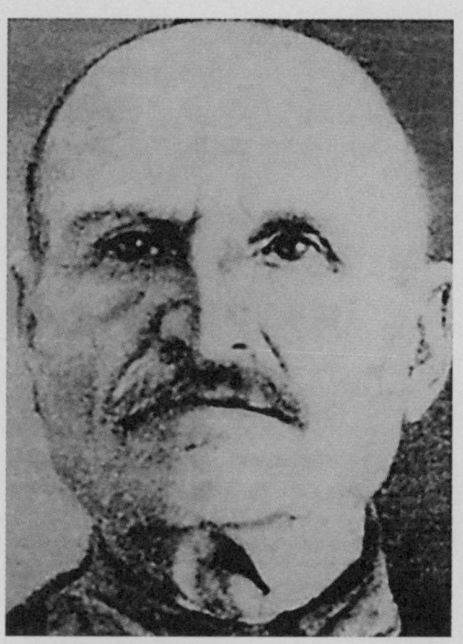

Chin with a transverse groove

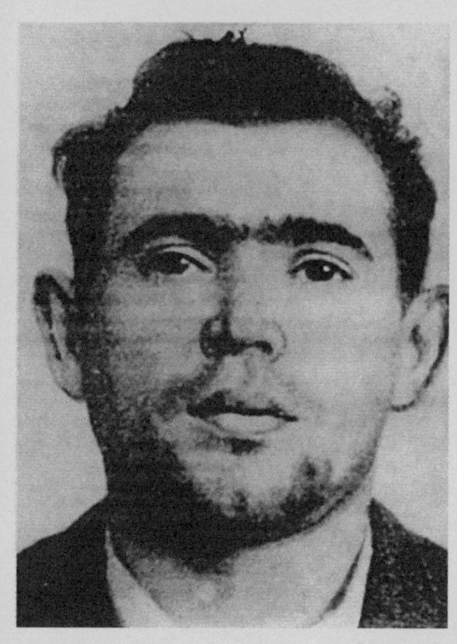

Unibrow

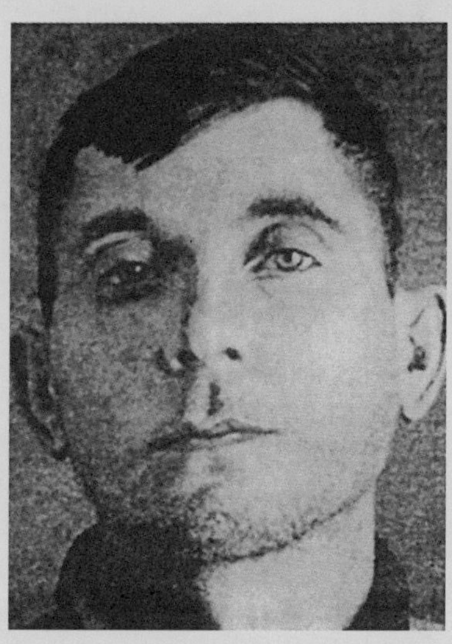

Spaced eyebrows

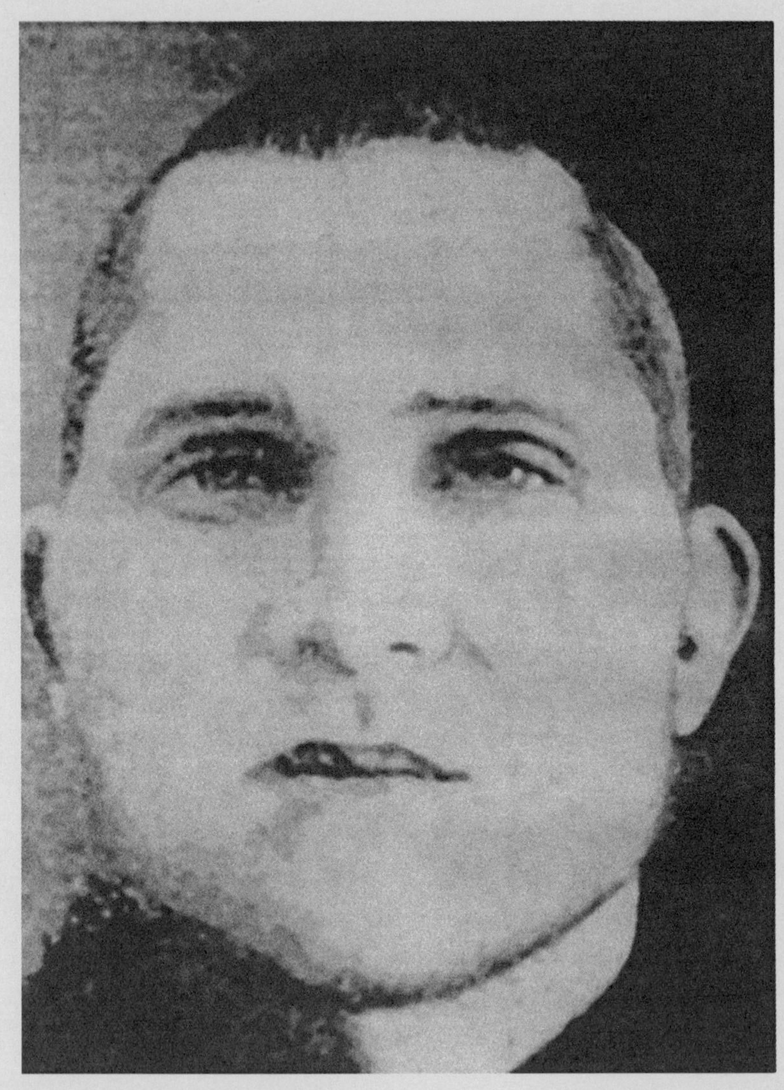

Narrow forehead

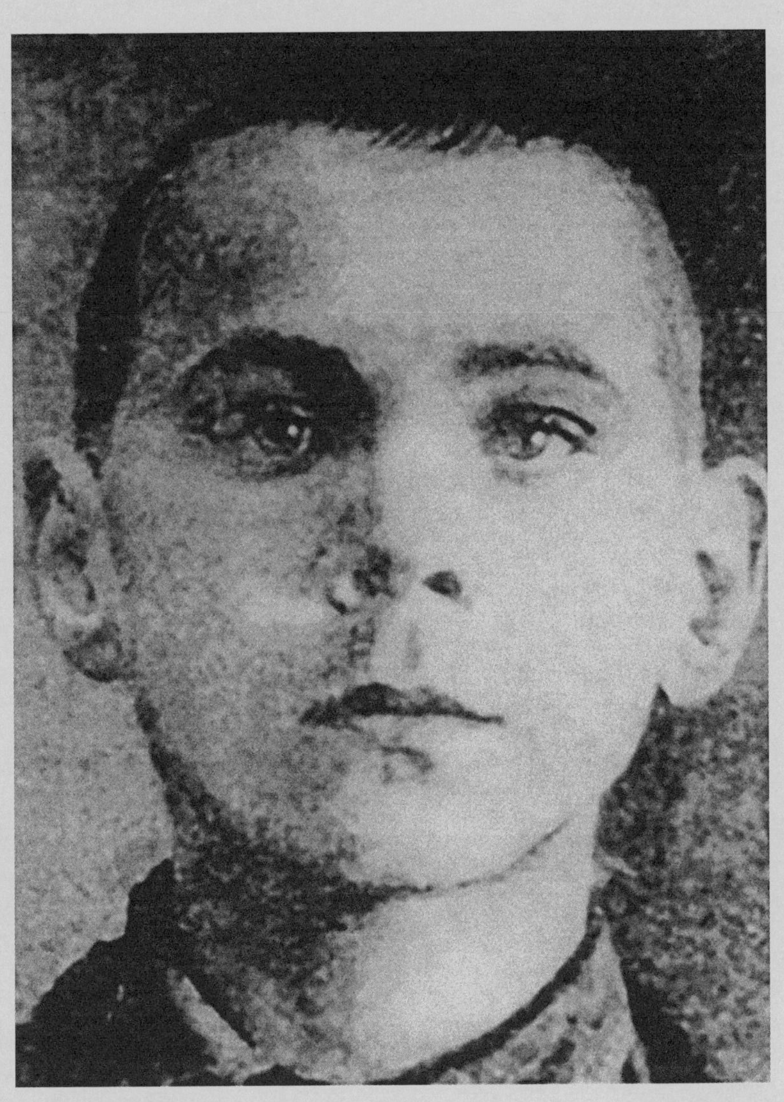

Average width forehead

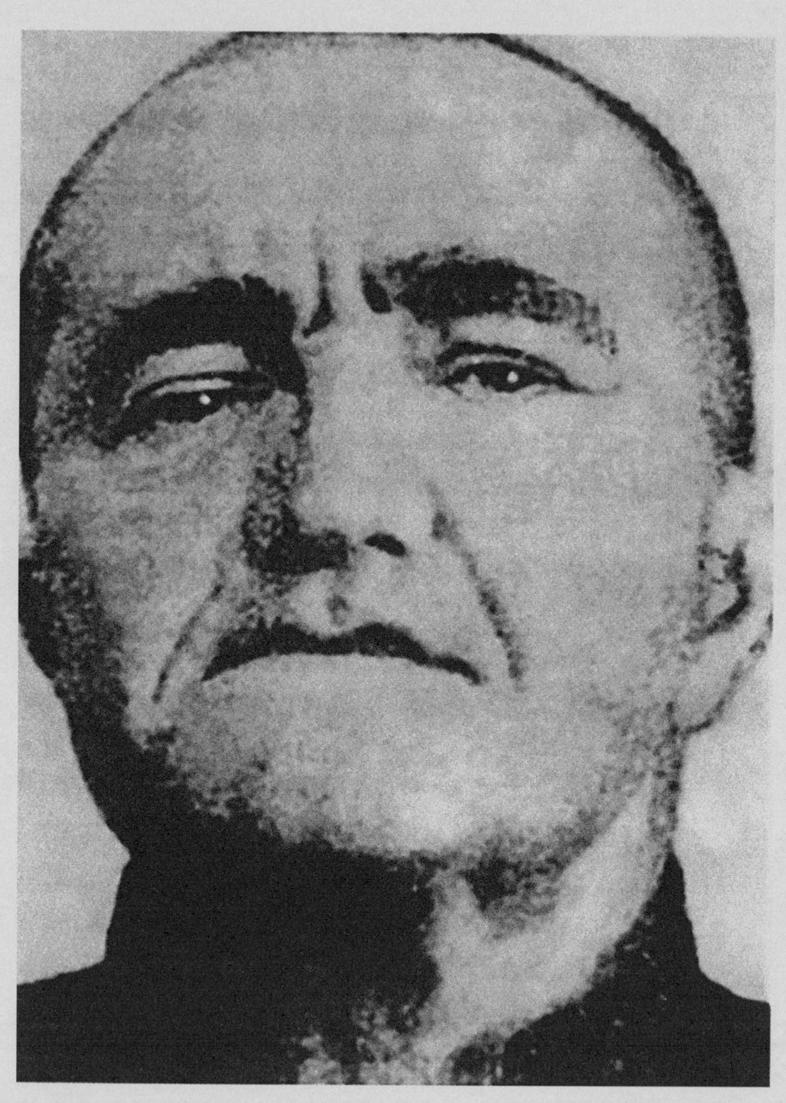

Wide eyebrows

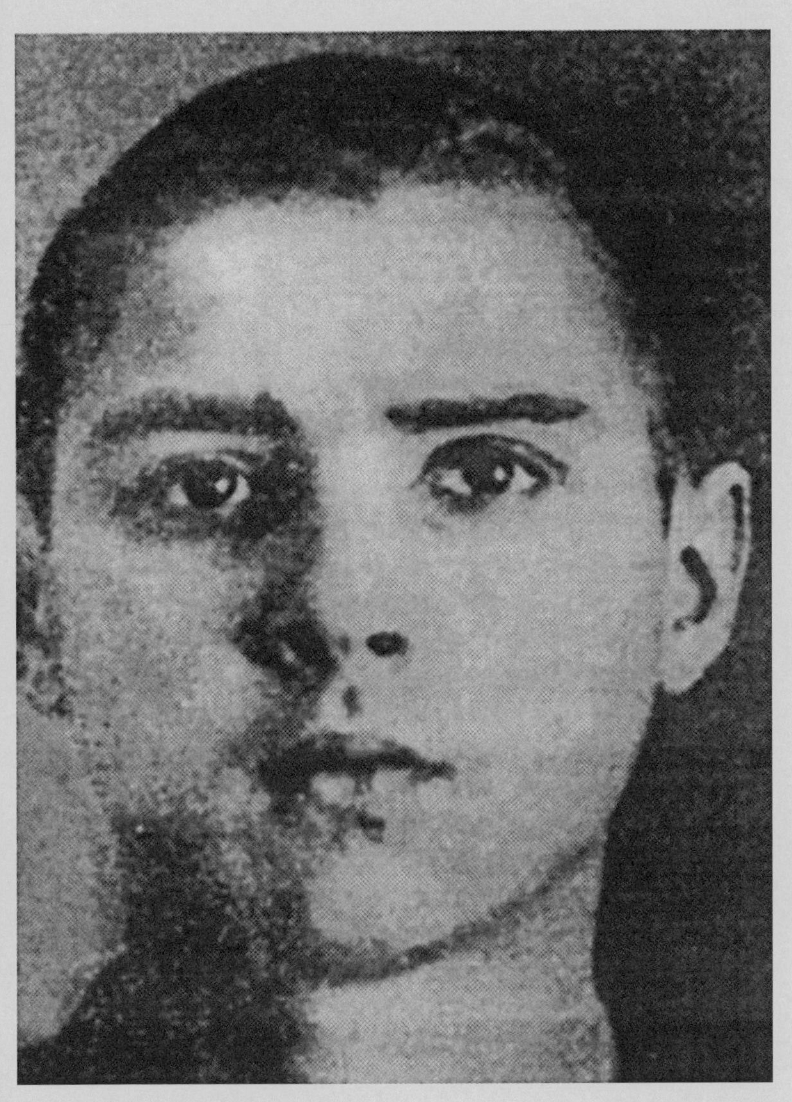

Horizontal eyebrows

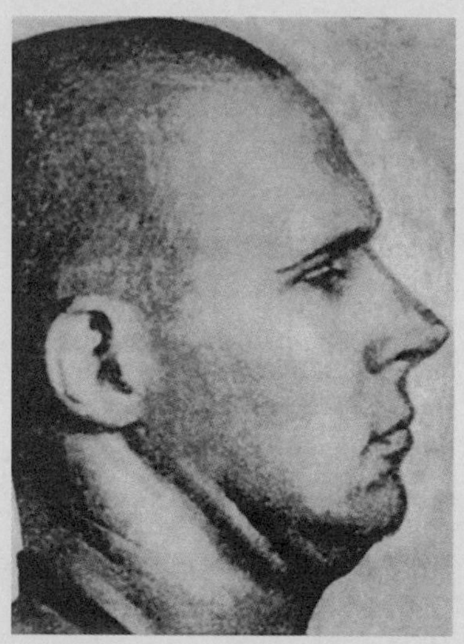

Sharp nose tip

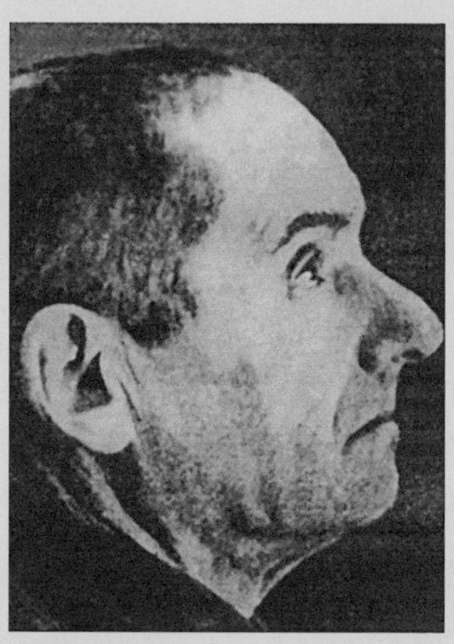

Vertical nasal base

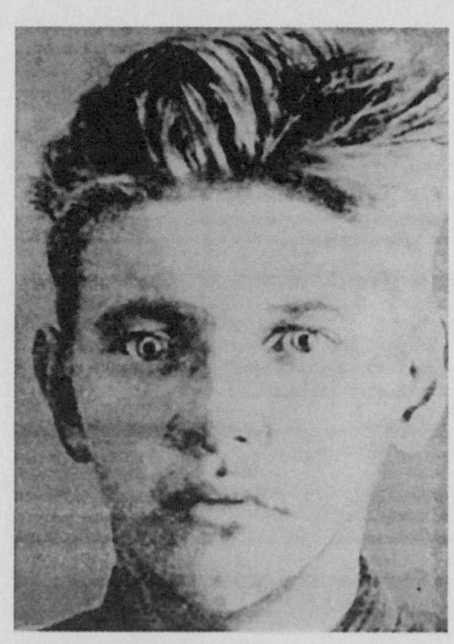

Triangular chin

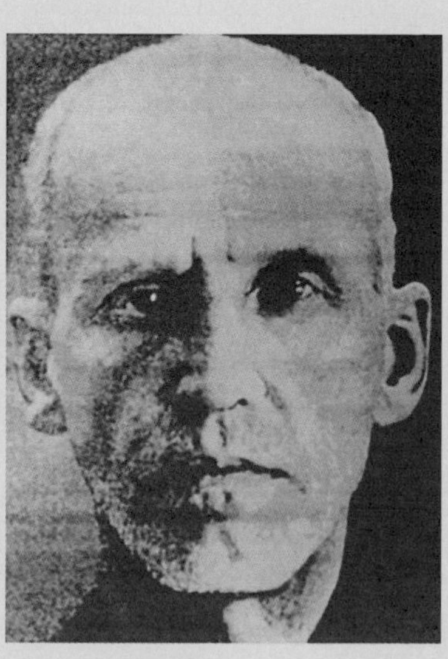

Rectangular chin

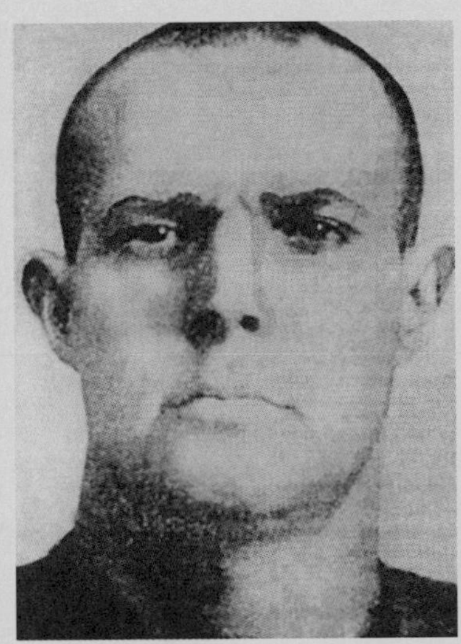

Protrusion of the upper ear

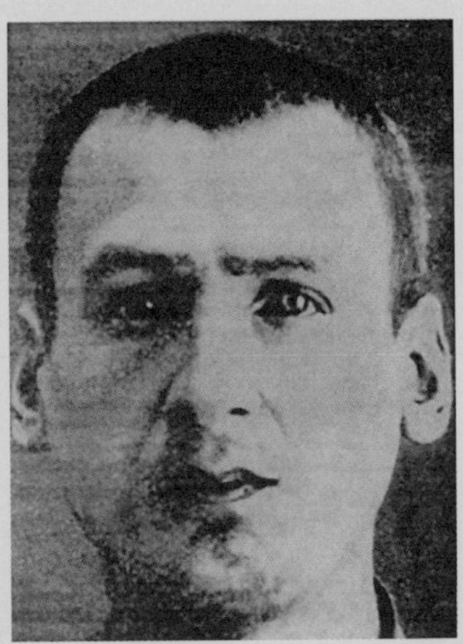

Protrusion of the lower ear

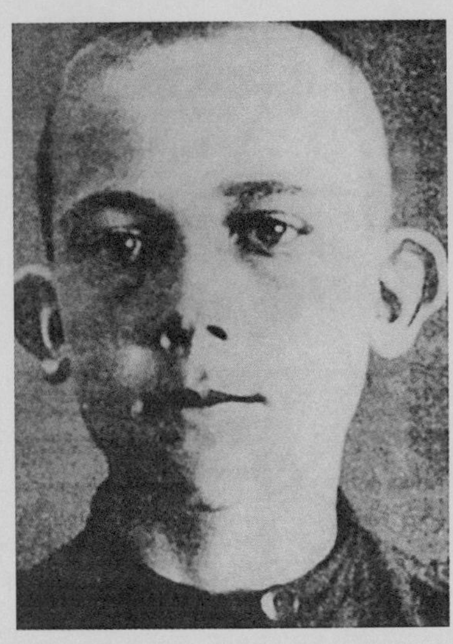

Protrusion of the whole ear

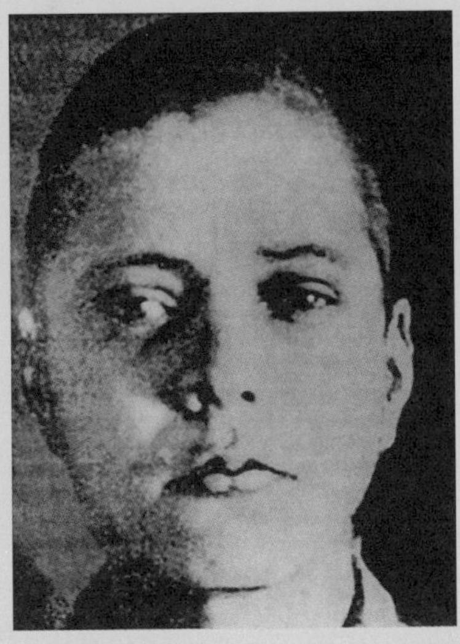

Closely adhered ears

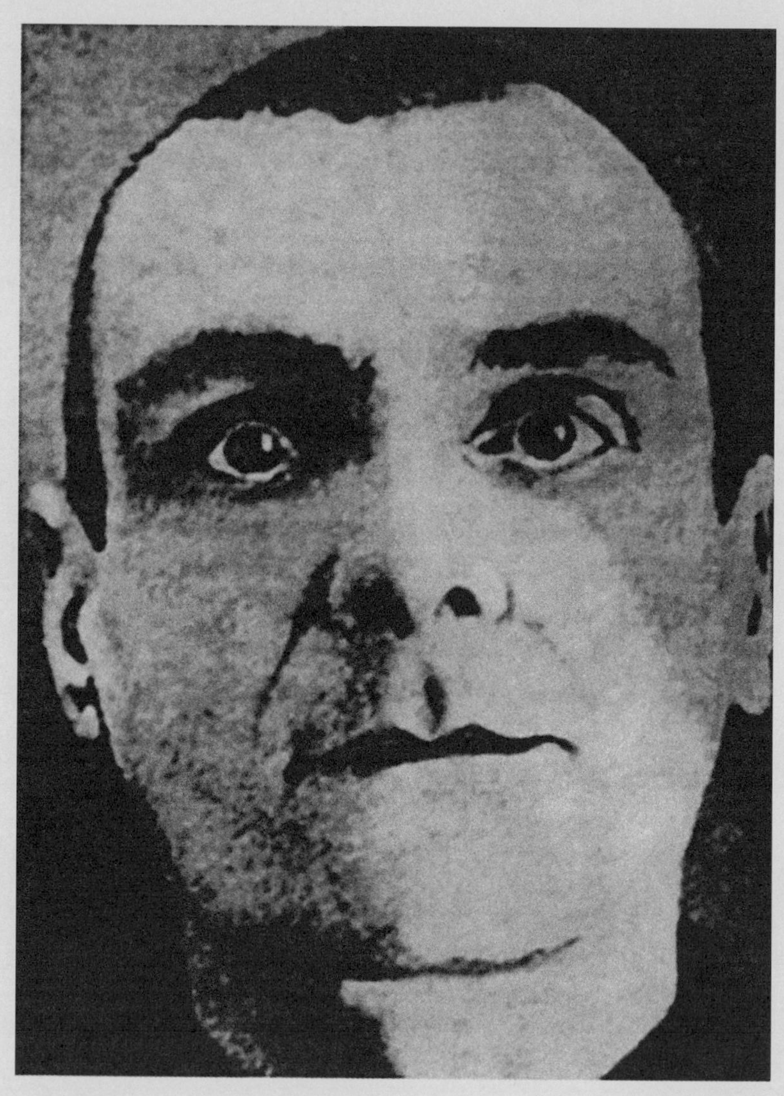

Large eyes

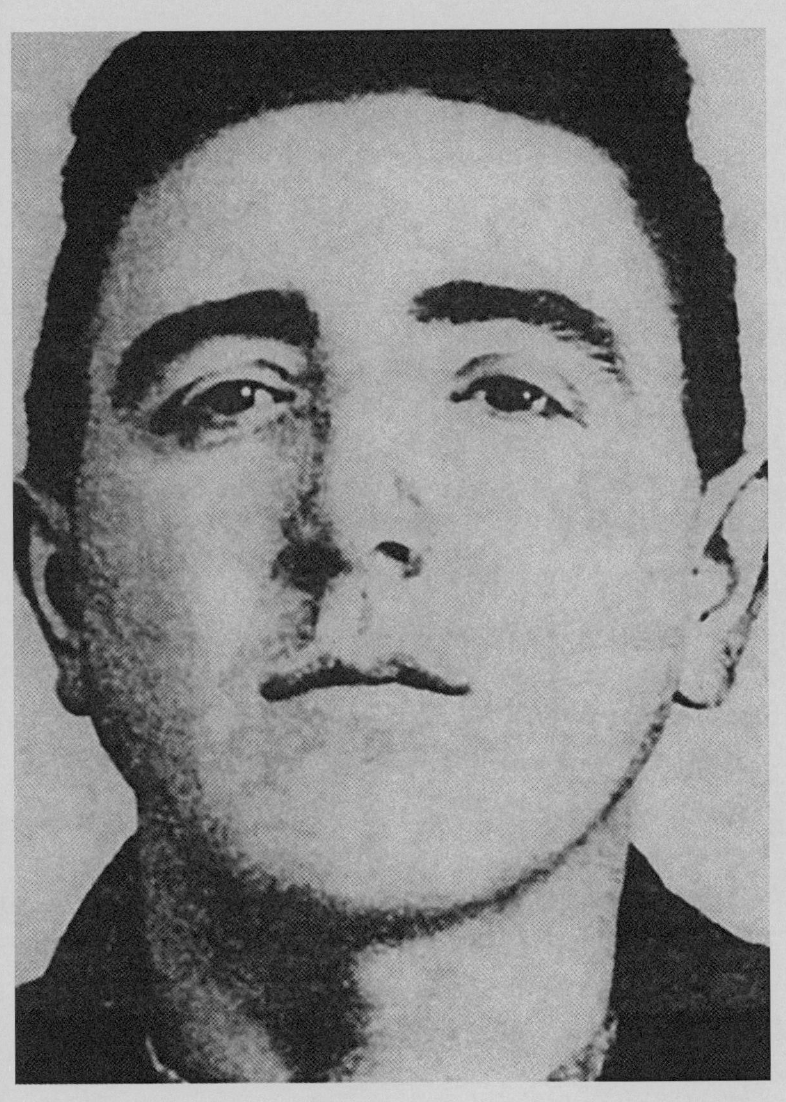

Downturned eyes

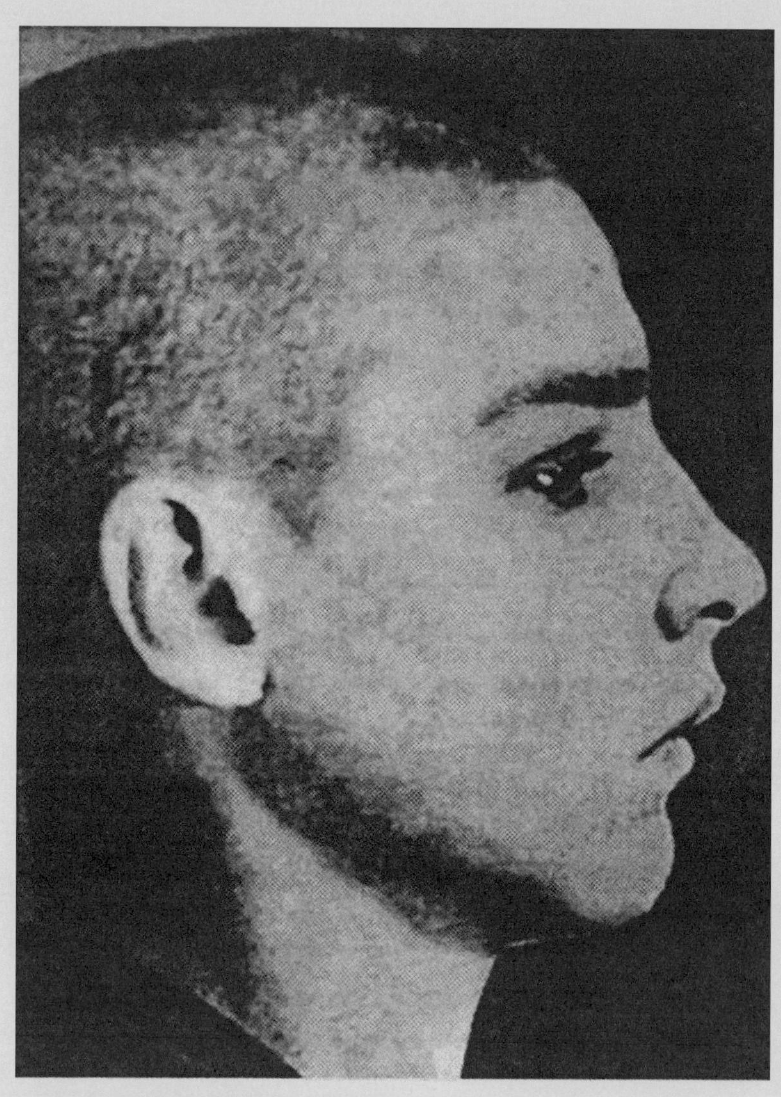

Protruding upper lip

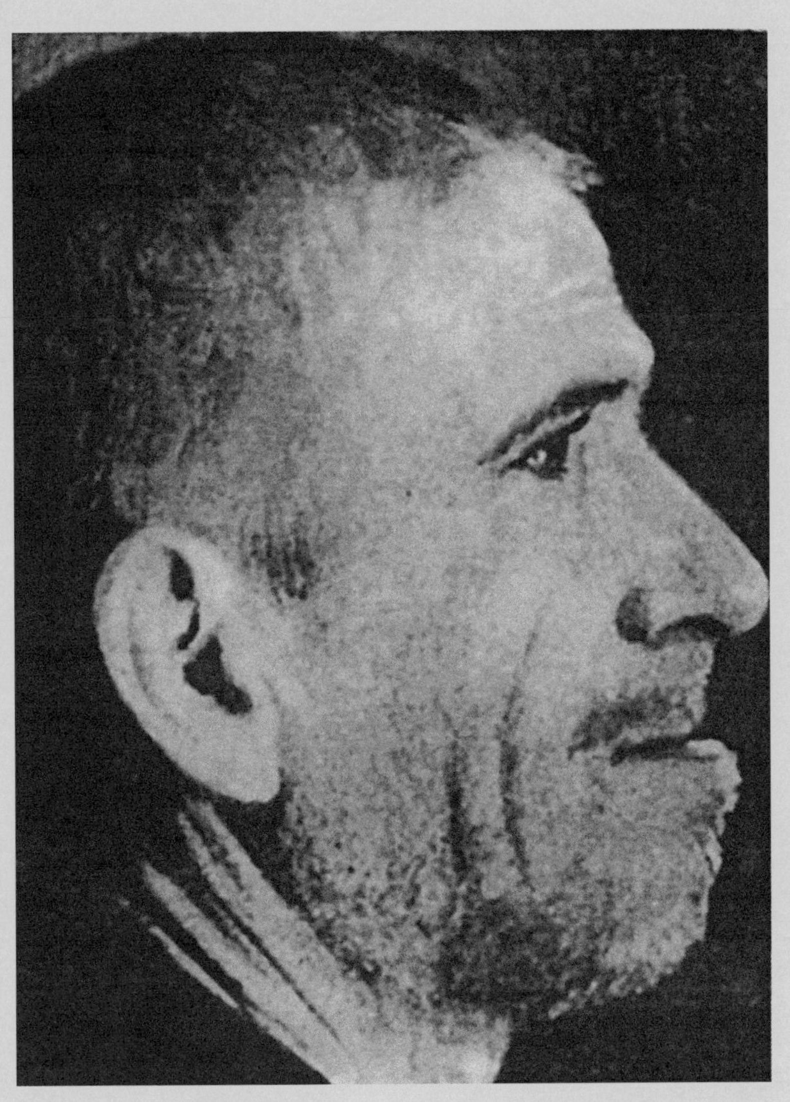

Protruding lower lip

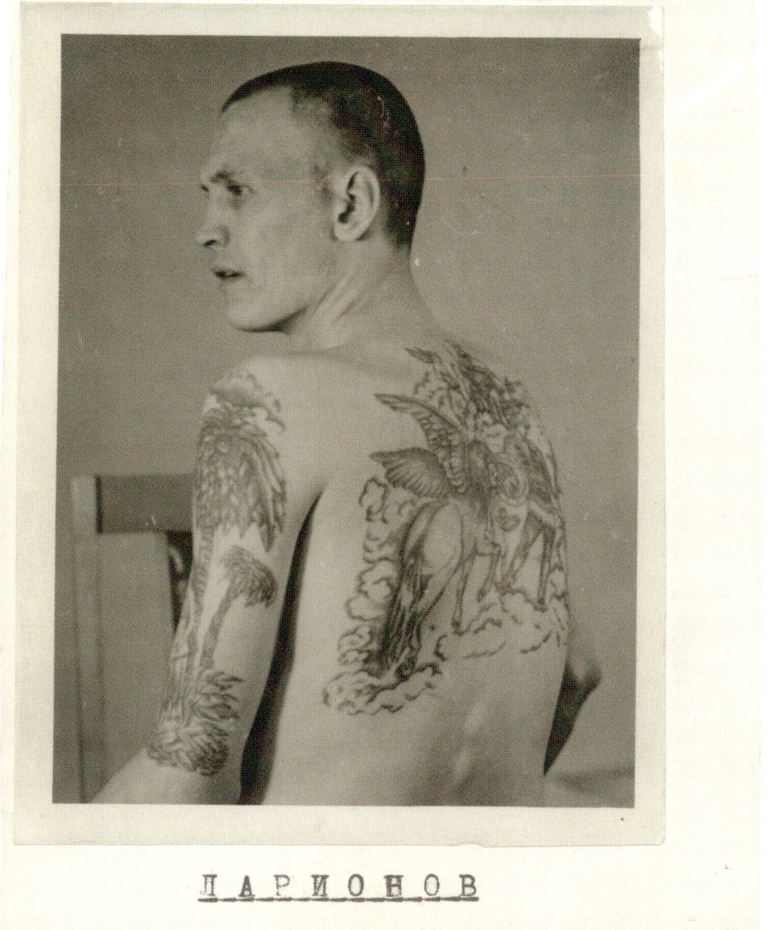

Vadim Aleksandrovitch Larionov

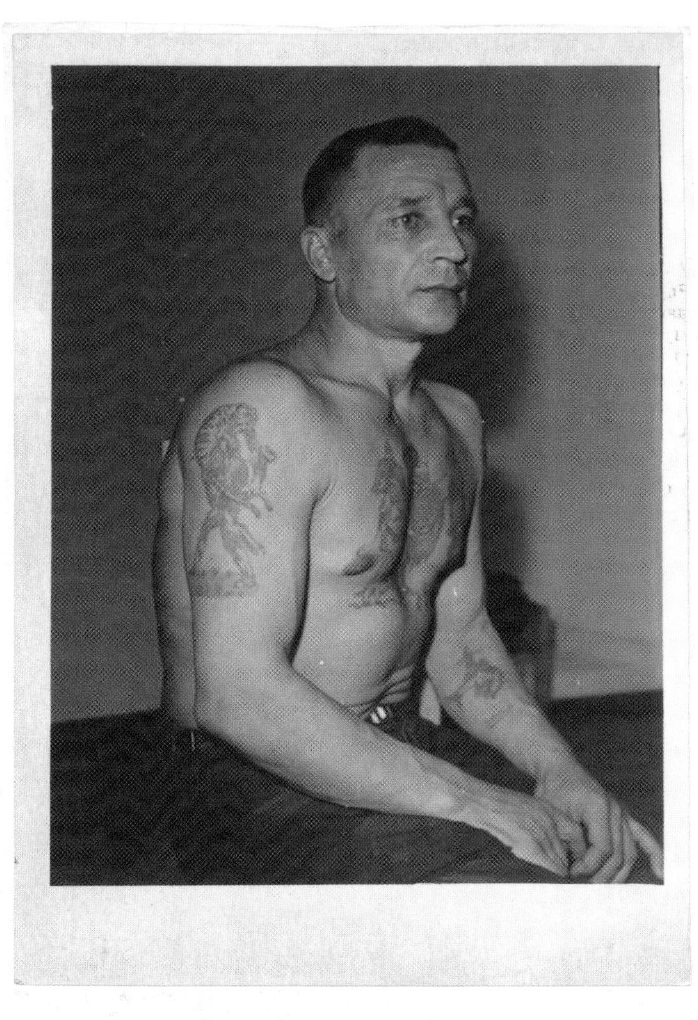

Vladimir Yefremovitch Yakovlev

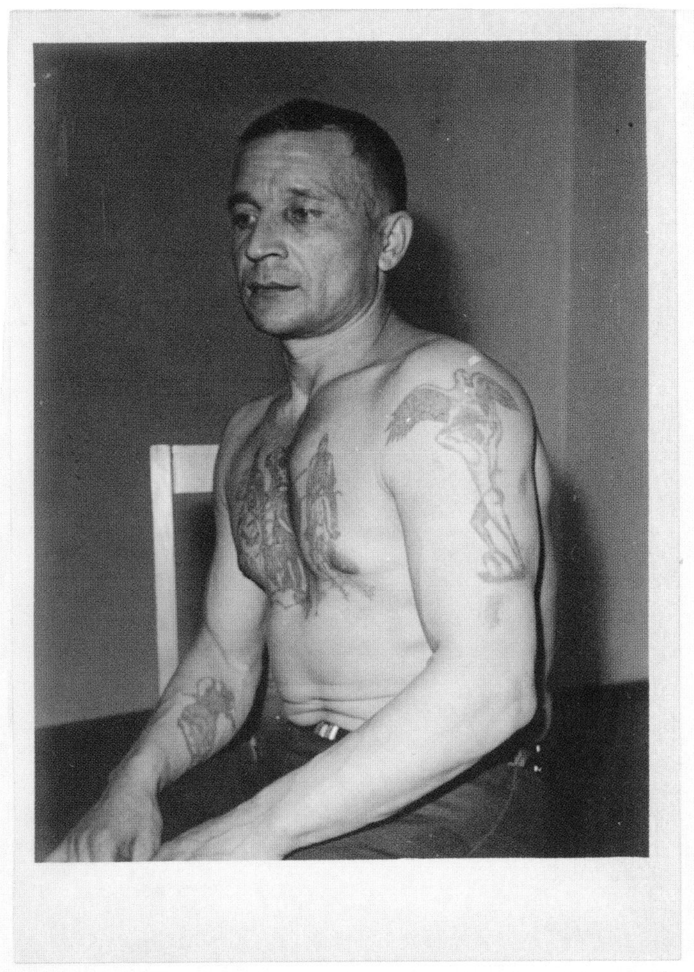

ЯКОВЛЕВ

ВЛАДИМИР ЕФРЕМОВИЧ

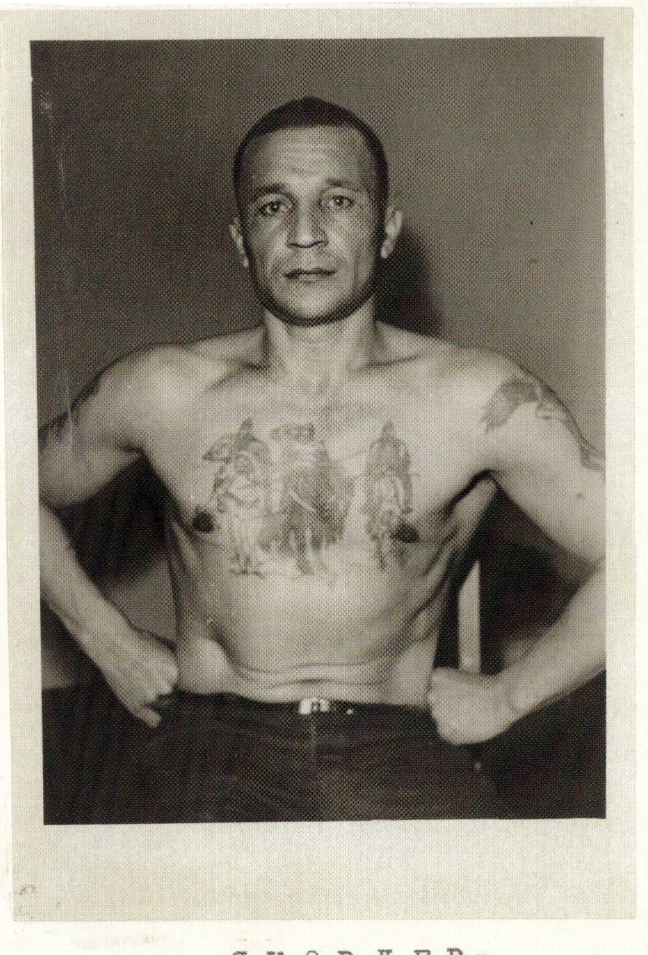

Vladimir Yefremovitch Yakovlev. Born 1938 in N-Krachkino, Chuvash, Autonomous Soviet Socialist Republic.

рачкино,
жден

Previously convicted under Article 89, Section 2 [theft of state and public property]; sentenced again under Article 89, Section 2 of the Criminal Code of the RSFSR (Russian Soviet Federative Socialist Republic) to five years' imprisonment.

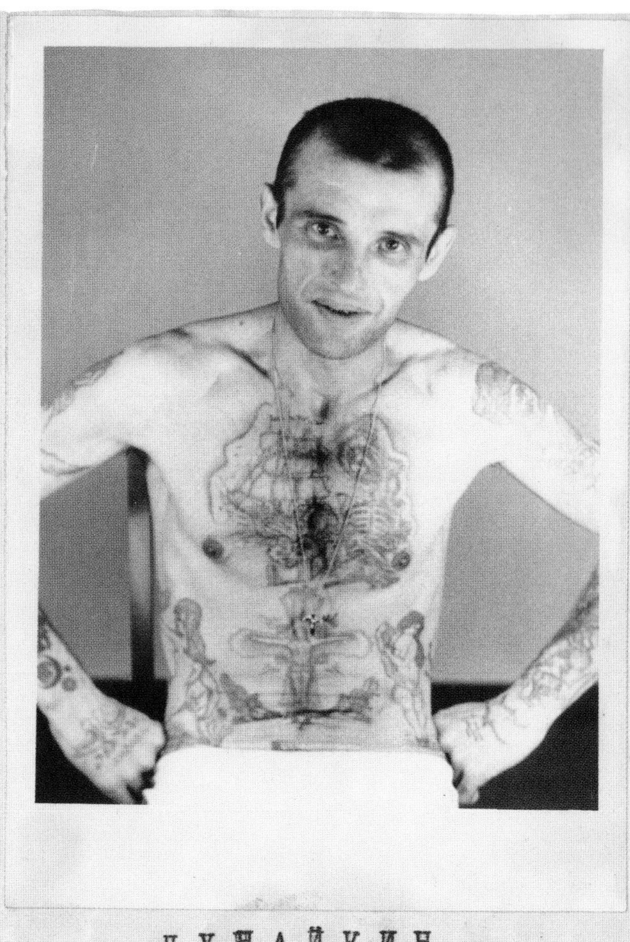

Adolph Ivanovitch Dunaikin. Born 1940 in Moscow.

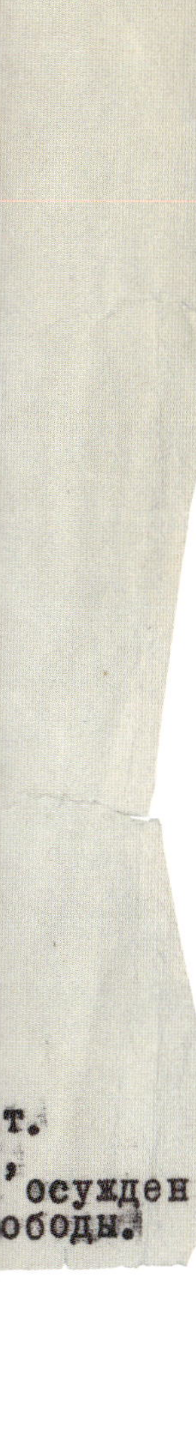

Previously convicted under Article 73, Section 1 [for failing to appear as a witness without valid reason] on 04. 06. 47; Article 82, Section 1 [the escape by the arrested individual from custody or imprisonment]; Article 182, Section 4 [for refusing to give or evading the giving of testimony]; Article 2, Section 2 [socially dangerous acts] on 04. 07. 47; Article 77, Section 1 [the insurrection of recidivists in penal institutions]; Article 218, Section 2 [the theft of firearms and ammunition by robbery, committed by an organised criminal group] of the RSFSR Criminal Code. Sentenced to ten years' imprisonment.

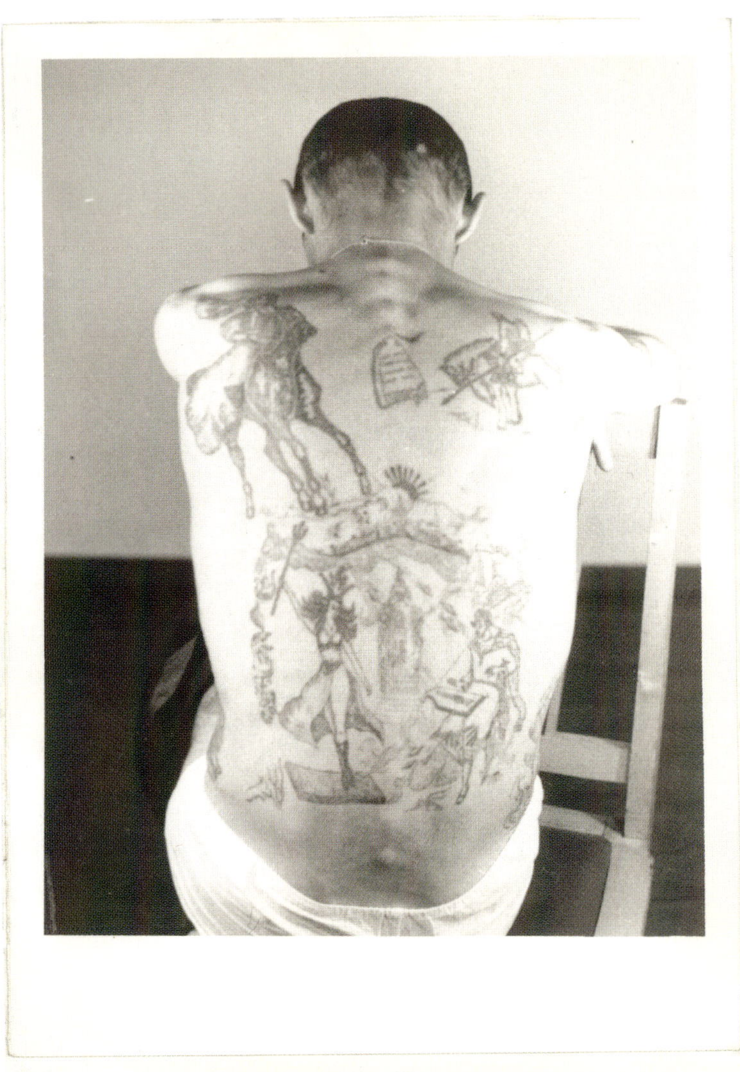

Adolph Ivanovitch Dunaikin

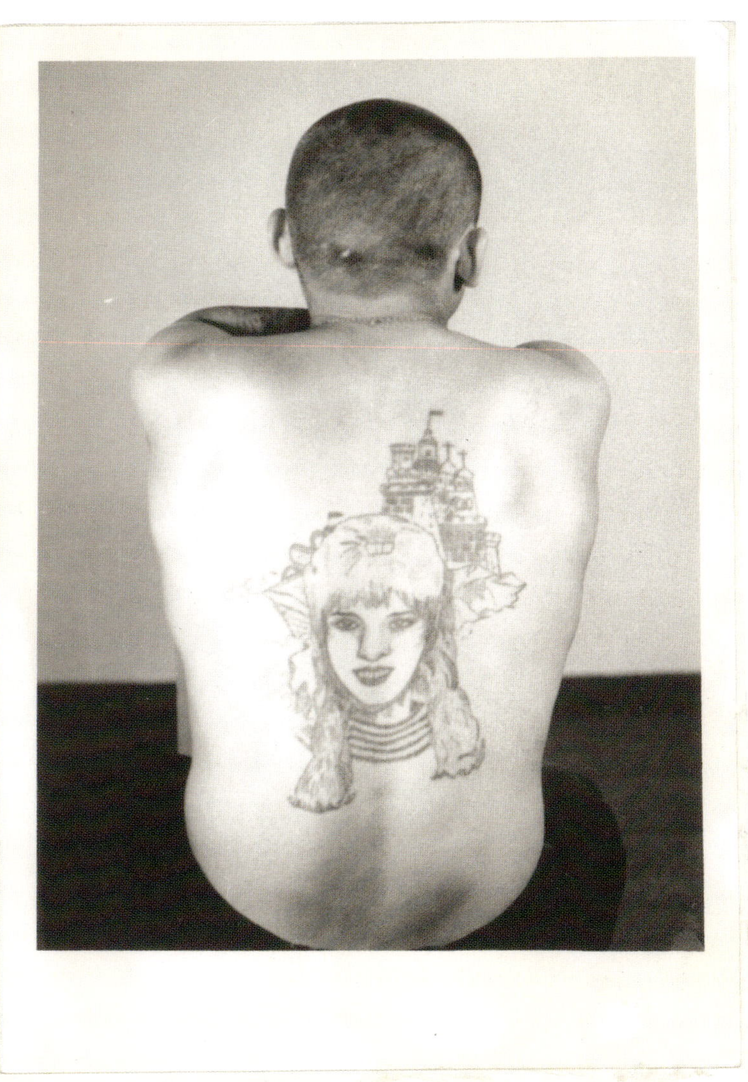

Andrei Ivanovitch Shubin

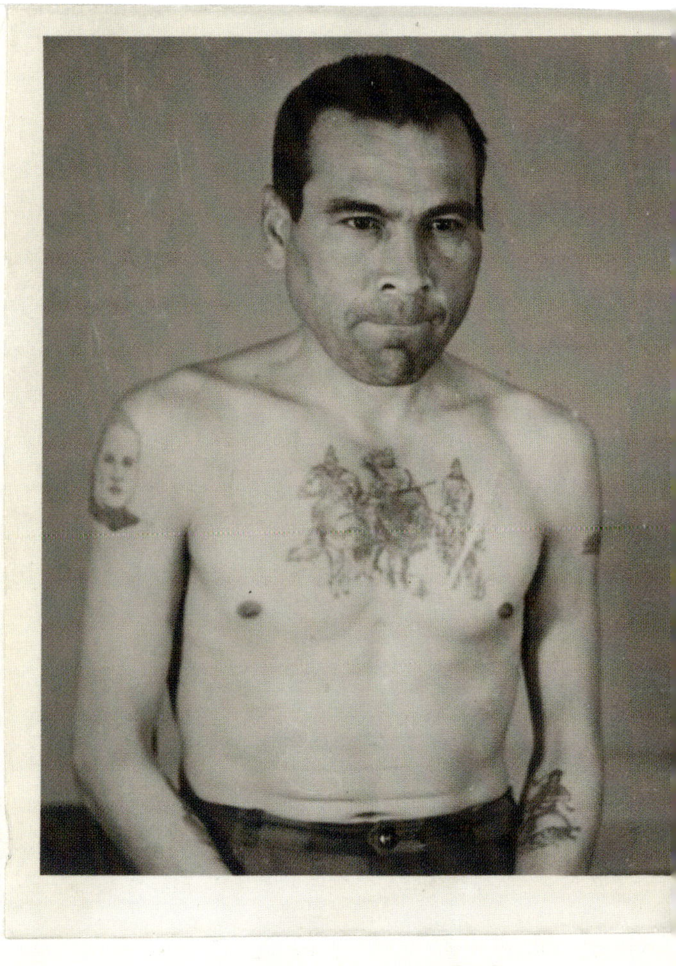

Felix Ivanovitch Larionov. Born 1938 in Tarkhany, Batyrevsky region, Chuvash, Autonomous Soviet Socialist Republic.

р-на, ЧАССР,
УК РСФСР,
да лишения

Previously convicted under Article 206, Section 2 [aggravated hooliganism];
later again under Article 206, Section 2 of the RSFSR Criminal Code.
Sentenced to four years' imprisonment.

Yuri Vasilyevitch Gavrilov. Born 1947 in Kimry, Kalinovsky Oblast, Russia.

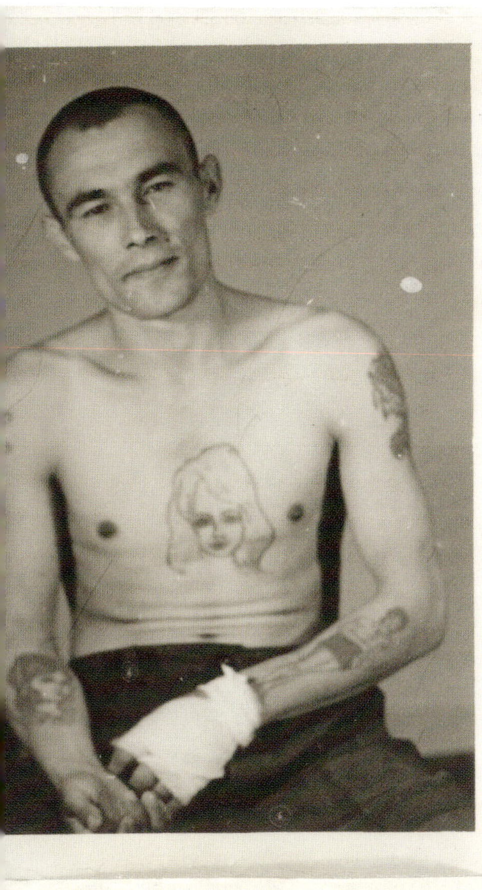

Previously convicted under Article 146, Section 2 [assault with intent to rob]; Article 102 [intentional homicide under aggravating circumstances]; Article 206, Section 3 [aggravated hooliganism]; Article 191 [an attempt on the life of an officer of the militia (police) in connection with the exercise of their duties for the preservation of public order]; Article 206 [hooliganism] of the RSFSR Criminal Code. Sentenced to fifteen years' imprisonment.

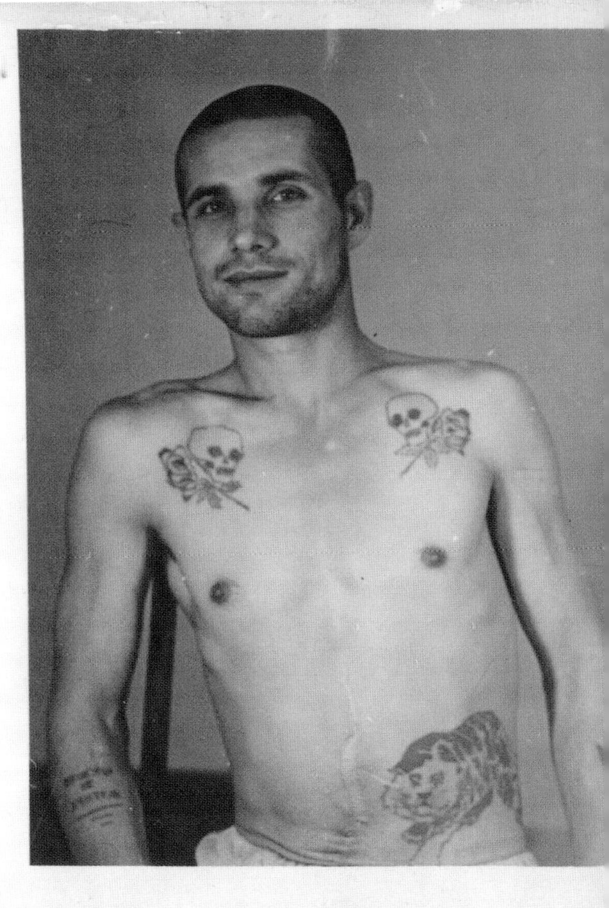

Pavel Yurievitch Rukin. Born 1953 in Novo-Devitchye, Novodevitchy region, Kuybyshev Oblast.

...ичьевского р-на,
...ч.2, 108 ч.1,
...г лишения свободы.

Previously convicted under Article 89, Section 2 [theft of state and public property]; Article 108, Section 1 [intentional infliction of grave bodily injury]; Article 77, Section 1 [the insurrection of recidivists in penal institutions] of the RSFSR Criminal Code. Sentenced to fifteen years' imprisonment.

These cards are used at the prison roll call which takes place daily. The face of each prisoner is checked against the standard mugshot photograph as it appears on his card.

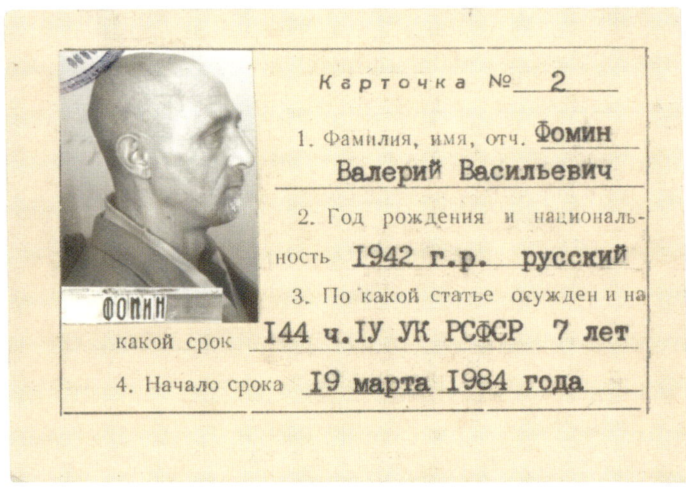

Card No. **2**

1. Family name, first name, patronymic:
Valeri Vasilyevitch Fomin
2. Year of birth and nationality:
Born in 1942   Russian
3. Under which Article sentenced and for how long:
Convicted under Article 144, Section 1 [the theft of personal property]
of the RSFSR Criminal Code. Sentenced to 7 years
4. Start of sentence:
19 March 1984

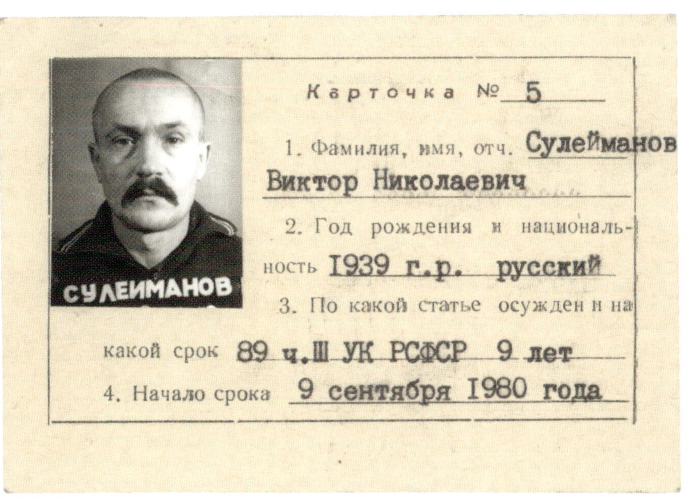

Card No. **5**

1. Family name, first name, patronymic:
Viktor Nikolaevitch Suleymanov
2. Year of birth and nationality:
Born in 1939 Russian
3. Under which Article sentenced and for how long:
Convicted under Article 89, Section 3 [the stealing of state or social property on a large scale] **of the RSFSR Criminal Code. Sentenced to 9 years**
4. Start of sentence:
9 September 1980

Text on the hand reads **'Tania'** (a woman's name).

A snake around the neck is a sign of drug addiction. Most inmates are either alcoholics or substance abusers. Their crimes are often committed while in a state of intoxication. The stars on the clavicles and epaulettes on the shoulders show that this inmate is an authority. The Madonna and Child is one of the most popular tattoos worn by criminals, and it can have a number of meanings. It can symbolise loyalty to a criminal clan; it can mean that the wearer believes the Mother of God will ward off evil; it can indicate that the wearer has been in the jail system and behind bars from an early age.

The trousers worn by the inmate are part of the uniform of a special regime colony, the strictest type of regime in the Soviet Union. Criminals sent here are known as *osobo opasnim retsidivistom* (especially dangerous recidivists), who have carried out grave offences such as murder or paedophilia. They are assigned to harsher and more restricted regimes of detention than other prisoners, and are not subject to be released on parole. For the general strict regime population, the uniform is a plain dark grey with no stripes. Only particularly dangerous criminals are made to wear striped clothing, partly as an aid to identification in the event of escape.

The prisoners are divided into castes. One of these castes is made up of the criminal elite called *blatniie**. They are commonly known as 'blue'†, because their bodies are blue from the tattoo dye that covers them. These are experienced criminals who have committed many crimes and have many previous convictions. Another large caste is *muzhiki*; 'fellows' or 'peasants' in Russian. They are not criminals as such, they may have been sentenced for economic offences, fraud or road-traffic accidents. In any standard prison they normally constitute up to half of the total number of inmates. The caste at the very bottom of the hierarchy and most despised is the so-called *opushenniie*, meaning 'lowered'. They are, in a manner of speaking, men who have been converted into the rank of women. They are often forcibly tattooed with 'beauty spots' on the neck, nose and ear lobes, and tattoos of naked women on the body. They might also have a tattoo of the sun on the buttocks, interpreted as 'in the circle of friends'. Or the tattoo of a stoker throwing coal into the anus, or a mouse, or a rat, usually applied forcibly. While the majority of inmates willingly get tattoos, the lowered do not.

* A person cannot become a *blatnoy*, or even be accepted into the criminal world simply by committing a crime. To join the ranks of the professional criminals any candidate must have a good knowledge of *fenya* (the criminal argot) and adhere to the 'correct understandings' (*ponyatiy*). Any relations with the authorities, even coincidental, would immediately close the door to the criminal world.
† The Russian word *goluboi* (blue) may be forcibly tattooed on to the face or body of a pederast in the prison, lowering the bearer to the *opushenniie* cast.

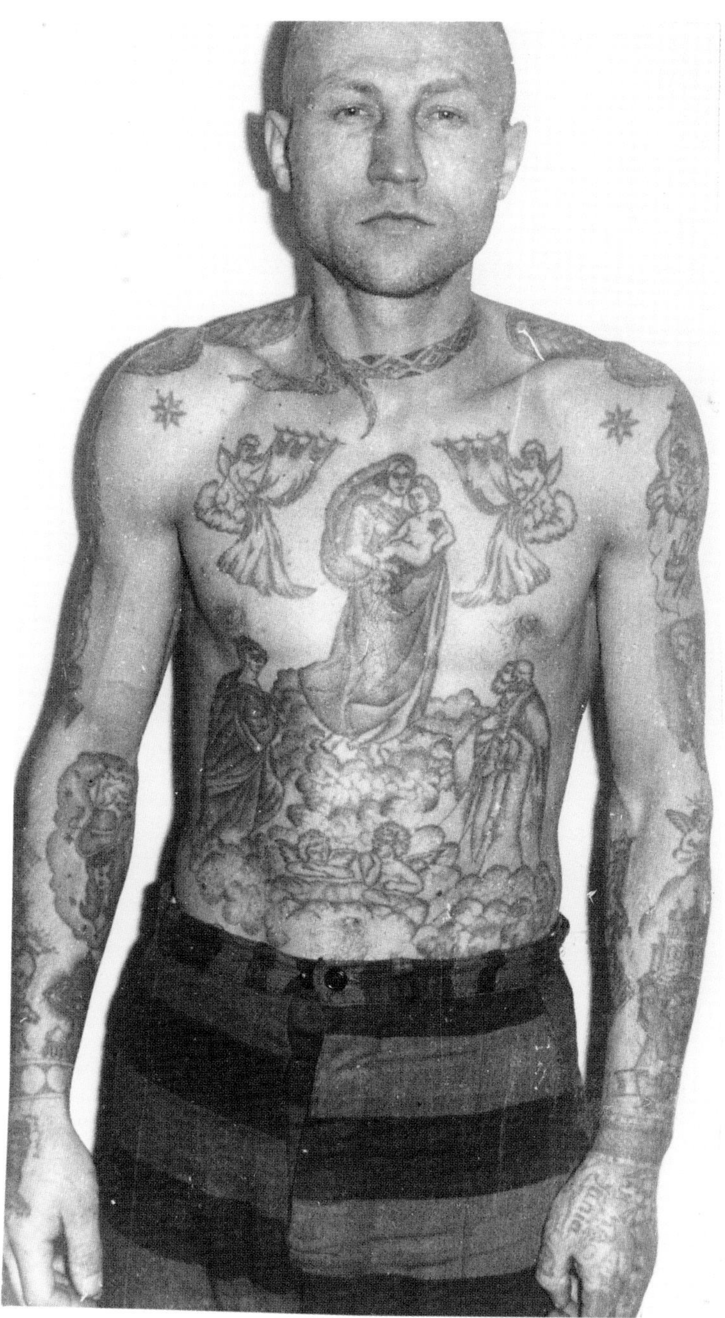

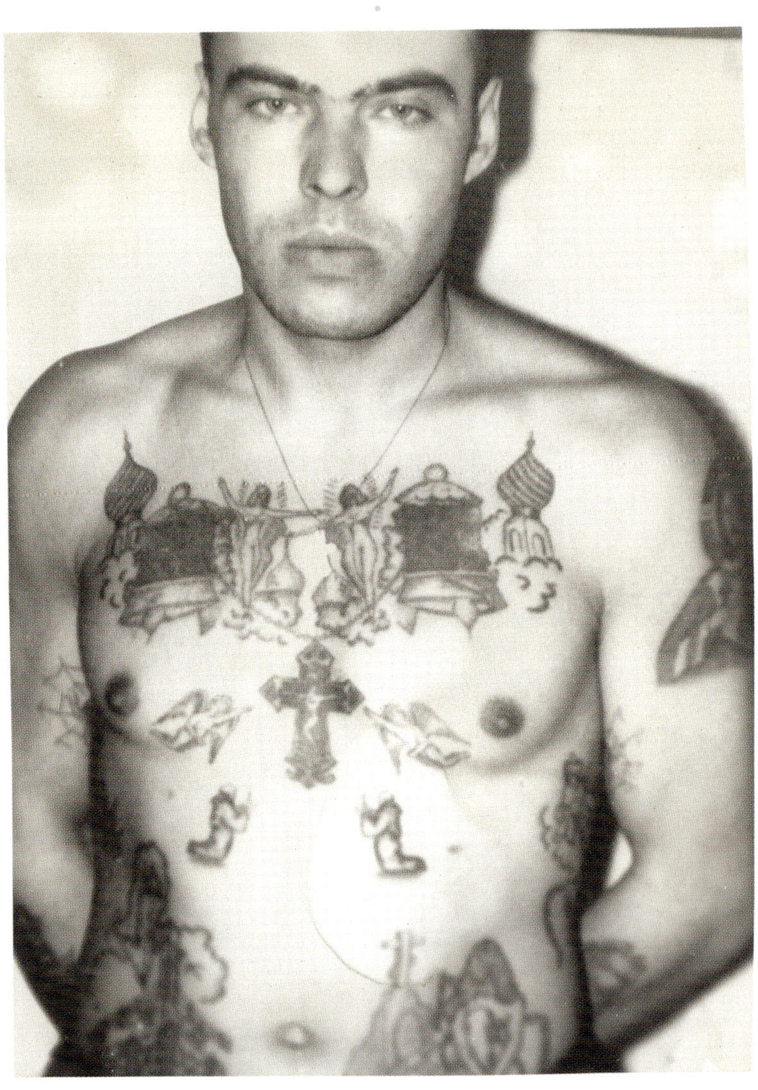

right: The stars on the shoulders show that this inmate is a criminal 'authority'.
The medals are awards that existed before the Revolution and as such are a
sign of antagonism and defiance towards the Soviet regime. The eyes on the
stomach denote a homosexual (the penis makes the 'nose' of the face).

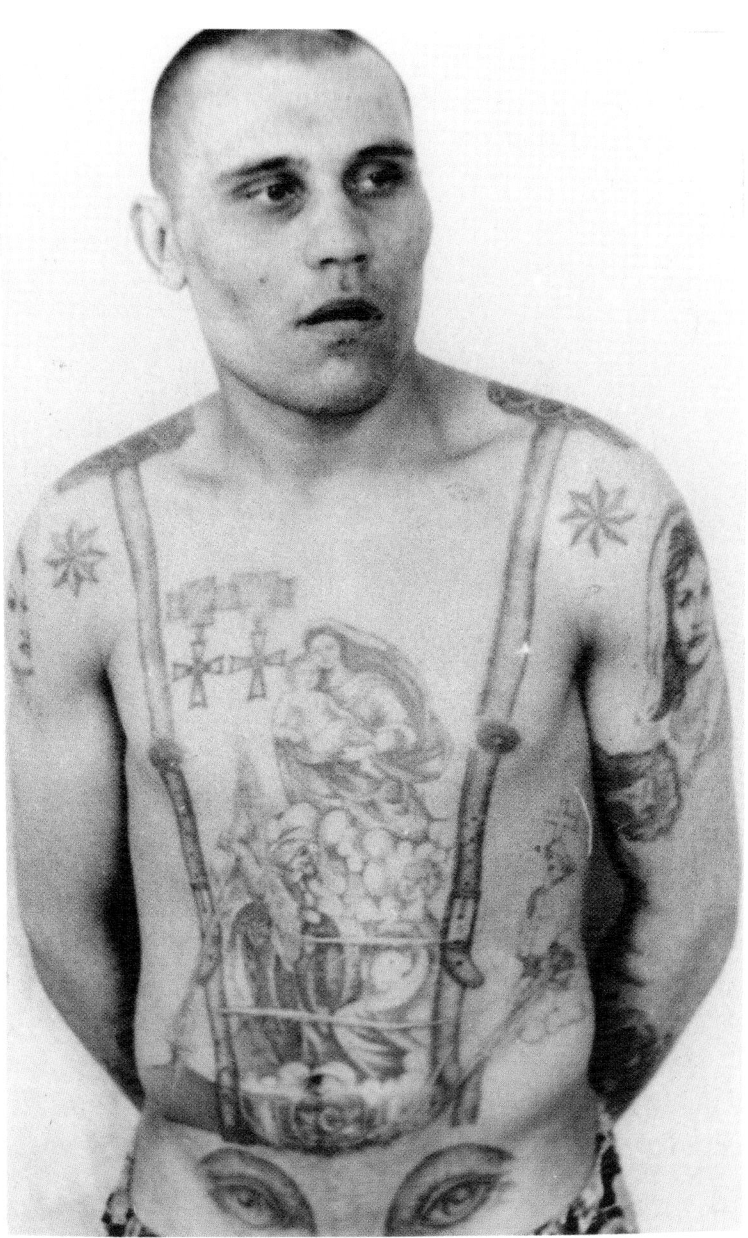

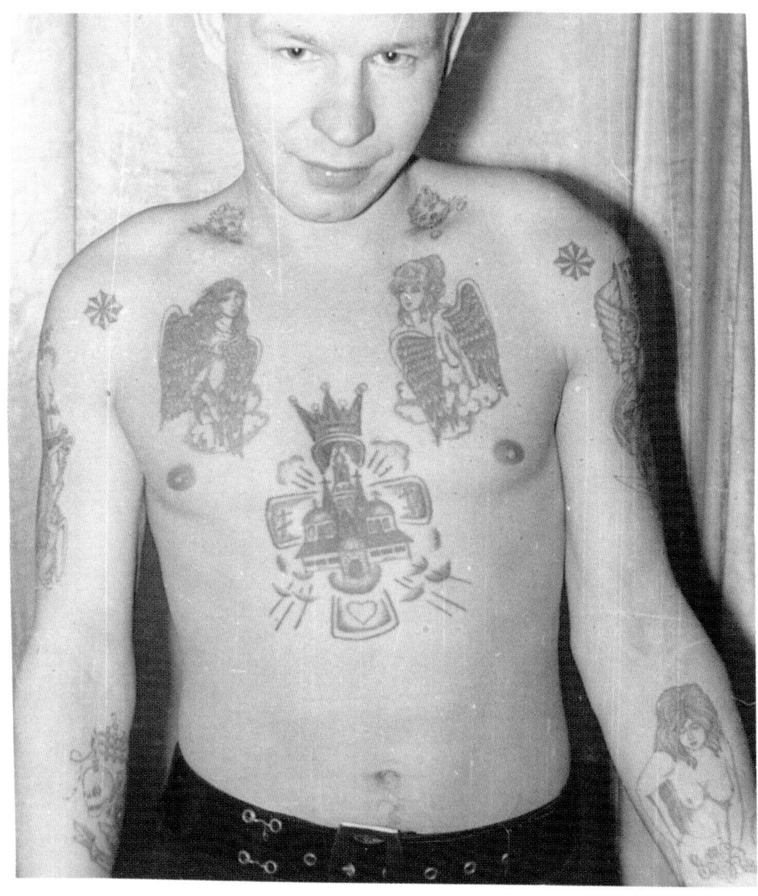

A prisoner's attitude is crucial to his survival in the zone. On arrival he must be able to judge immediately who to avoid and who to approach. In turn he will be assessed by *smotryashchiy* (watchers) who will report the newcomer's status to the cell's thief-in-law. It's not unusual that cells built for thirty-eight people would actually hold fifty-five or sixty. Many prisoners are locked up for twenty-four hours a day, others receive only an hour's 'exercise' in a three-by-five-metre walled concrete 'yard'. This severe overcrowding means that inmates have to take turns at sleeping and standing. The amount of time a prisoner has to wash at the (single) sink, use the (single) toilet, or even stand by the window, is greatly reduced. This is where the hierarchy of the cell is crucial: the higher the status of the inmate, the easier his life. Inmates who have been 'lowered' are not allowed to sleep in a bunk and have to make do with the floor.

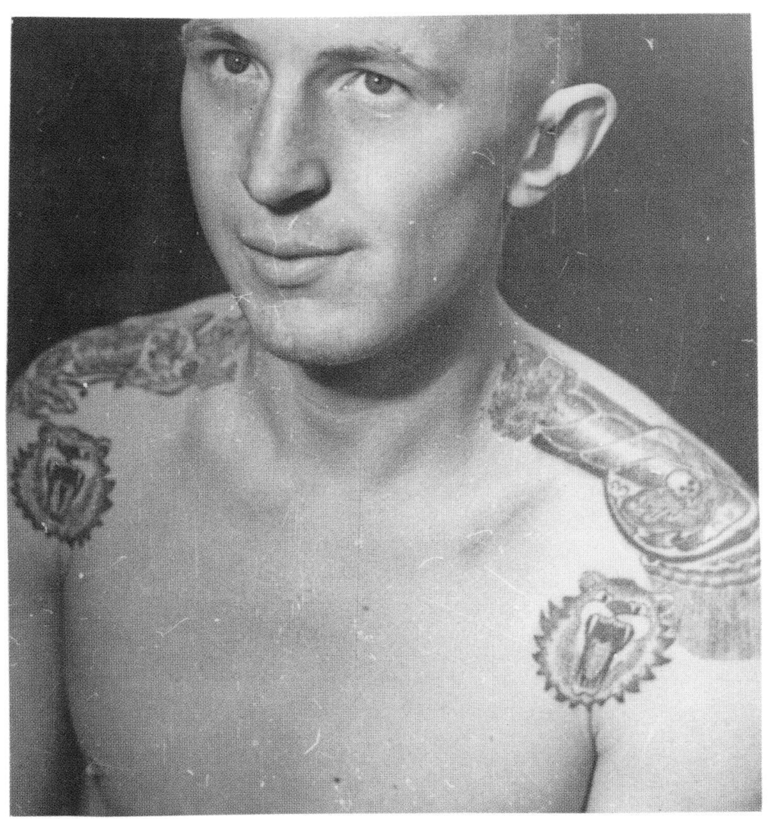

The uniform-style epaulettes tattooed on the shoulders of a thief reveal his convictions and status. The skull tattooed here means this prisoner has a negative attitude towards the system. He has no authoritative stars – this is his first conviction, so it's likely he will get more tattoos. The head of a bear with its mouth open is a 'grin of power' – the wearer considers himself to be a vicious criminal, hating law-enforcement workers.

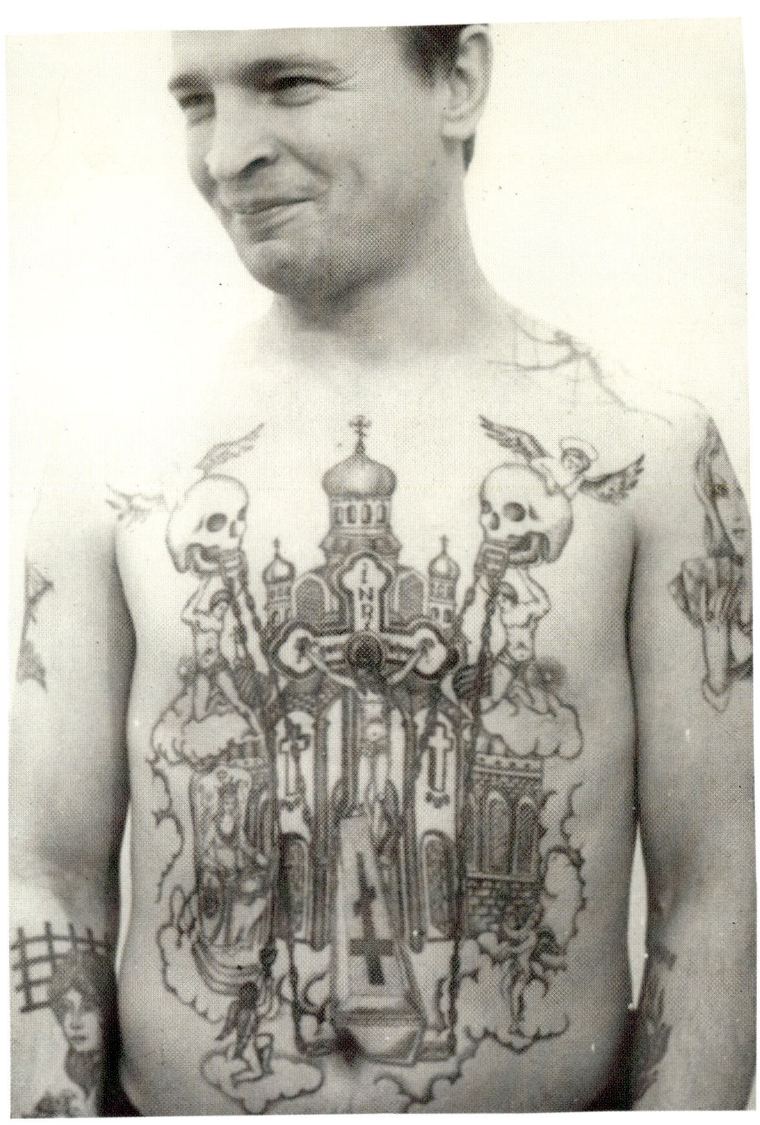

Images of monasteries, churches, cathedrals, the Virgin Mary, saints and angels predominantly found on the chest and back display a devotion to the world of thieves and its customs. The skulls tattooed on this inmate, sometimes seen with an angel flying away, indicate a conviction for murder. The coffin also represents a murder – they are burying the victim.

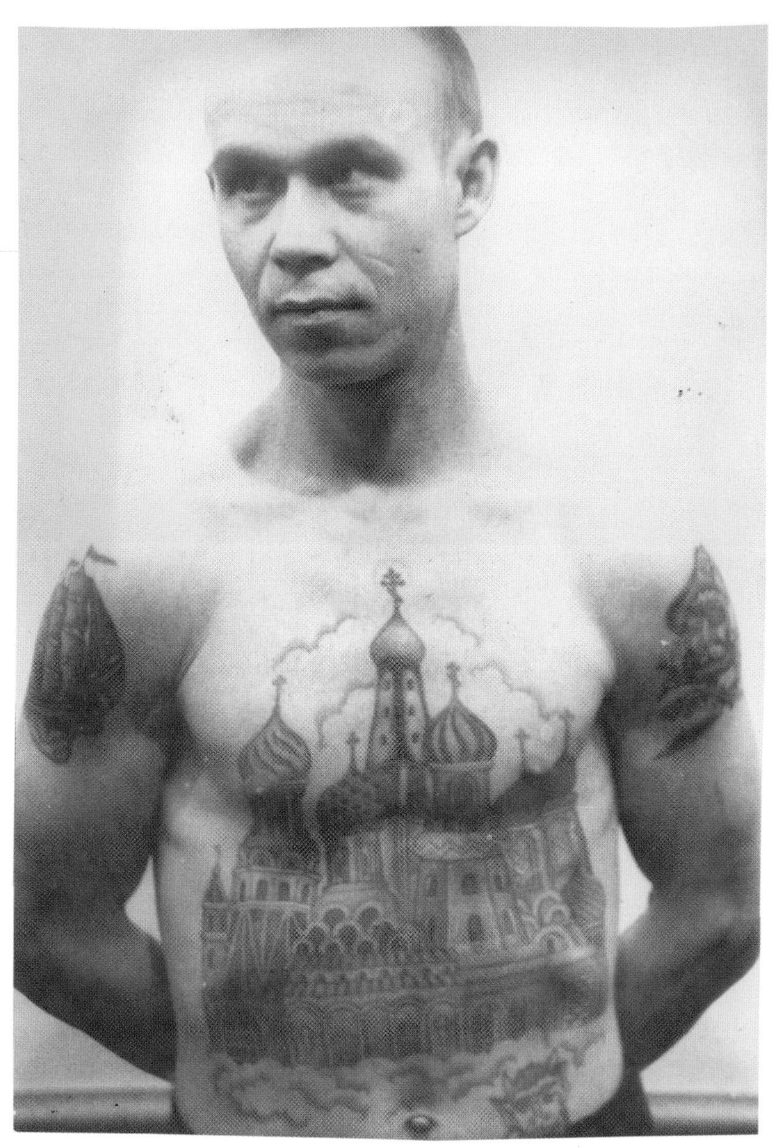

Text across the chest reads **'Live in sin, die laughing'**.

This criminal is tattooed in the traditional style, with the most important
motif appearing in the centre of the chest: a typical 'thieves' cross', flanked
by angels. Images of saints and crosses are often accompanied by indecent
and vulgar texts. Humorous tattoos or 'foolishness for the prison's sake'
reflect the world of the elite convicts or *blatniie*, as they – just like holy
fools – have their own whims and mockeries. The Virgin Mary can be depicted
naked or the crucified Jesus Christ can be substituted by a naked woman or
a man with emphasised genitals. The cross on a chain can be carried by
devils, cats or skeletons instead of angels. Mockery and obscenity in tattoos
with biblical subjects is a certain calque of holy foolishness that is very
common, especially among the marginal *blatniie*.

The doves carrying olive twigs tattooed on to the shoulders are a symbol
of deliverance from suffering, see also page 183.

On the arms are the Hare and Wolf from the Russian cartoon series
Nu, Pogodi! (*Well, Just You Wait!* [1969–2006]); the Wolf character was
portrayed with criminal habits and became a popular tattoo motif in the
prisons and camps, see also pages 77, 177 and 204.

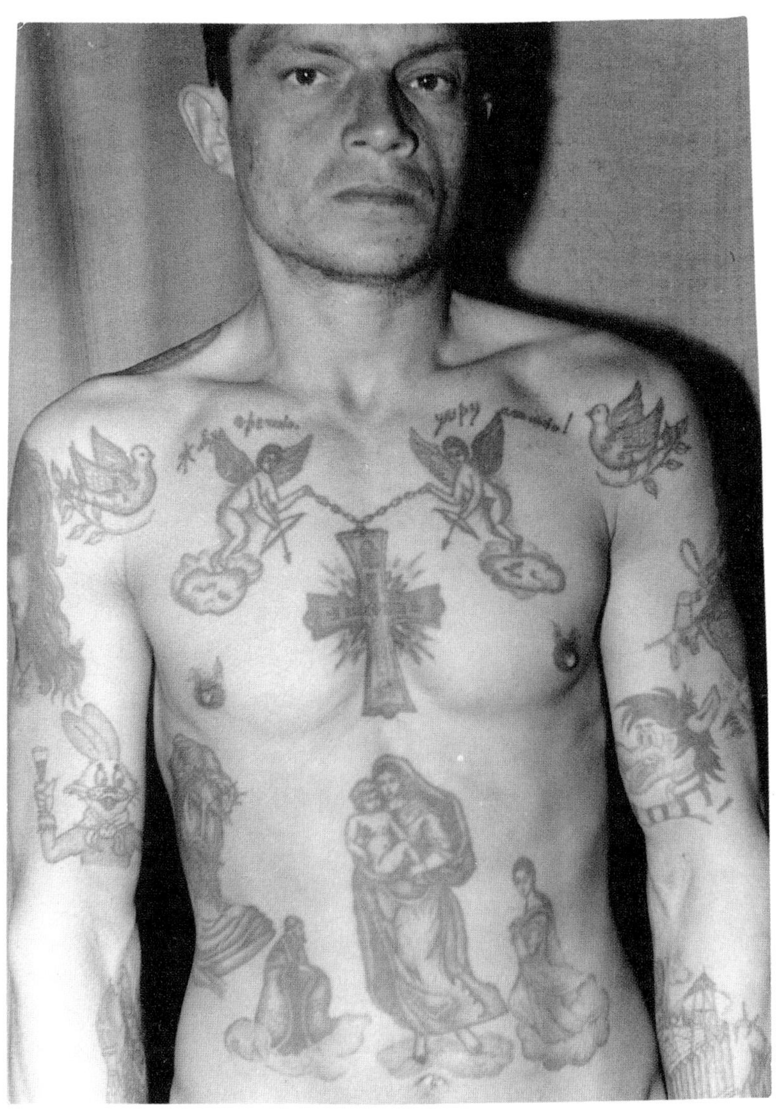

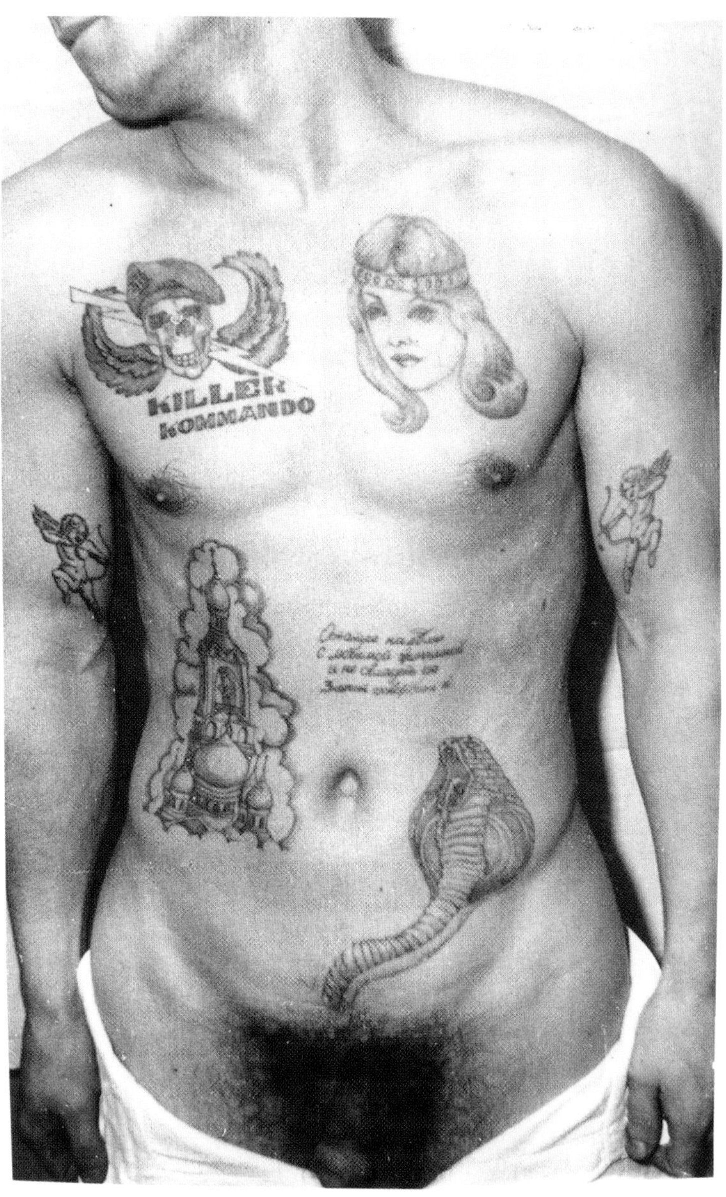

KILLER
KOMMANDO

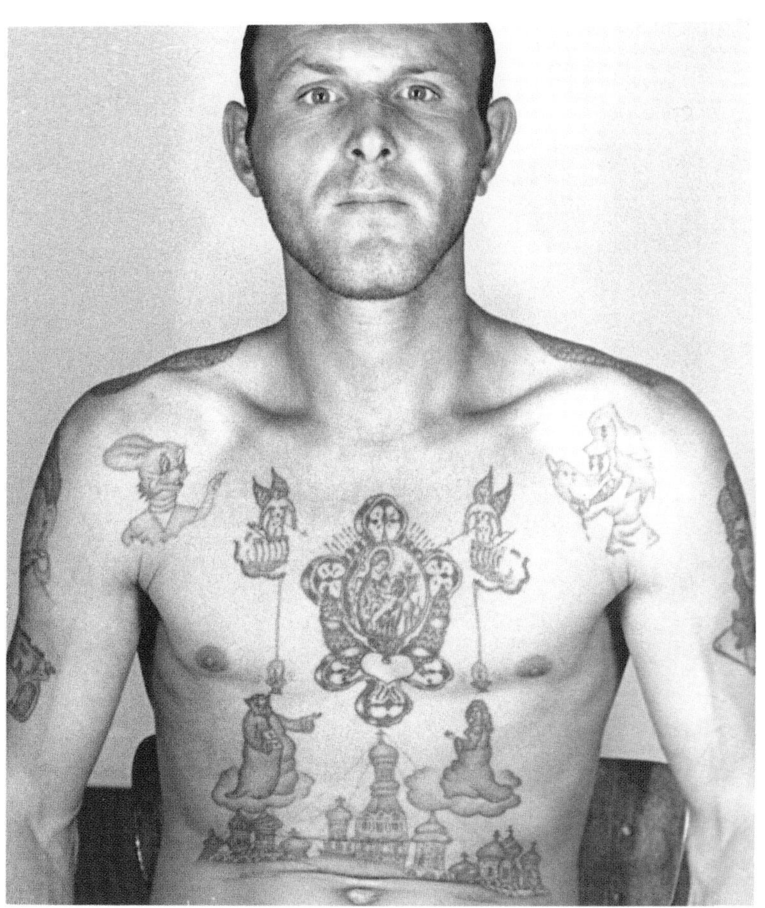

above: The number of domes reveals this inmate is a recidivist thief who has been convicted eleven times. He is also tattooed with the cartoon characters from *Nu, Pogodi!* (*Well, Just You Wait!* [1969–2006]), see also pages 75, 177 and 204. The pistol tattooed on his right arm is a display of aggression.

left: **'Killer Kommando'** with a skull and lightning bolt clearly labels this prisoner as a murderer. Text on the stomach reads **'To have moments alone with the woman you love and not to take her is an insult to her'**.

On the arms cupid sending an arrow symbolises the faith that the beloved woman will wait for the wearer to be released. The prisoner's penis is tattooed on to the stomach in the form of a snake about to bite.

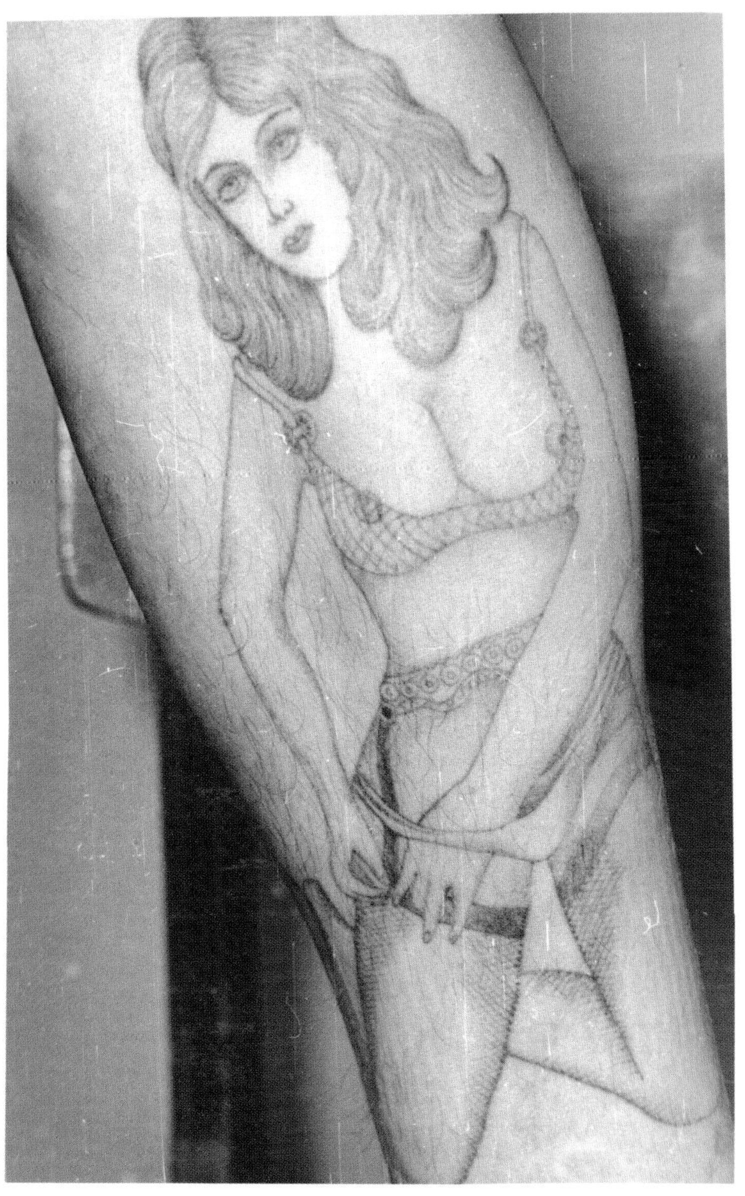

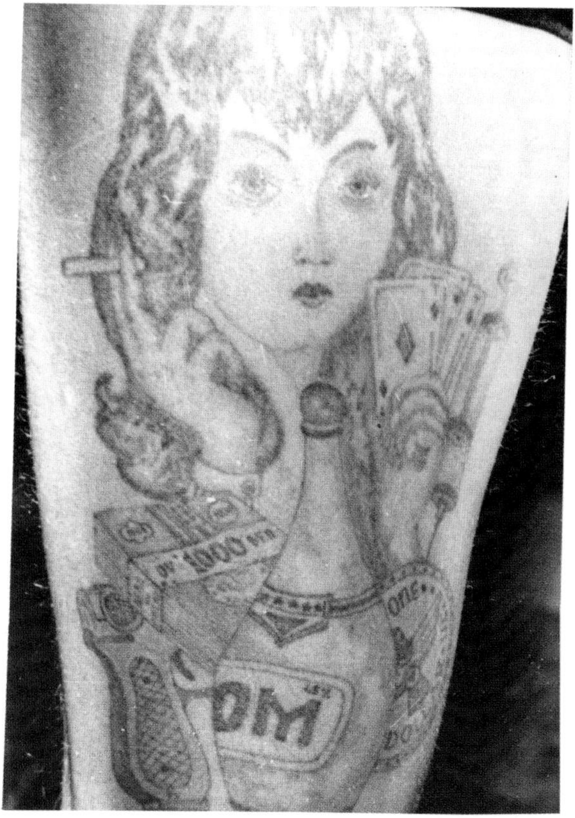

above: On the thigh is a woman smoking, playing cards, a bottle of cognac, a gun, a syringe and some money. This tattoo is commonly interpreted as 'This is what we love, this is what ruins us'. It shows that the bearer has a tendency towards wild living.

Sailors often get tattoos over the course of their voyages; these are generally viewed as a mark of their profession. There was a case of a sailor in Arkhangelsk who had a naked woman tattooed on his thigh during a sea voyage. Eventually he left the sea, got married and settled down. One day he went to a beach, where there was also a gang of *blatniie* hanging out. The *shesterka* [literally 'six' in Russian meaning a 'bag-carrier'] reported to the *pakhan*, 'There's a skirt on the beach.' So they tried to sexually abuse the young man. He explained that he hadn't known what the tattoo meant, and fought back, but they beat him, knocked out his teeth, then killed him.

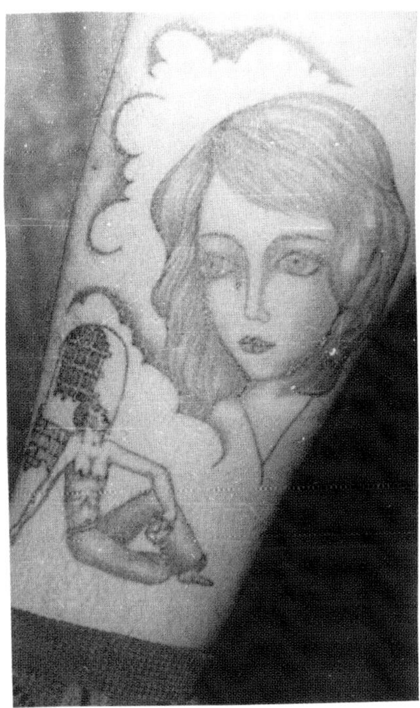

above: A tattoo showing longing for a wife or girlfriend.

right: Text on the leg reads **'Prison for a *zek* is a university of crime'**.

This tattoo means that an ordinary person who is sentenced for a minor offence will inevitably improve his criminal skills in prison, as professional criminals share their experience. For example, pickpockets reveal how to make sure the victim feels nothing as their pockets are emptied of valuables. Even if a person has committed a crime in error, when he leaves prison he will be more likely and able to commit crimes purposefully and professionally. The reality is that penal institutions don't correct inmates, even though they were once called 'Correctional Labour Institutions'. Today they are known as 'Institutions for the Execution of Sentences', so they are no longer required to deal with the problem of correction.

overleaf: Text across both forearms reads **'No blood / only chifir'** (a type of strong tea with a high caffeine level typically drunk by inmates); this indicates an addiction to drugs. German text on the wrist under a tattoo of a gun reads *Jedem das Seine*, **'To each what he deserves'**. English text on the gun reads: **'TIGER'** a sign of aggression. Latin text on the right leg reads: *Memento Mori*, **'Remember that you will die'**.

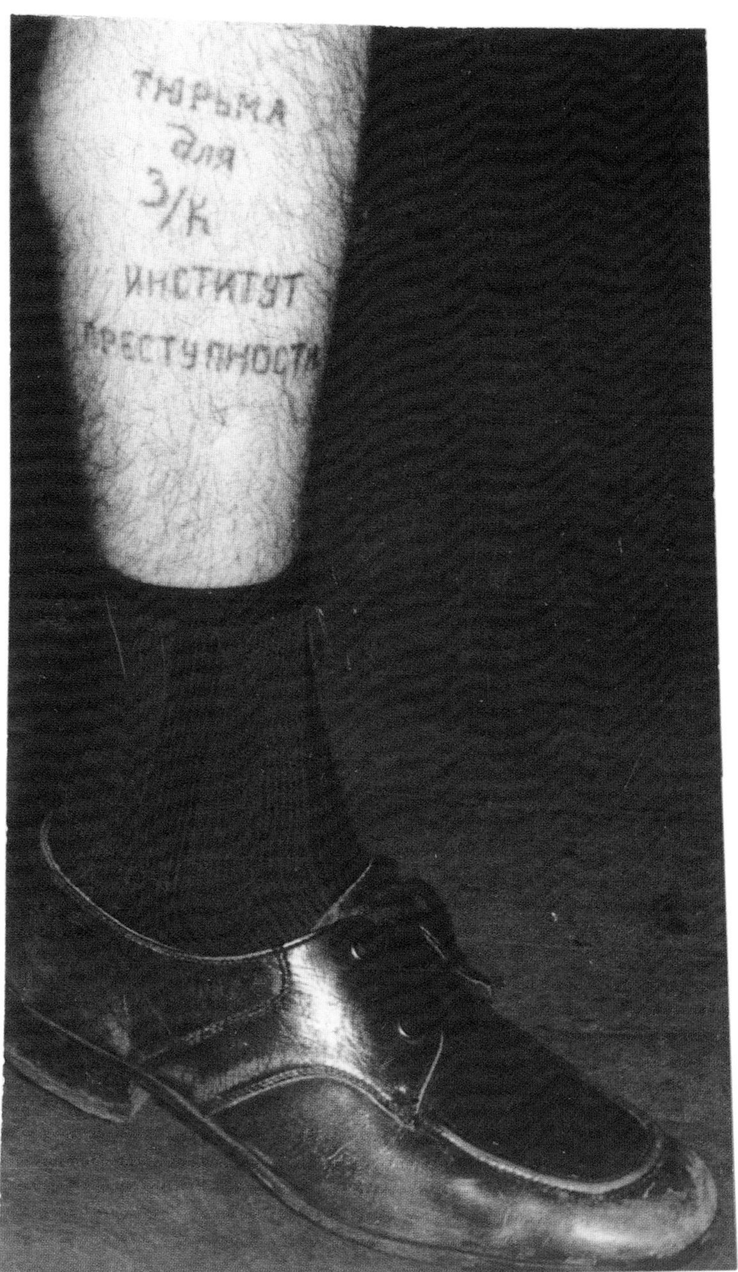
ТЮРЬМА
для
З/К
ИНСТИТУТ
ПРЕСТУПНОСТИ

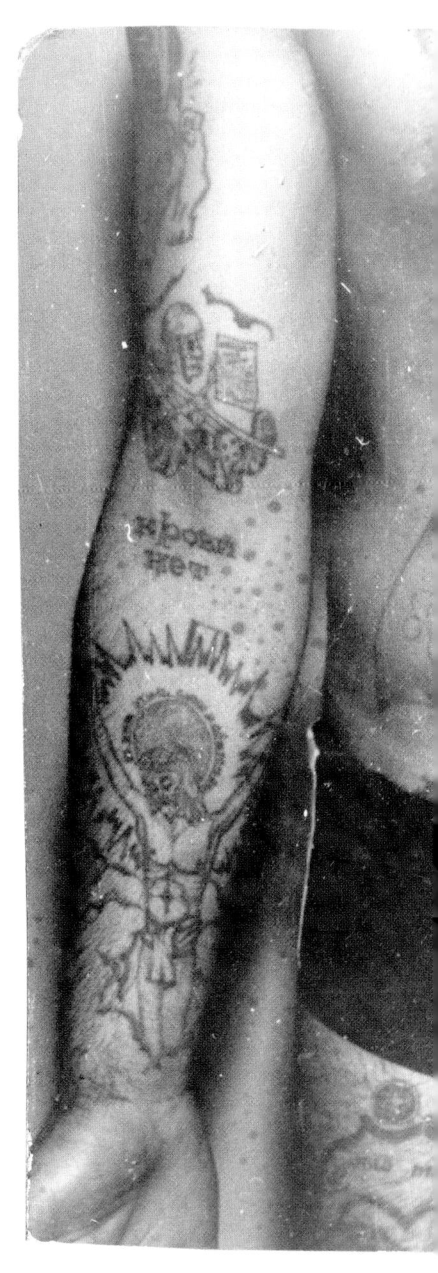хрена
нет

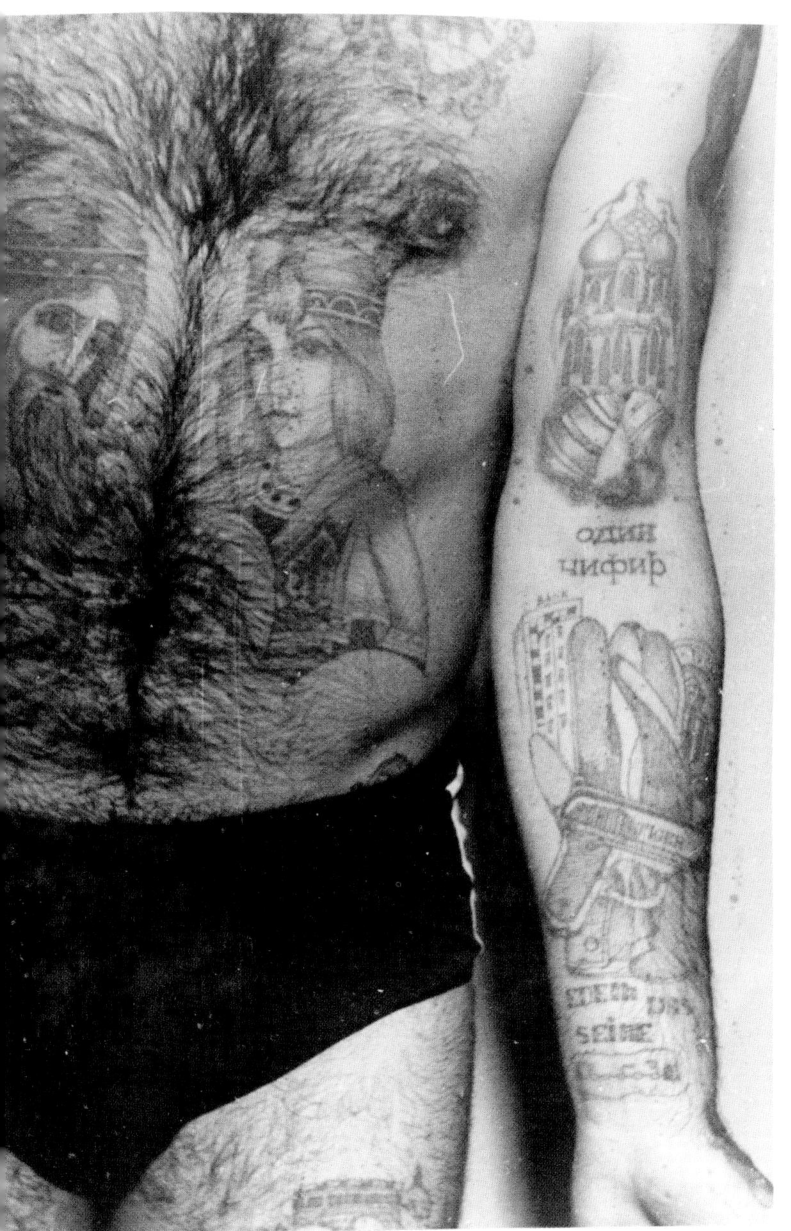
один
чифир

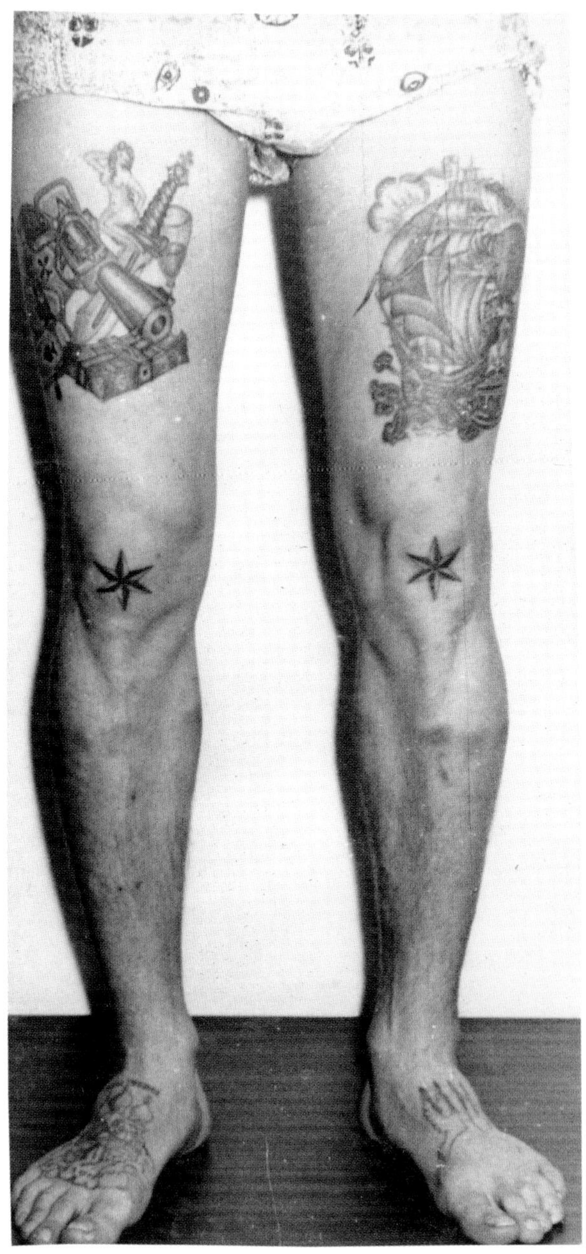

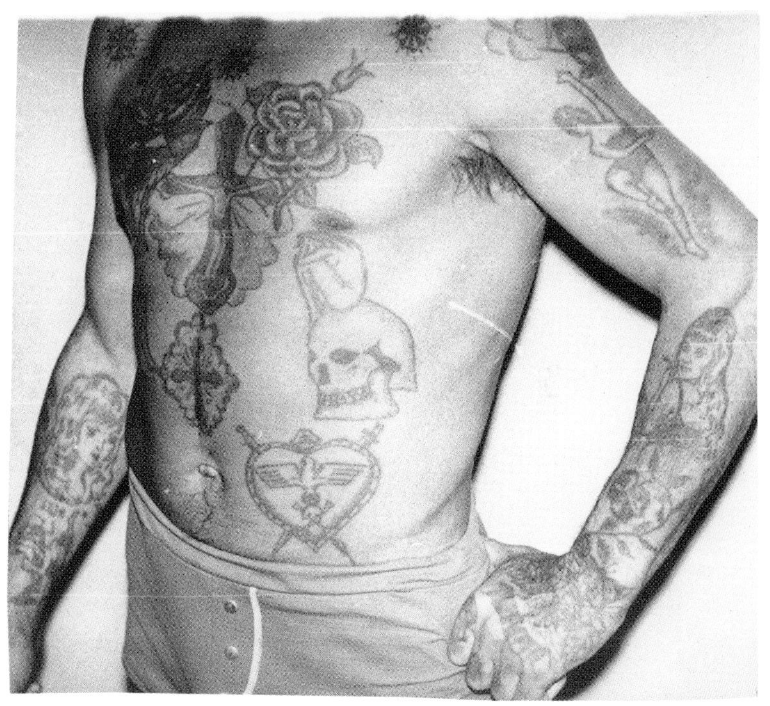

above: A rose can sometimes be tattooed in colour (red rose with green leaves and stem), meaning faithfulness to a beloved one, in memory of affection, a symbol of love.

left: Eight- or six-pointed stars tattooed on the knees mean 'I won't kneel in front of the law or follow orders from the administration', while stars on the chest or collarbone show the bearer is an authority in the criminal world.

On the inmate's right thigh are tattooed a gun, a syringe, a knife, money, cards, drink and a naked girl: all are meant as symbols of a life of crime. This is a version of the tattoo 'This is what is destroying us' and its meaning is 'This is what makes life worth living – to commit crimes'. (Only the black suits – the criminal suits – of spades and clubs are shown on the cards in the tattoo.)

A sailing ship on the thigh has a number of interpretations. Generally it means that the inmate is an 'eternal tramp' or an 'eternal wanderer': a travelling thief. The number of masts can indicate the number of convictions. If the thefts are committed on public transport (train, tram, bus or coach) the criminal is known as a *transportnik*. The tattoo also means that the bearer is prone to escape from penal colonies. It is necessary to keep inmates with this type of tattoo under close surveillance.

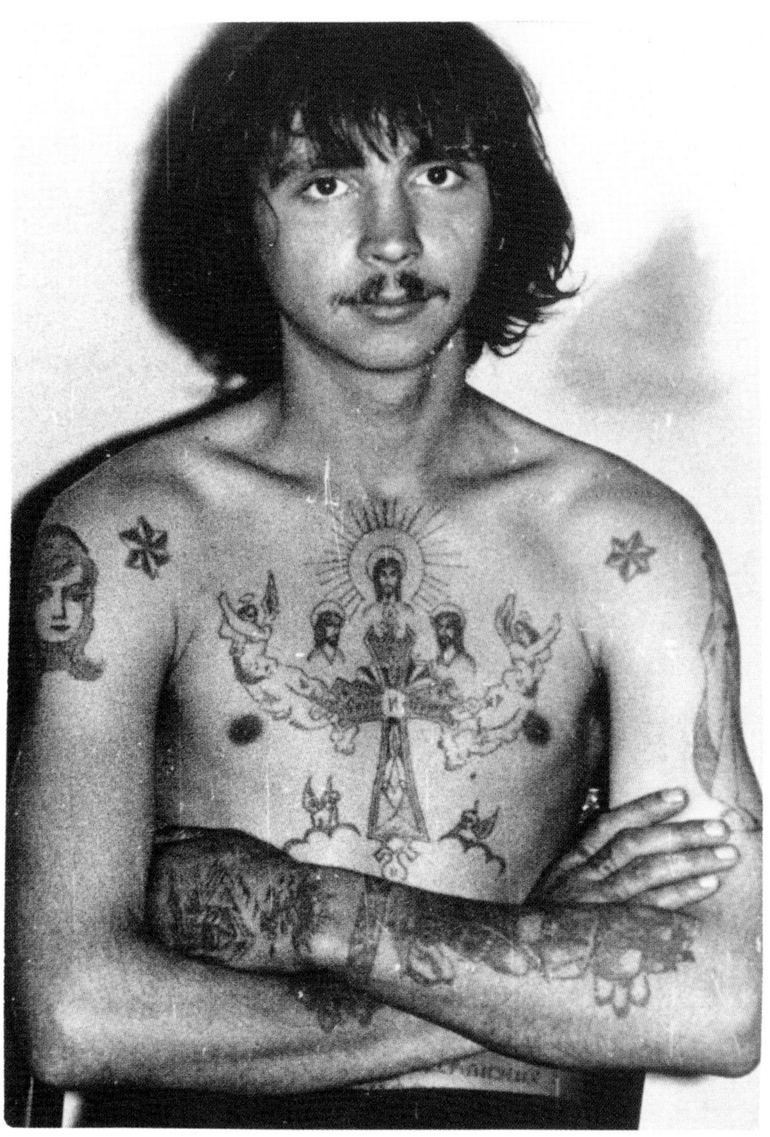

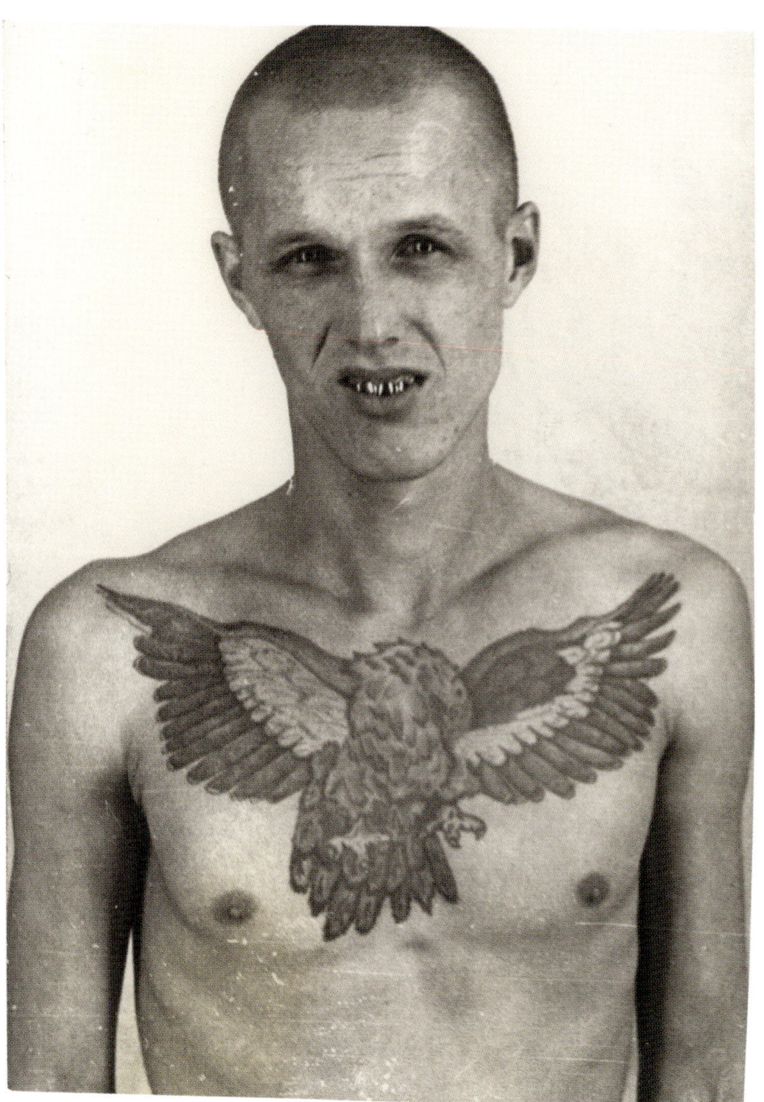

Traditionally eagles on the chest (as well as crucifixes, cats' heads and thieves' stars) denoted an authoritative criminal. Today the original meanings have been lost. Criminals might tattoo naked women, dollar bills, and so on simply as indications that the bearer belongs to the criminal class and intends to persist in a life of crime. [Arkady Bronnikov states that any tattoo of an eagle on the chest denotes that the bearer is a rapist.]

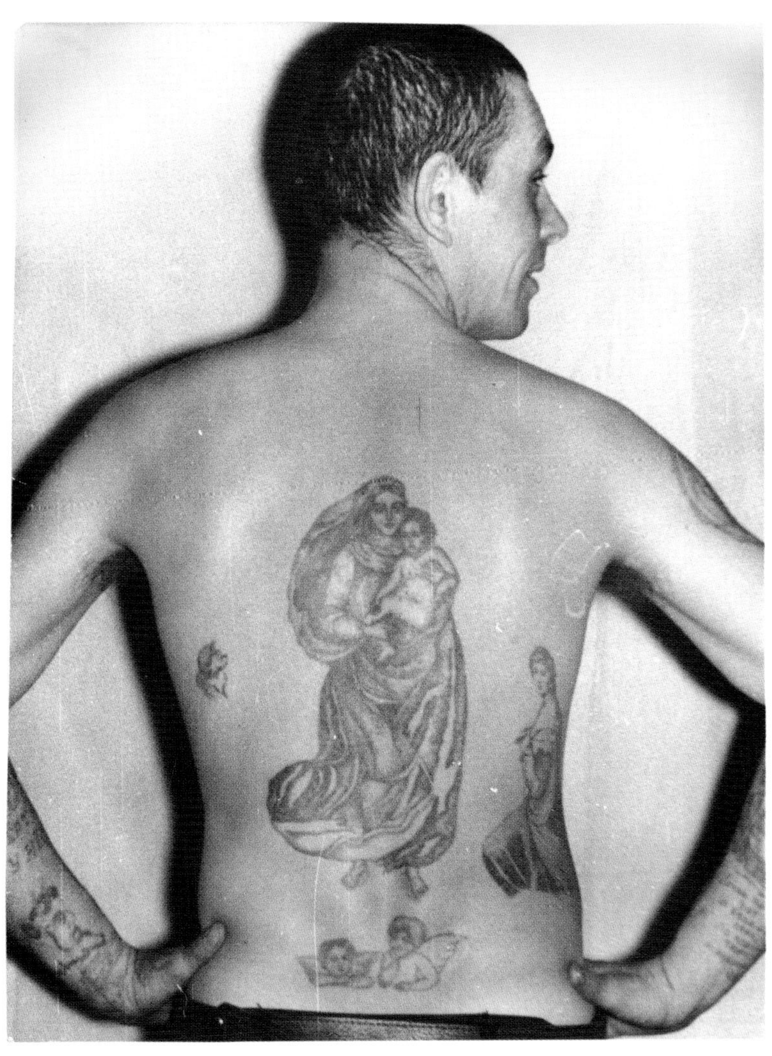

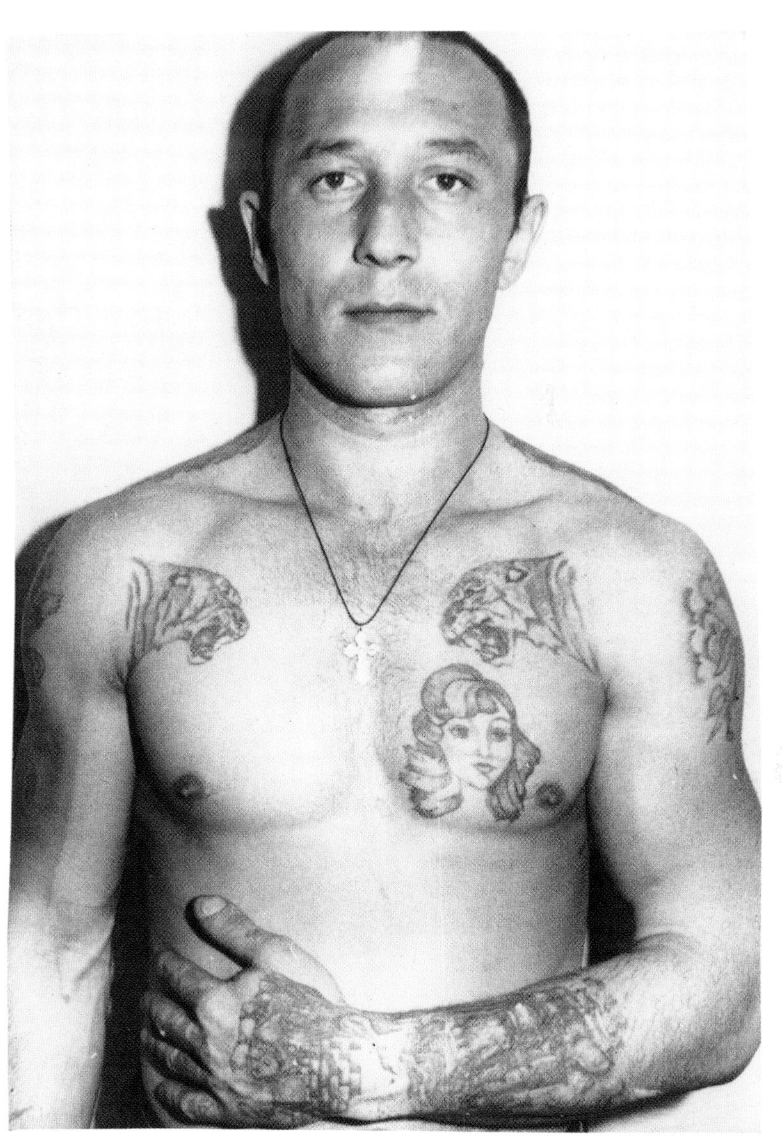

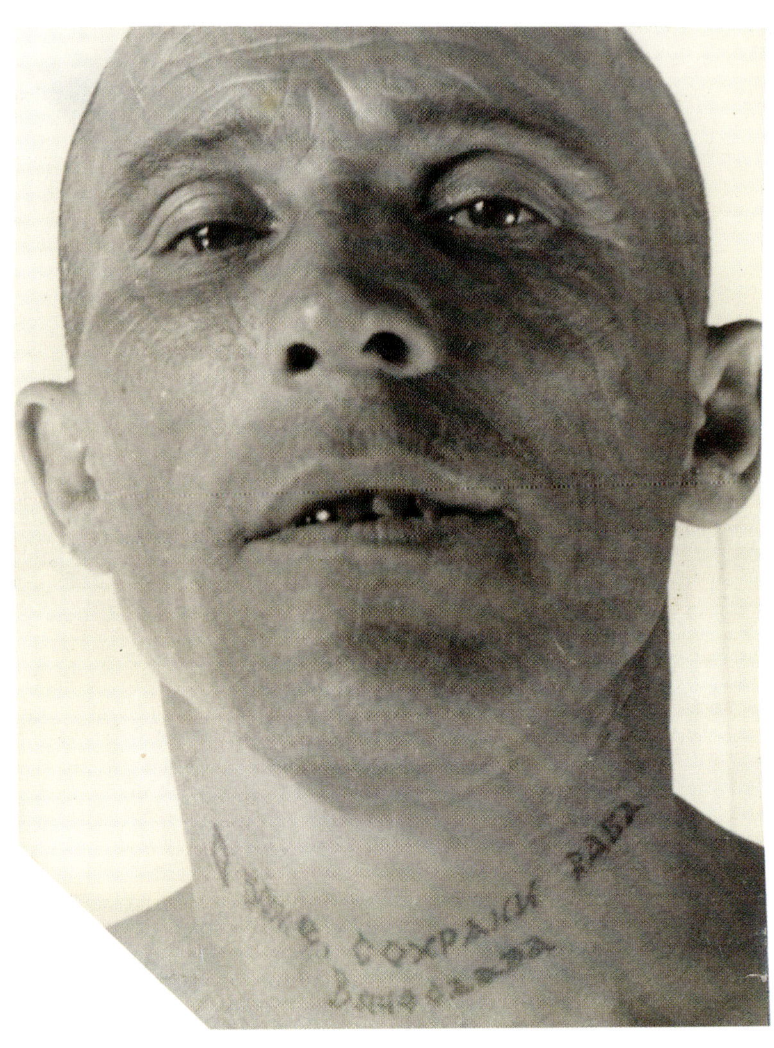

Text across the neck reads **'Lord, protect your servant Viacheslav'**.

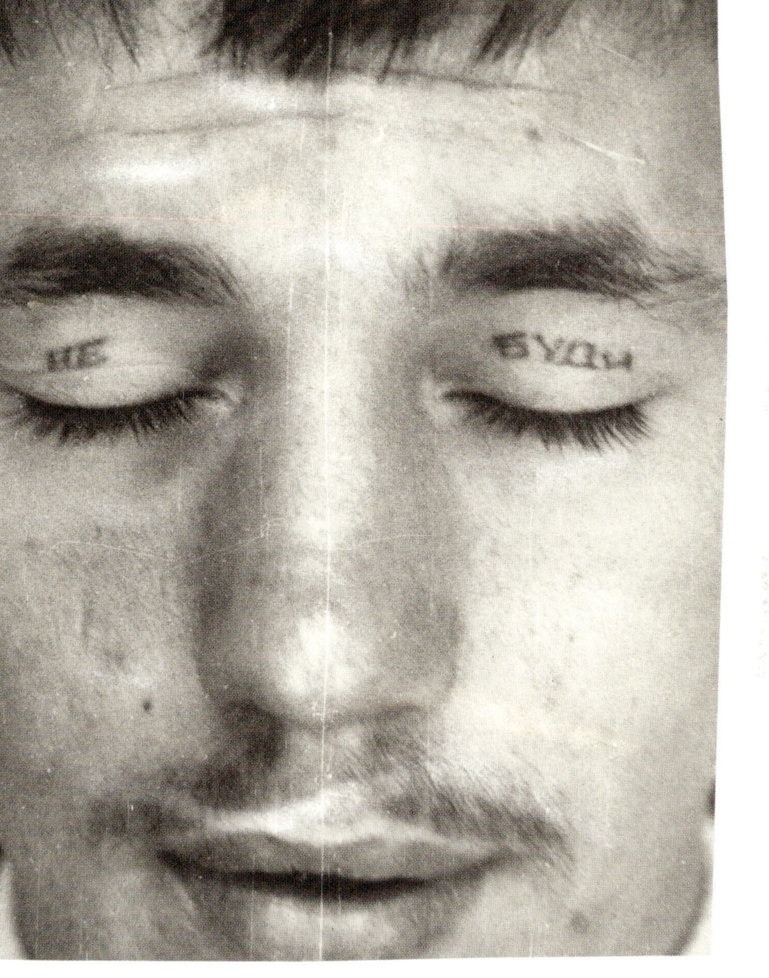

Text across the eyelids reads **'DON'T / WAKE'**.

Eye tattoos are made by inserting a metal spoon under the eyelid so that the 'needle' doesn't pierce the eye.

Text above the waist reads **'The key to a woman's heart'**, see also page 105.
English text reads **'Made in USSR'**. Latin text on the right arm reads *Memento Mori*, **'Remember that you will die'**. Latin text on the left arm reads *Dum Spiro Spero*, **'While I breathe, I hope'**.

The following statement was given by a prisoner, born in 1948, reconvicted in 1973 for robbery, sentenced to eight years in custody and serving his sentence in a special regime colony.

'I had lived in the city of Perm with my parents up until the latest arrest. I have spent ten years in penal colonies. Had my tattoos done the first time I was in prison. It was a reinforced regime colony and I truly believed it was only the police who were to blame. When I saw the tattoo of one of the inmates reading "ZLO" [meaning 'evil', 'vice'] and learnt that it was an abbreviation standing for "I'll get revenge on the gundogs", I had it tattooed on my left wrist. I also liked it because it read "evil", and you obviously don't tattoo such words for nothing. I was eighteen at the time and I wanted to show off. I thought, when I got out of prison and people saw the tattoo they would think, "This man has seen a lot of evil in his life". I wanted to create the impression that I was a man who had gone through the mill, as they say. Then I got a tattoo on the right wrist depicting a handshake with crossed daggers and the text: "A hand to the thief, a knife to the prosecutor". I did it under the influence of *blatniie* songs and *vory v zakone* [thieves-in-law] although I personally had no grudge against the prosecutor. *Vory v zakone* were the stuff of legends, they really affected people like myself, we considered them to be like heroes. This tattoo was done only for the colony. Another tattoo that I got on the left forearm showed the Olympic rings and torch. 1980 was the year of the Olympic Games in Moscow, and there was a lot of talk about them in the colony. So my tattoo was really of the moment. I got the next two tattoos under the influence of a mate who had tattooed his body all over. He drew a lot of attention, everybody was looking at him with curiosity.

I was also imagining that I'd go to the beach and everybody would be gazing at my tattoos with admiration. In our colony images of crucified Christ were in fashion. I didn't want to lag behind and did it on a thigh together with the text: "God is not some sucker – he'll cut everything down." The image on the right thigh shows a man with a lion's head and a bottle of vodka in his hand. I also have the year of my birth tattooed on the fingers of my left hand with a skull instead of the last numeral. I was young and didn't want people to see the actual year of my birth, I wanted to look older.'

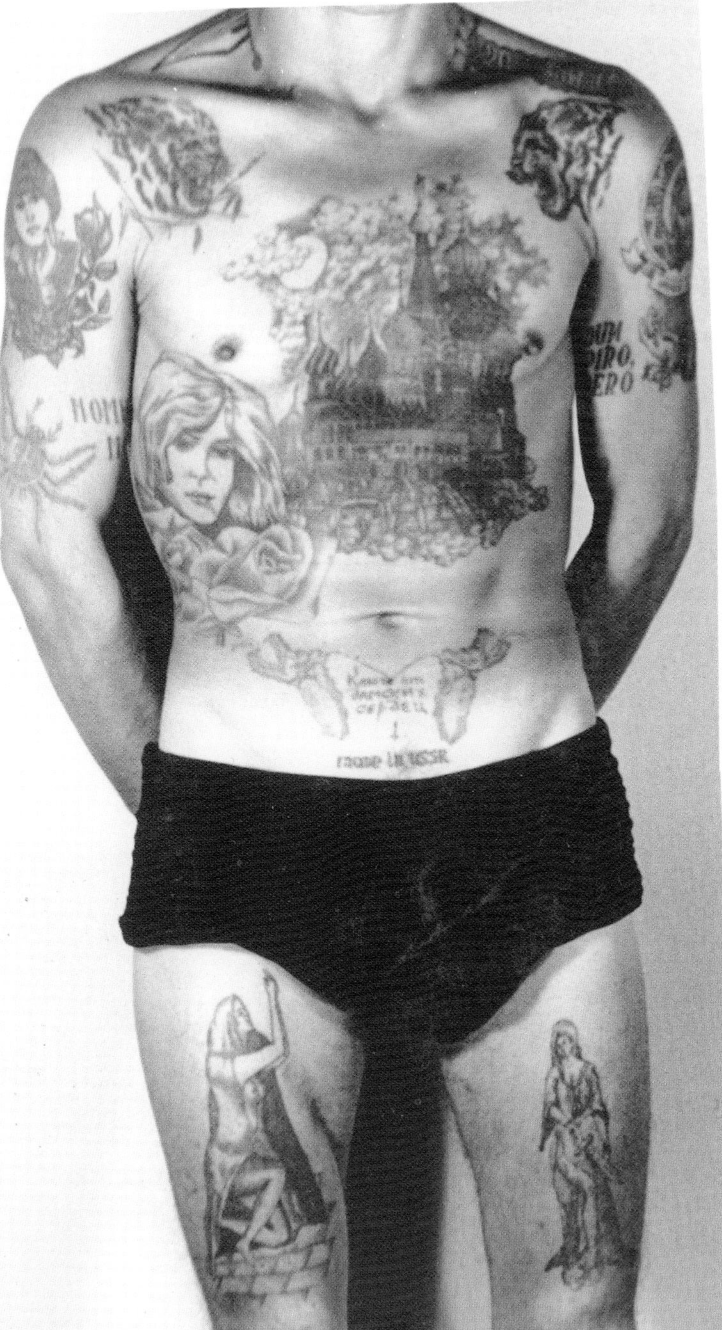

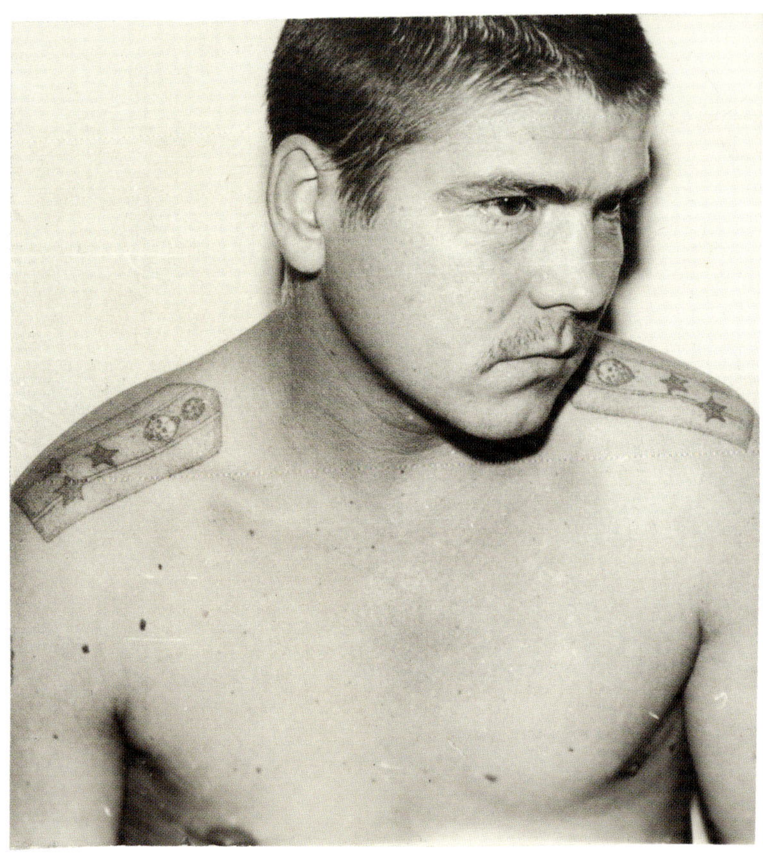

The newly imprisoned look up to tattooed inmates with respect and fear, admitting their privilege and authority. It is not only the air of romance that tattooed people with authority have, but significant material and moral privileges too, both in colonies and out of them. Those with authority or *avtoriteti* take the best bunk beds and the best food, they weasel out of hard physical work (getting *muzhiki* or the 'lowered' to do it). They take away packages and parcels and use other ways to oppress and humiliate those who are weaker and less experienced. One inmate stated: 'A tattoo for us is like a tail-coat with medals of distinction, the more tattoos we have the more respect we get. And the other way round, the person with no tattoos has no power, he is not regarded as a proper criminal, he is not respected by the gang.'

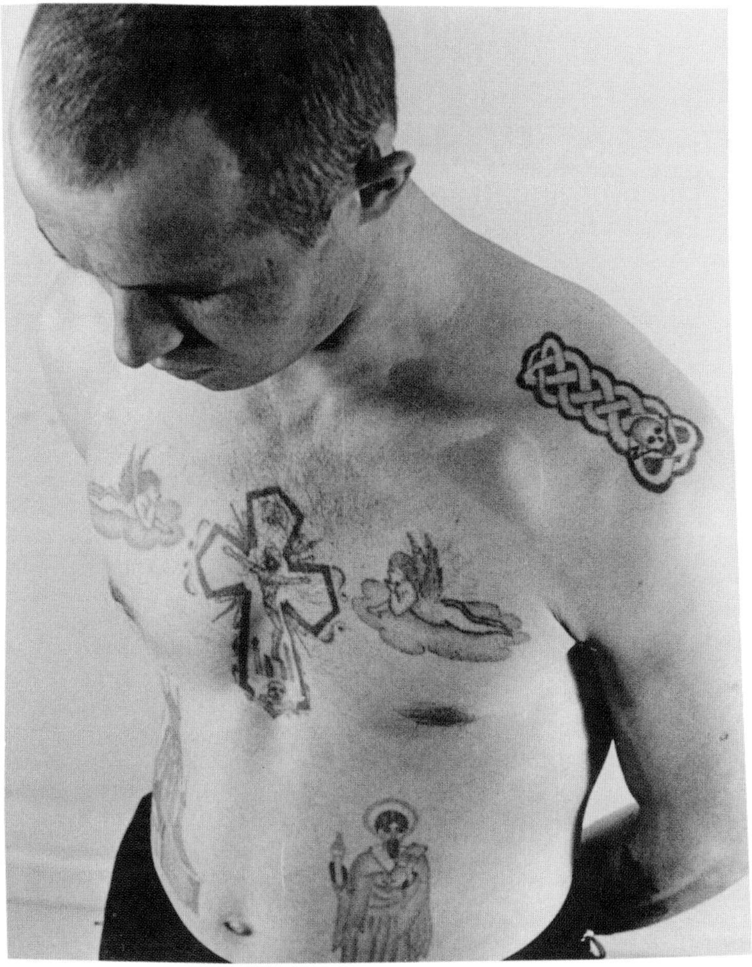

The design of epaulettes tattooed on to the shoulders is adapted either from a pre-Revolutionary uniform or an existing Soviet one; both indicate the bearer has a negative attitude towards the system. They are worn by high-ranking criminals who might also have a corresponding nickname such as 'major' or 'colonel'. Epaulettes with three little stars or skulls are deciphered as: 'I am not a slave of the camps, no one can force me to work'; 'I am captive, but I was born free'; 'I'm a colonel of the zone – I will not sully my hands with a wheelbarrow'; 'The strong win – the weak die'; 'Horses die from work'.

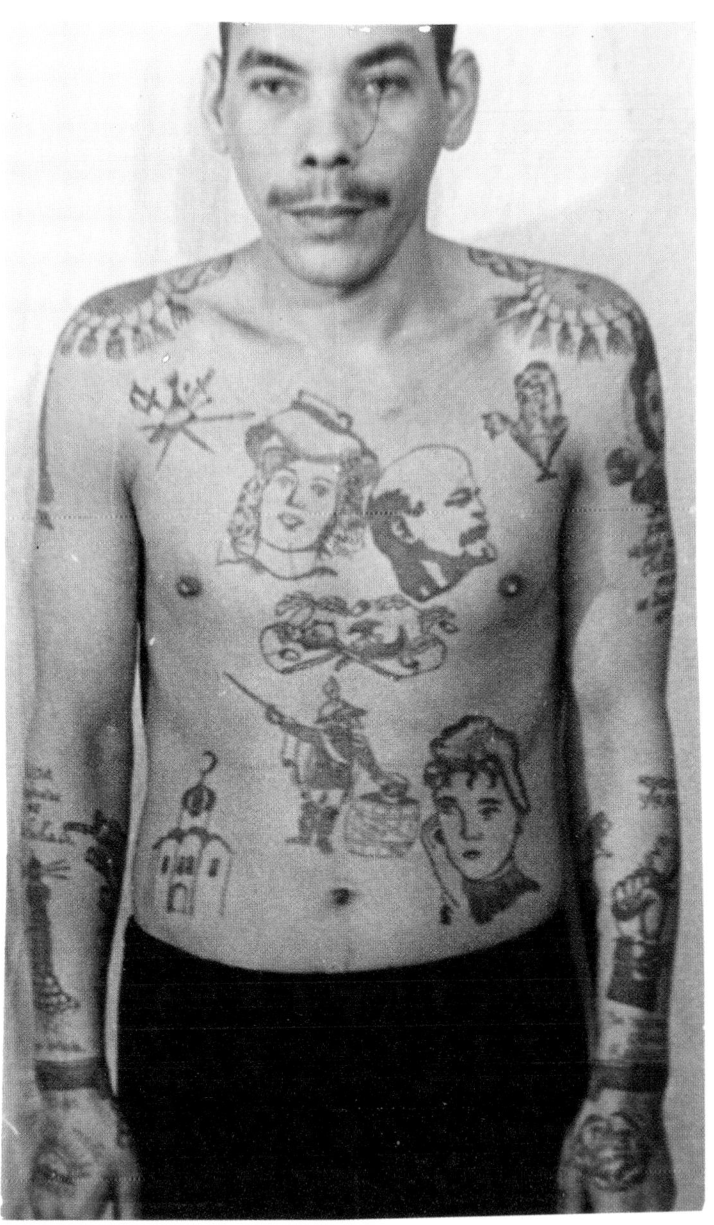

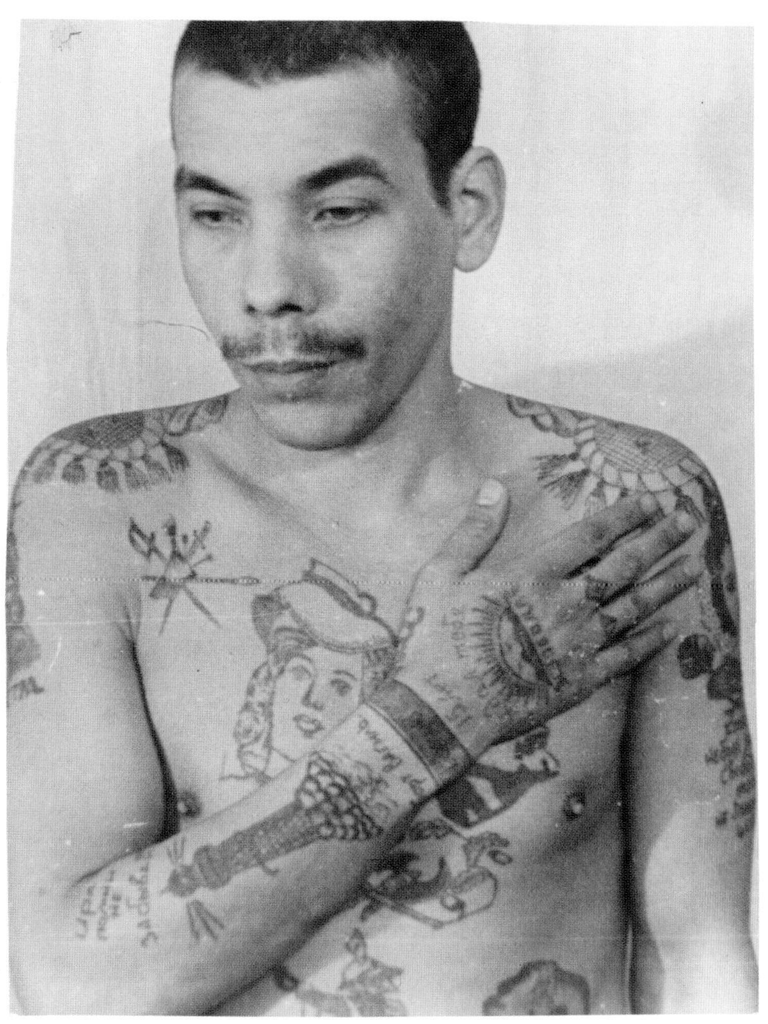

Text on the arm reads **'Remember me, don't forget me'** and **'I waited 15 years for you'**.

This man is a Muslim. On his stomach (left) is a religious building with a crescent moon; his features also indicate that he is not Russian. He is not an authoritative thief, but has tried to imitate them with his tattoos to increase his standing within the prison. The portrait of Lenin carries a dual meaning, see page 120. The lighthouse on his right arm denotes a pursuit of freedom. Each wrist manacle indicates a sentence of more than five years in prison.

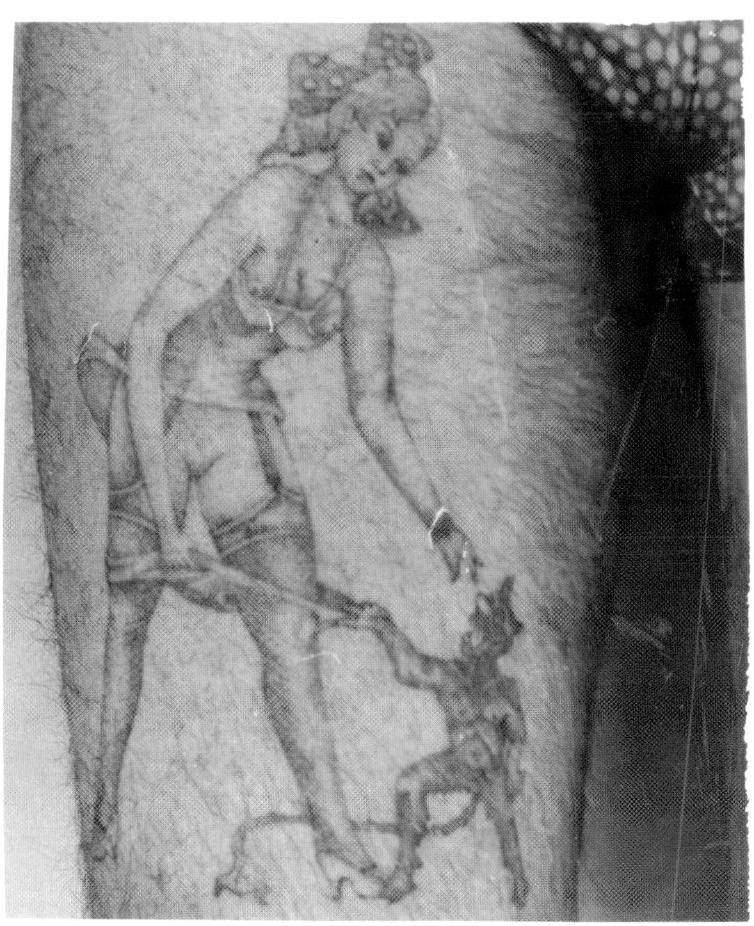

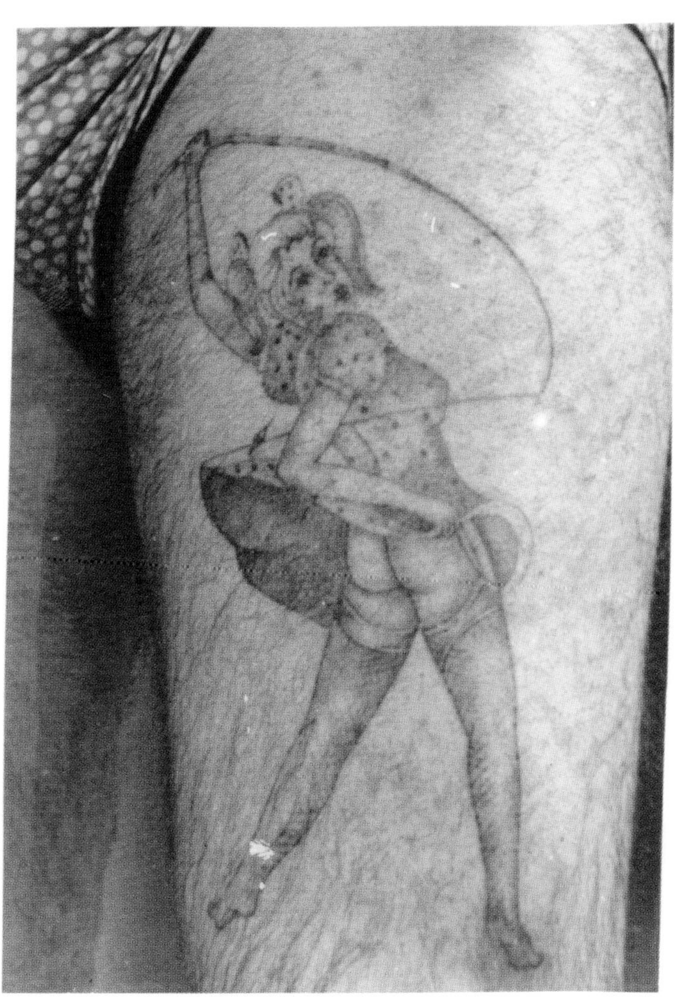

Tattoos depicting a devil lifting up a woman's dress and pulling down her underwear, or a woman hooking her dress with a fishing rod, are commonly worn by vicious hooligans and rapists, see also pages 131 and 217.

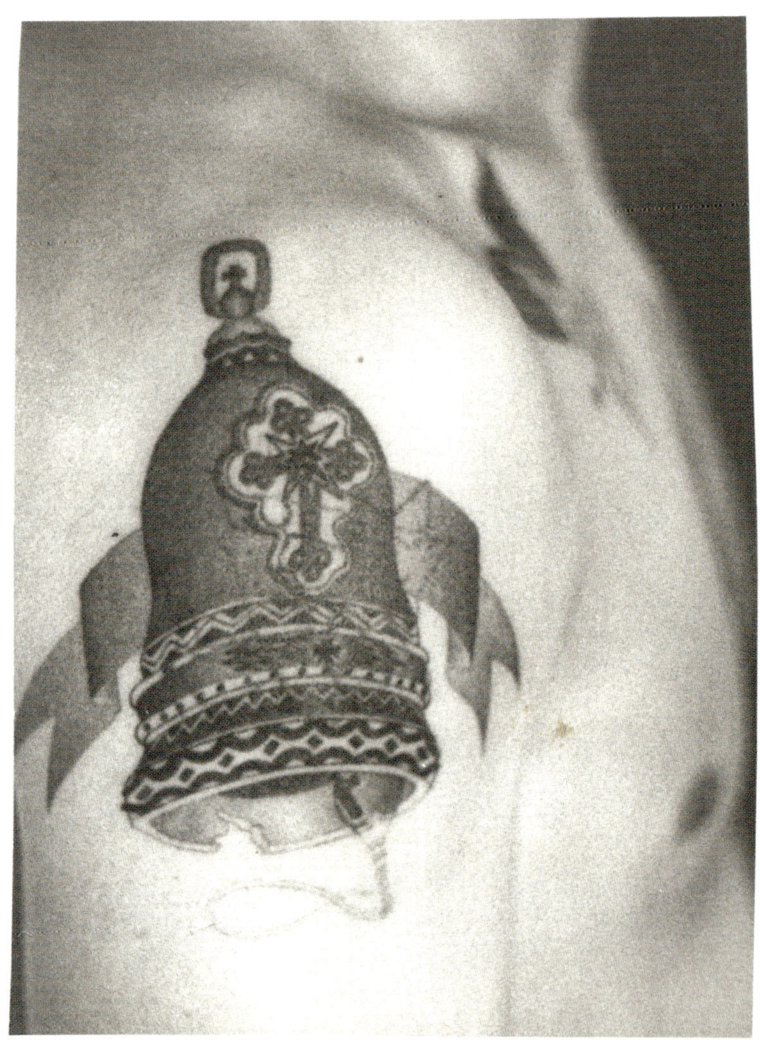

A church bell on a chain tattooed on the right shoulder is often made by pickpockets who have taken money from believers on church festival days. The number of chain rings corresponds to the number of convictions. If the rings are missing, the tattoo stands for: he served the sentence for the crime completely, 'from start to finish'.

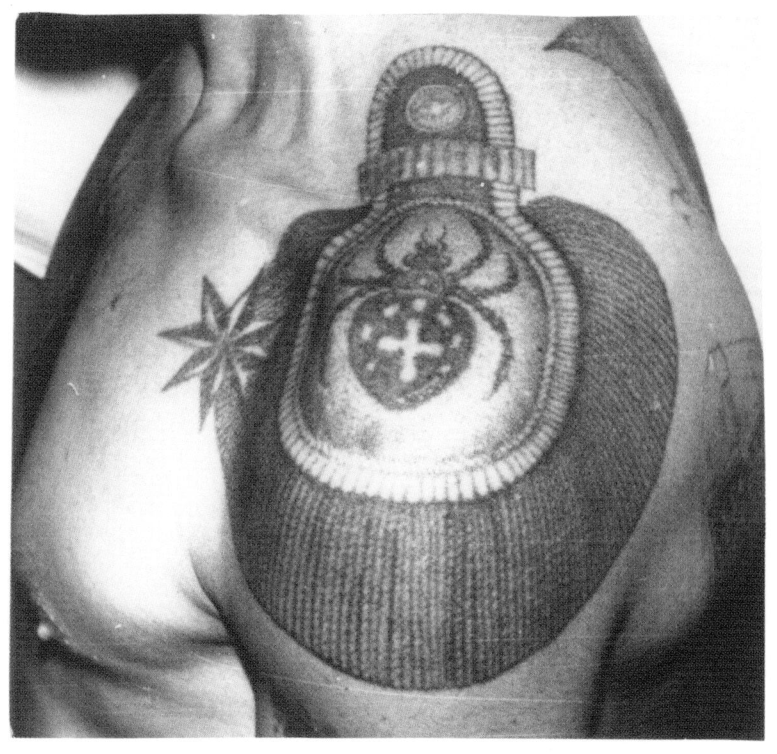

The epaulette tattoo of a criminal 'authority'.

'The young peasant who has become a prisoner sees that in this hell only the criminals live comparatively well, that they are important, that the all-powerful camp administrators fear them. The criminals always have clothes and food, and they support each other.'
Varlam Shalamov, *The Red Cross* (1958)

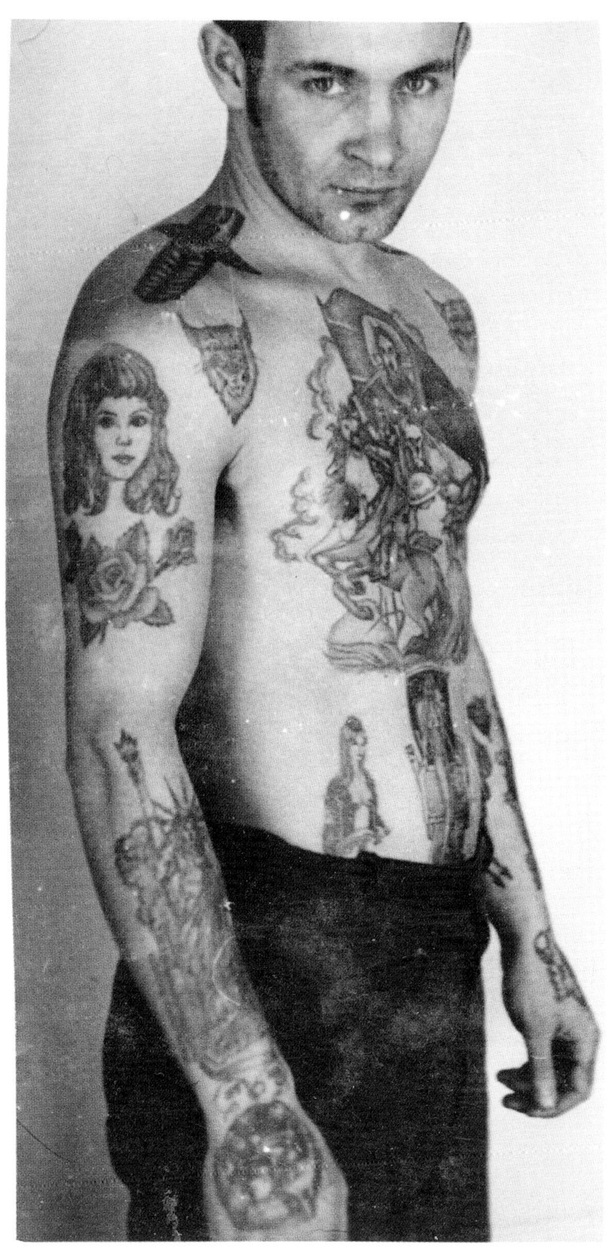

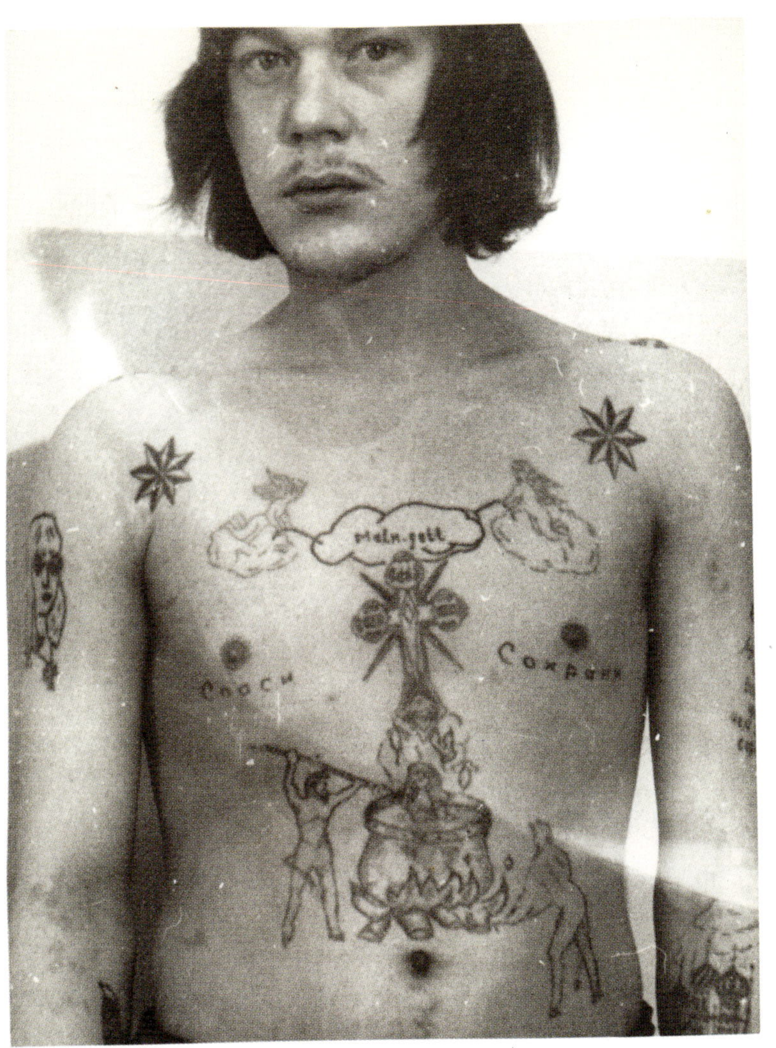

German text over the cross reads *Mein Gott*, **'My God'**. Text under the nipples reads **'Save'** and **'Protect'**.

A woman boiling in a pot (or burning at the stake, see page 113) indicates the crime was spurred on by a woman: 'Death to the bitch that betrayed me'. The number of logs on the fire denotes the custodial sentence given.

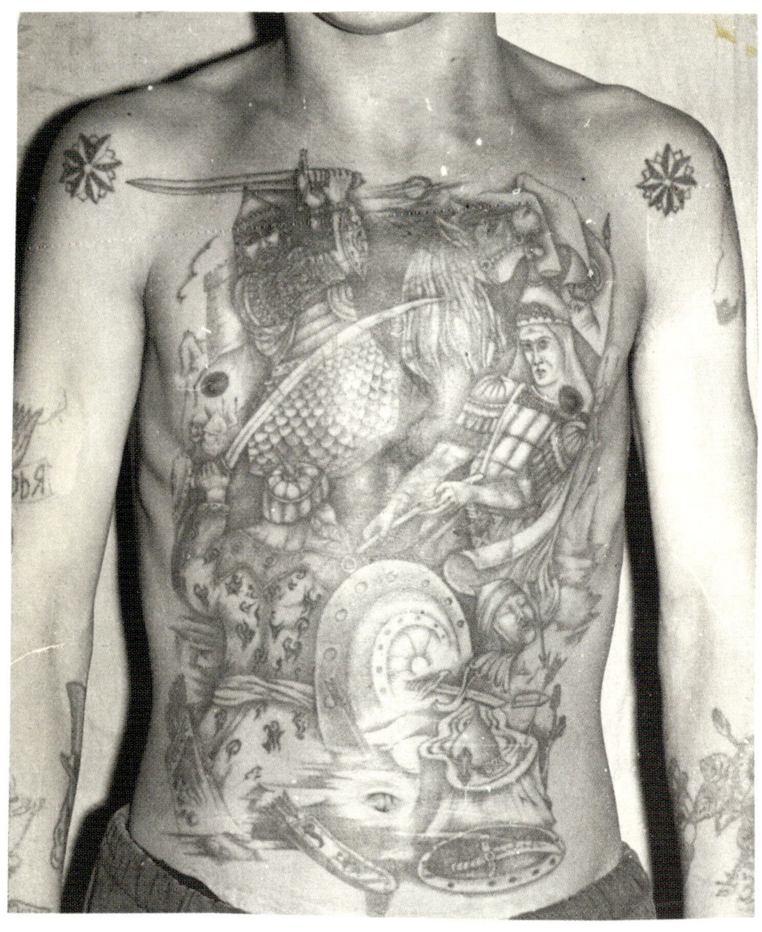

Battle scenes and knights in armour represent executioners or overseers sometimes known as 'fighters'. They act according to the commands of the *pakhan* (the head of a group of thieves, an 'authoritative thief'), beating up or raping other inmates. They may also murder other prisoners who have been found 'guilty' by the *pakhan*. Many of these tattoos are based on ancient Russian legends. In this scene medieval bogatyrs (warrior-knights) defend the steppe against Mogolian hordes. In this way the tattoo also denotes the bearer's aggression towards non-ethnic Russians.

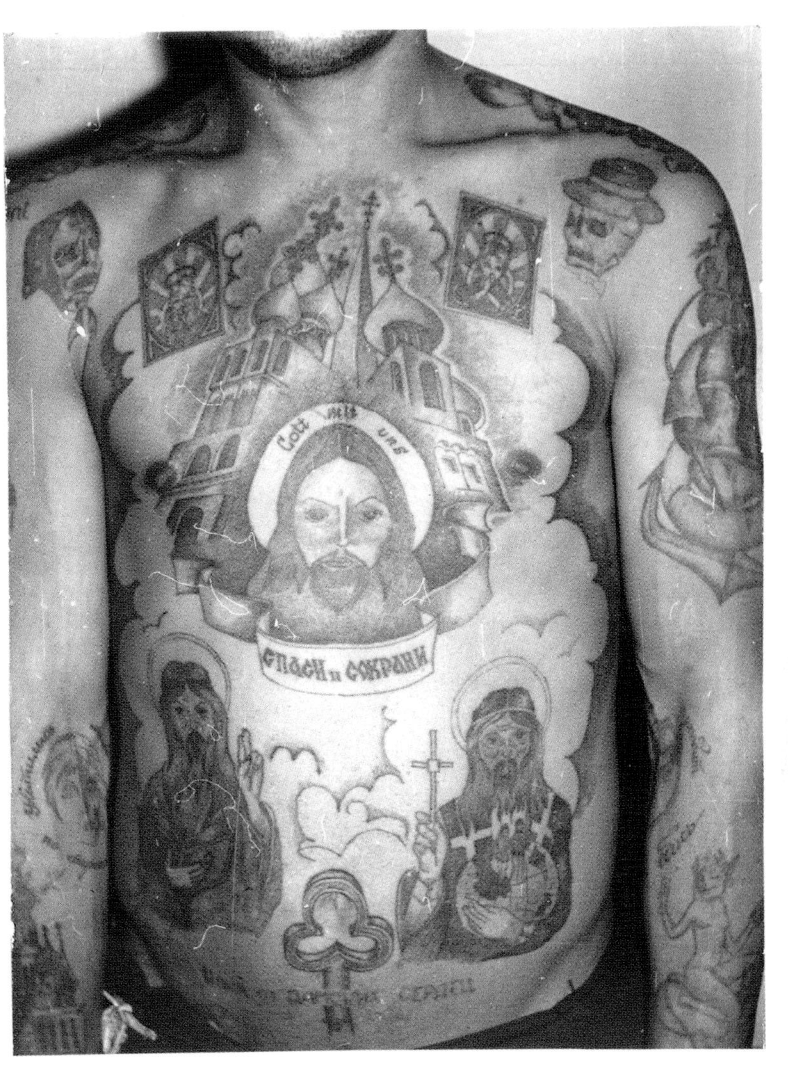

Text on the chest reads **'God be with us'** and **'Save and Protect'**. Text above the waist reads **'The key to a woman's heart'**.

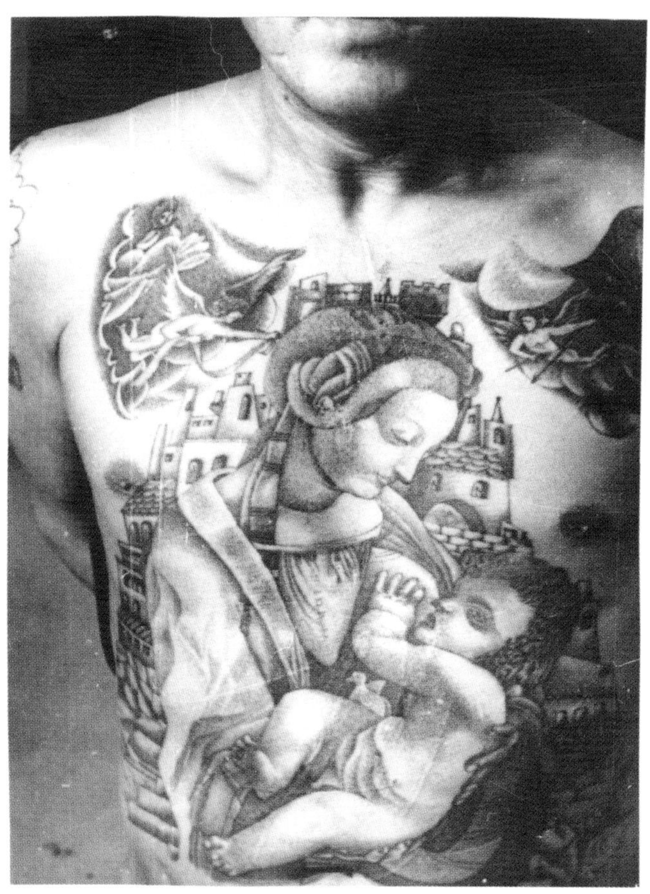

above: The Madonna and Child is a thieves' talisman, acting as a guardian from misfortune and misery. It also means that the bearer has been a thief from an early age: 'Prison is my home'; 'A child of prison'.

right: This man is an Estonian political prisoner with one star, meaning he has the status of a semi-authority. He is a nationalist who fought for sovereignty in the Baltic republics, a common practice in Latvia, Lithuania and Estonia following the collapse of the Soviet Union. He was imprisoned in the same colony as Aleksandr Solzhenitsyn and is mentioned in his writing.

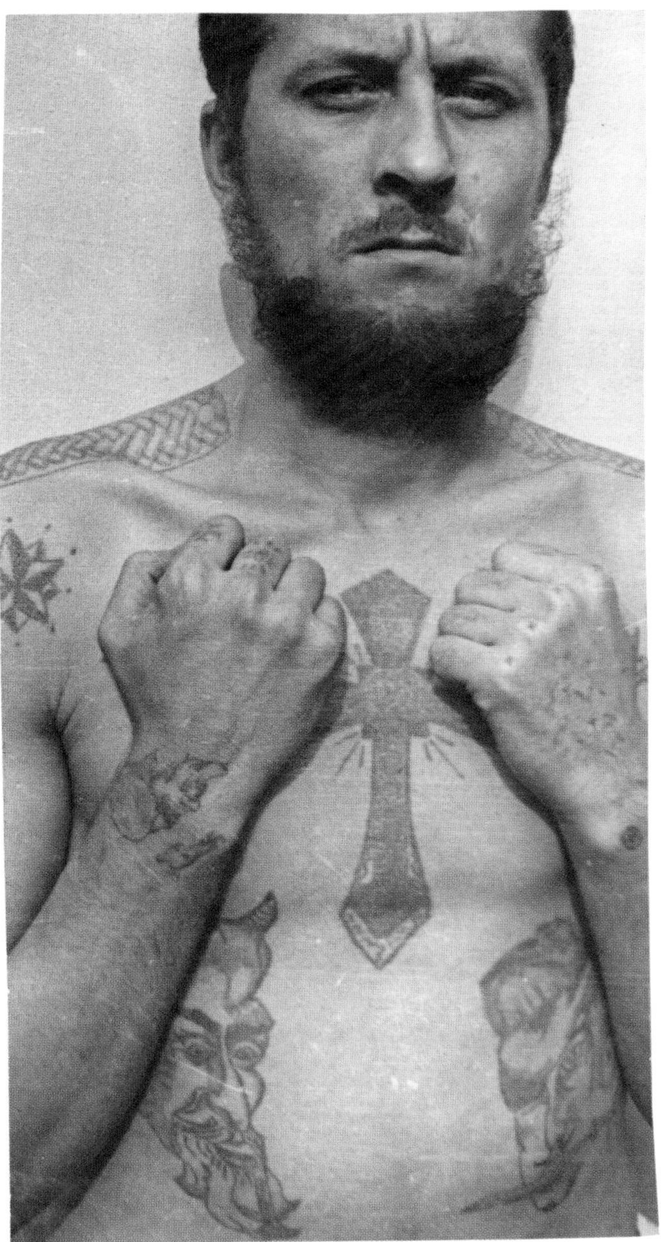

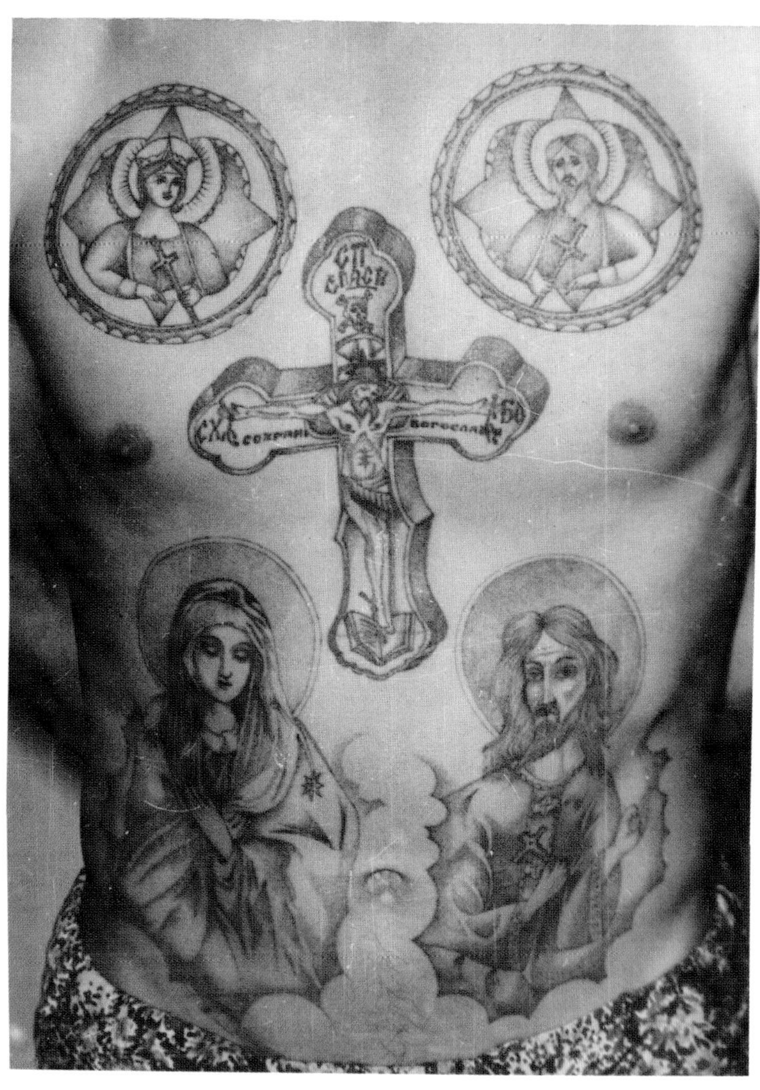

Text in the cross reads **'SA Save'**, **'PR Protect'** and **'BL Bless'**.

Thieves are the most organised, tight-knit group. All the others – hooligans, rapists – rank below them. Thieves hold the top position in penal colonies. All crosses indicate the caste of thieves.

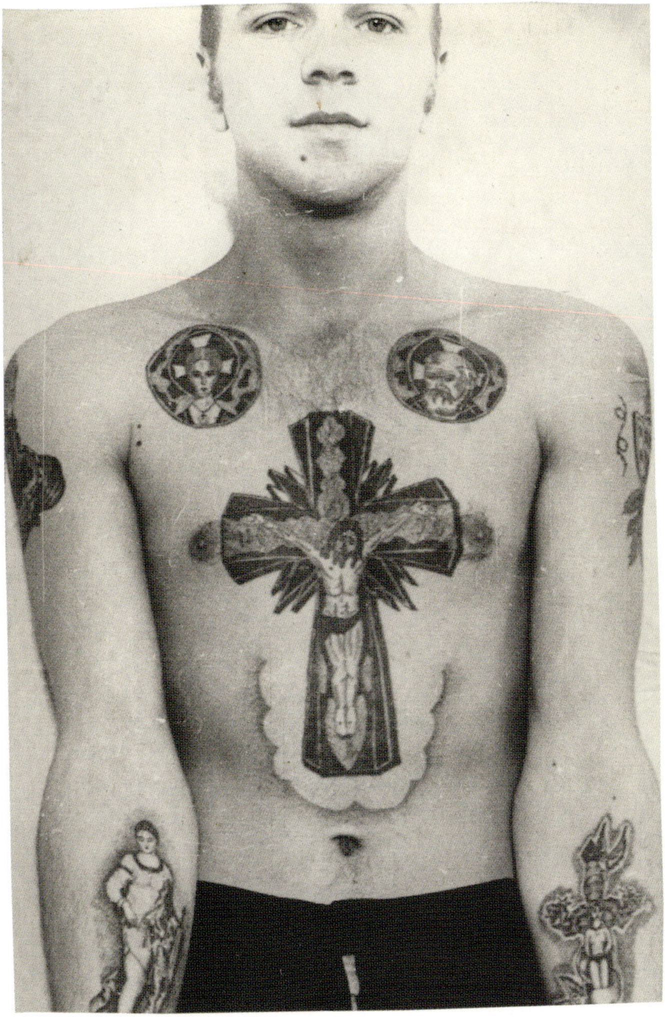

On the right forearm is a tattoo of the painting *Judith* (1504) by Giorgione, an Italian painter of the High Renaissance. 'Judith the beautiful widow' is a character from the Bible described as a rich and dangerous female. When her city is surrounded by the Assyrians she manipulates her way into the enemy's camp and seduces their leader. When they are alone, she beheads him with his own sword. In this context the tattoo means that the bearer believes he was betrayed by a woman.

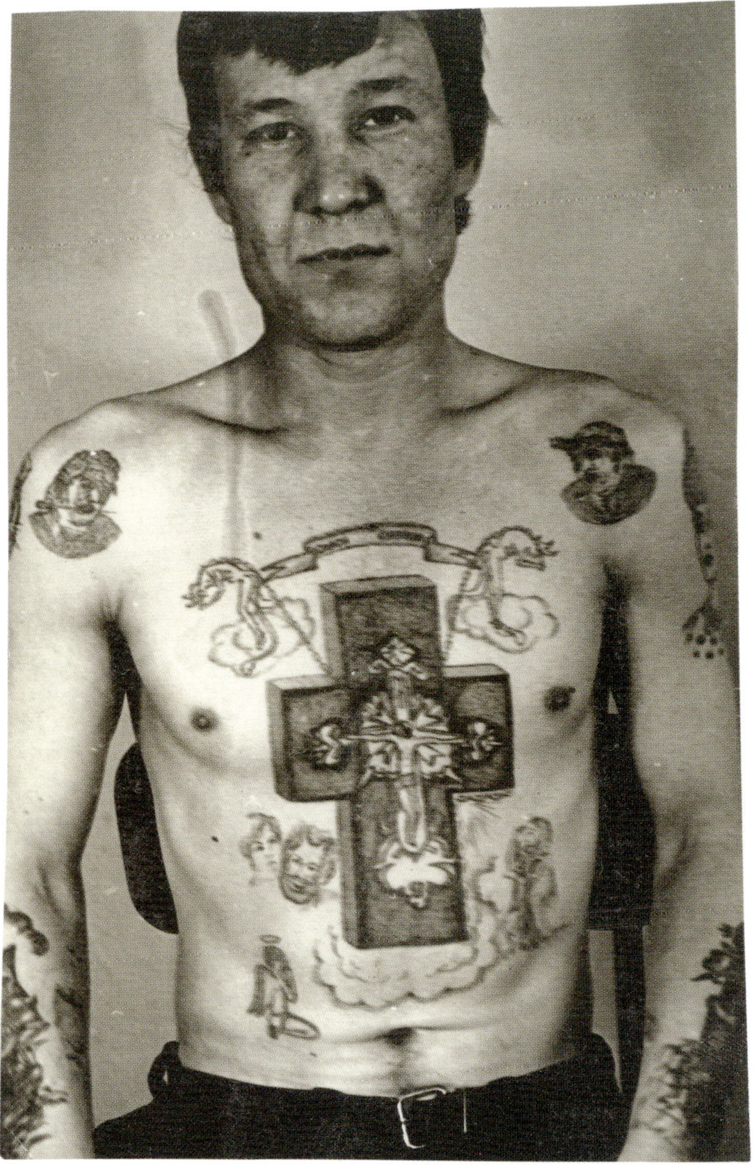

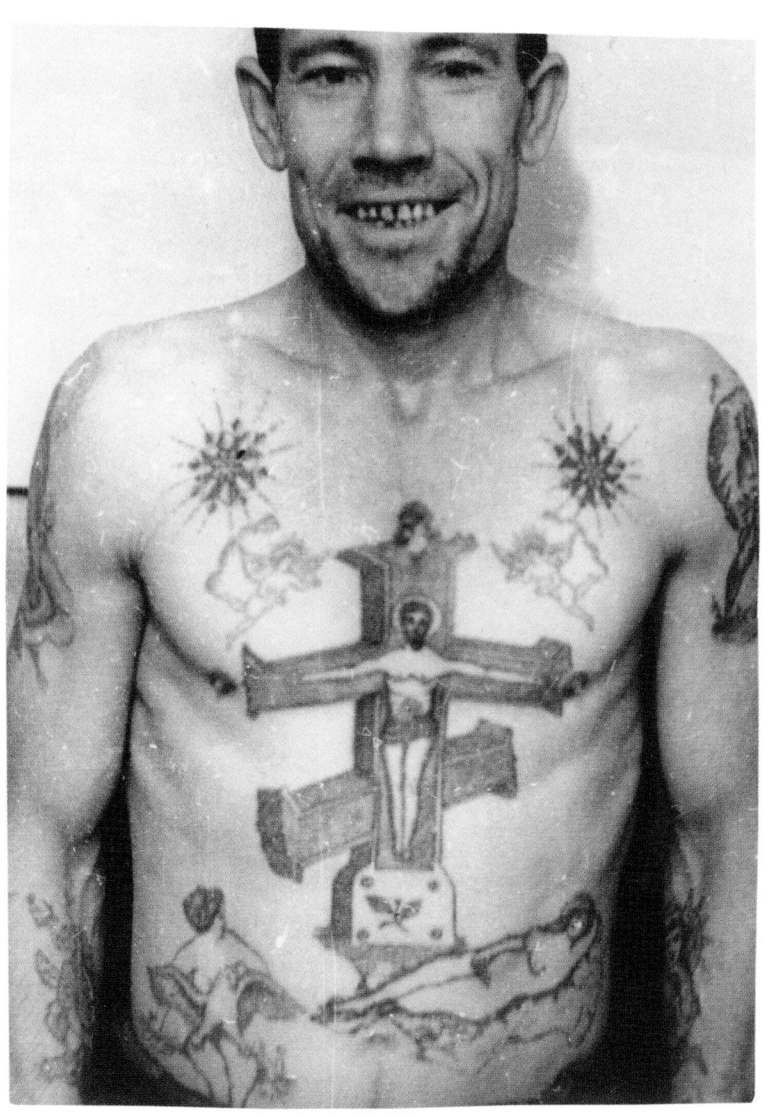

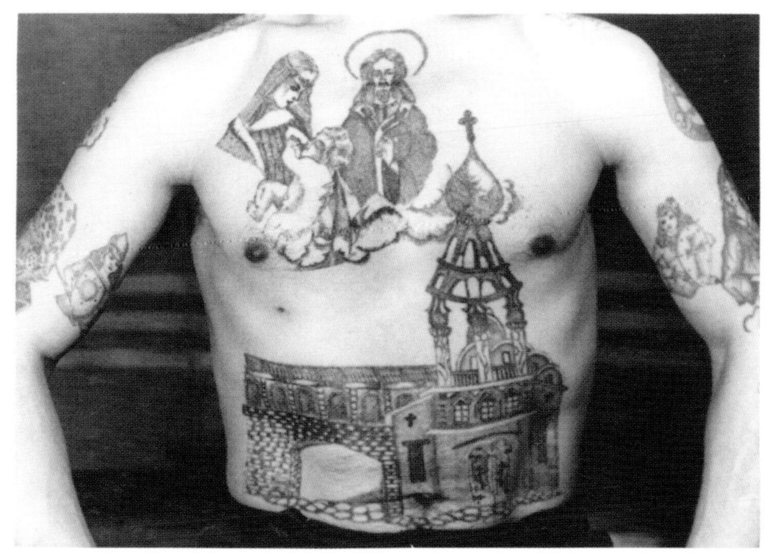

On the thigh a hooded executioner with an axe stands above a half-naked woman, a common tattoo on persons convicted of the murder of a relative (or relatives). Its secondary meaning is 'Death to traitors'.

The naked woman being burnt on a cross symbolises a conviction for the murder of a woman. The number of logs can denote the number of years of the sentence.

The naked woman entwined in a snake on the forearm refers to the ancient story of the serpent-temptress. This tattoo means that the owner was coerced into committing a crime by a woman. If this type of tattoo appears on the back it means the bearer is a *gunsel* (a passive homosexual). In that case the image is intended to give the active homosexual the illusion of copulating with a woman.

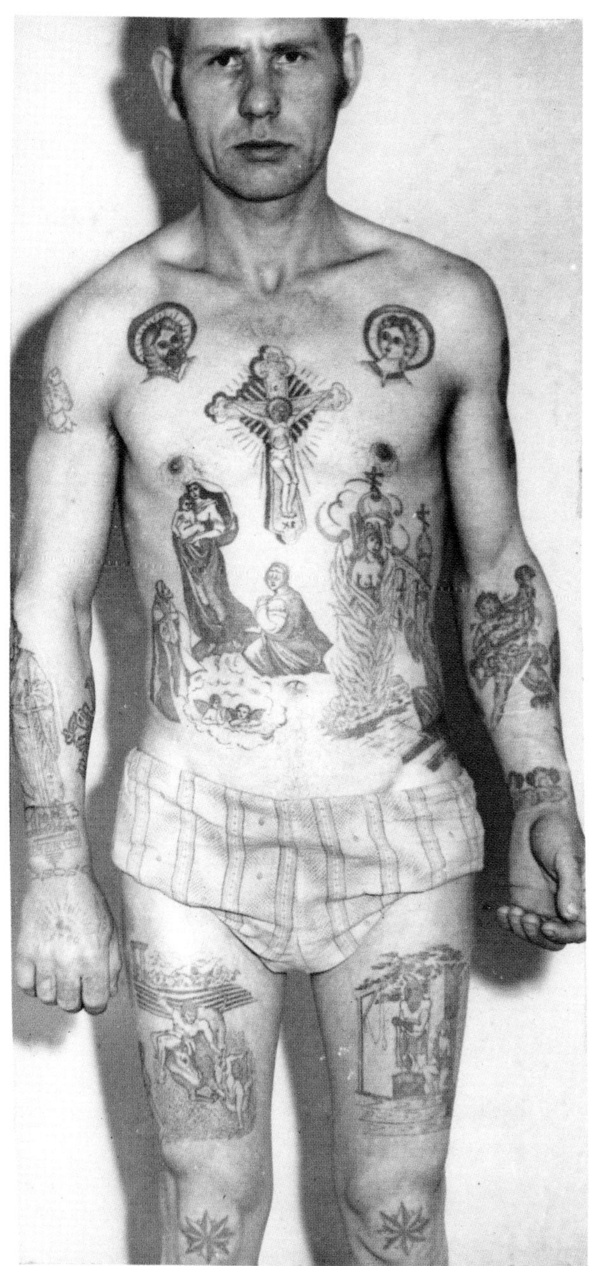

This prisoner is a victim of syphilis and has suffered severe scarring to his face, eyes and mouth. In the prisons and colonies male or female prisoners suffering from venereal diseases (such as syphilis) are known as *buketniki* (bouquet holders). They are also nicknamed after army ranks, depending on how advanced their condition is, for example, 'Kolka whored around without taking any precautions; yesterday the medic told me that he was already a "lieutenant".' (An inmate suffering from second-stage syphilis is known as a 'colonel', third-stage a 'general'). There are cases where people have contracted syphilis, AIDS and tetanus while having tattoos made under insanitary prison conditions. Tattooing is forbidden in the prisons and camps. Prosecuted and punished severely by the authorities, the practice has acquired more status as it is pushed underground.

The tigers on this inmate's shoulders are a 'grin' against the authorities, denoting someone who is aggressive towards the prison or camp regime. The figure of the writer is known as a 'scribe' and is worn by pickpockets who use sharpened objects to help them commit their thefts. Sharpened rings, coins and razors are used to slice open the bags and pockets of their victims without their knowledge. The burning candle is a traditional thieve's motif and carries the messages 'The quiet life melts like wax', or 'My destiny is the light of one candle. I live until my candle burns out'. The grille of the cell window means 'I was born in prison' and 'My destiny – the big sky in squares'. The pirate on the arm means that he is inclined to sadism, and has a negative attitude to those who embark on a path of correction. The cowboy on the other arm displays a tendency towards risk-taking and adventure.

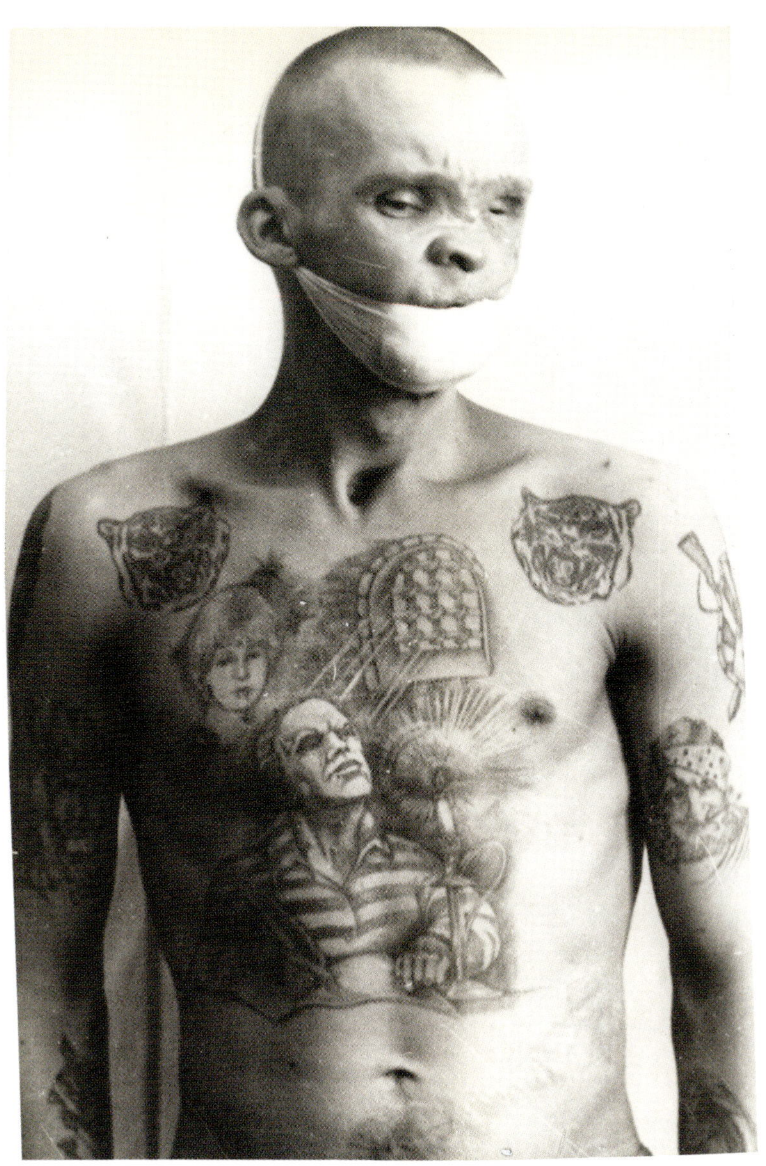

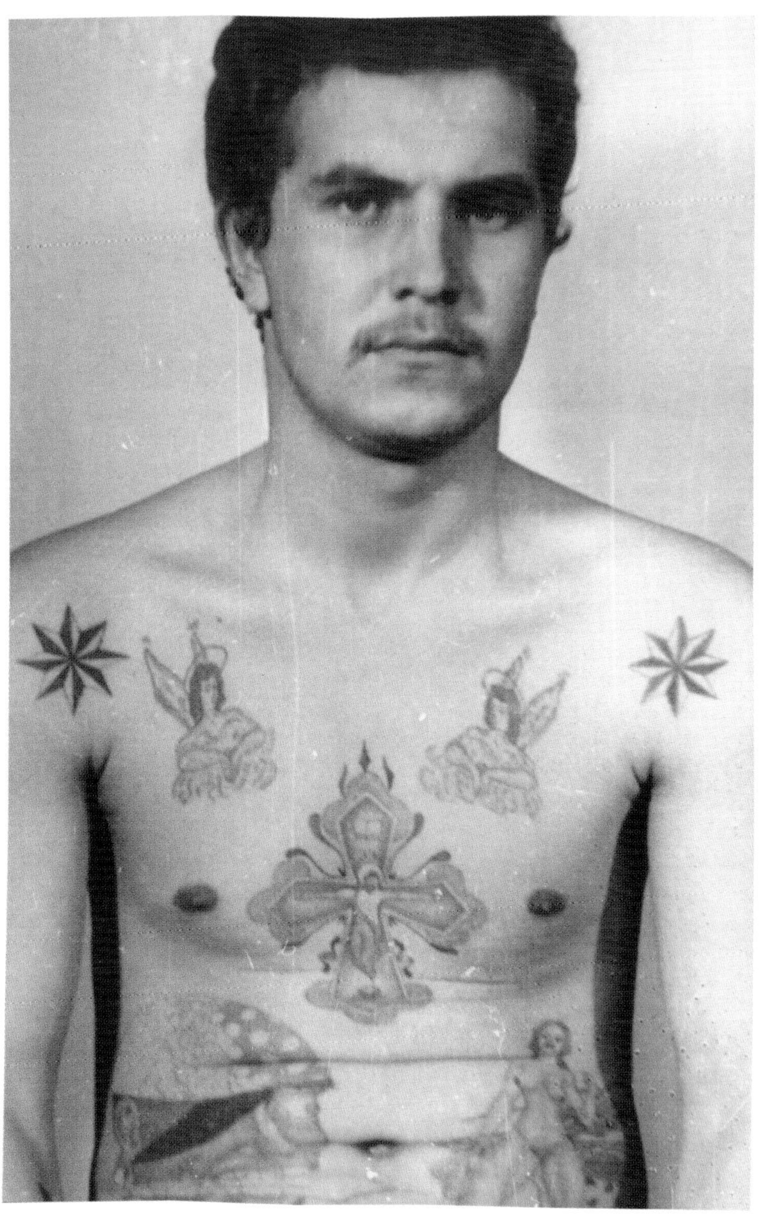

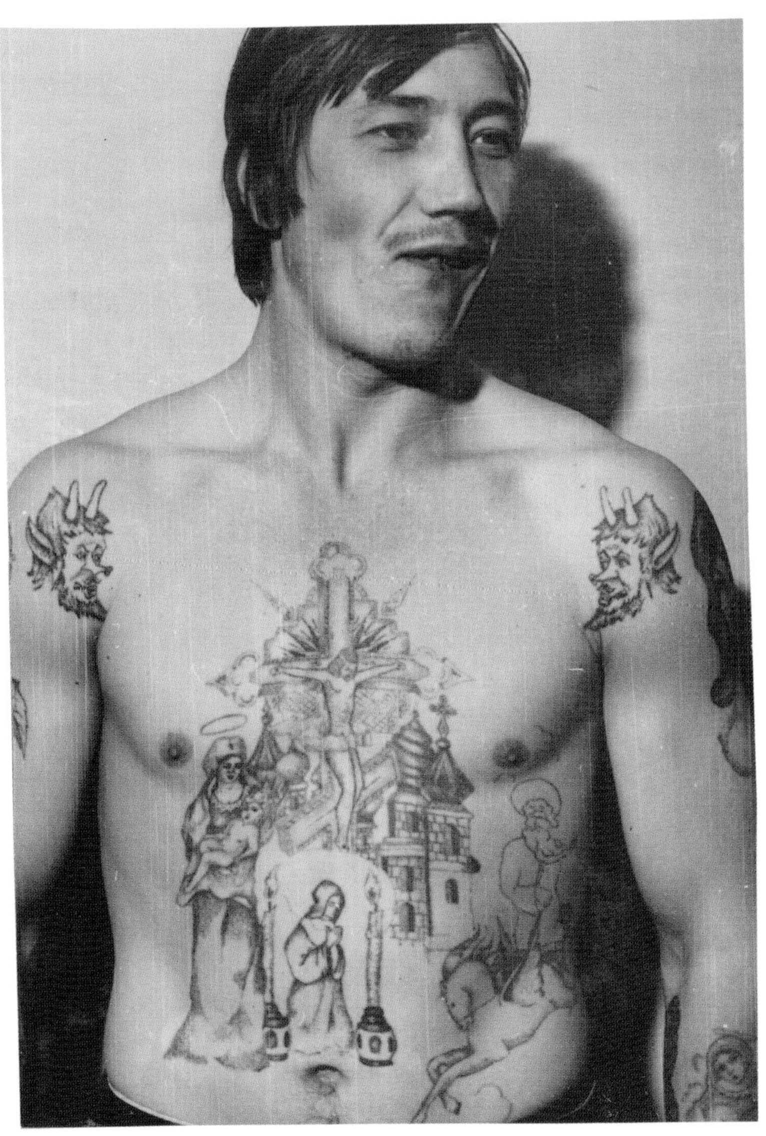

The 'devils' on the shoulders of this inmate symbolise a hatred of authority and the prison structure. This type of tattoo is known as an *oskal* (grin), a baring of teeth towards the system. They are sometimes accompanied by anti-Soviet texts.

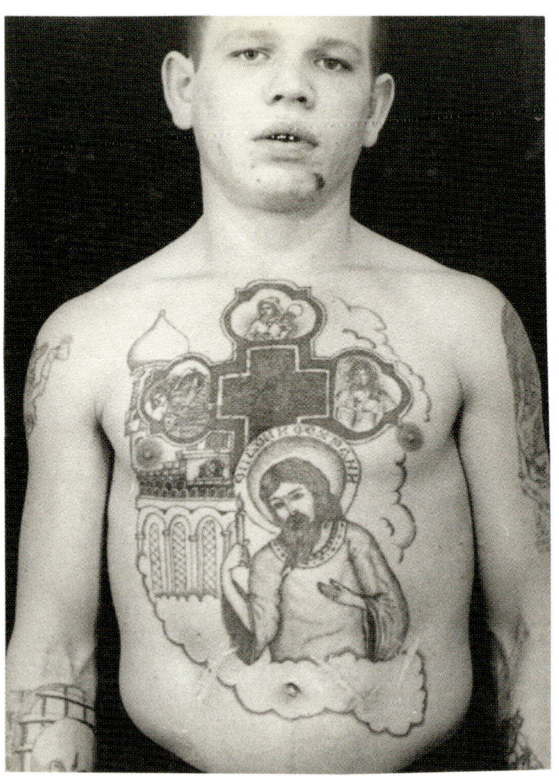

above: Text on the chest reads **'Save and Protect'**.

right: German text on the chest reads *Gott mit uns*, **'God with Us'**. German text on the wrist reads *Jeder ist seines Glückes Schmied!*, **'Everyone has his own fortune!'**

The words *Gott mit uns* served as a rallying cry of both the Russian Empire and the Third Reich; this tattoo is a stand against Soviet authority. The eight-pointed stars show that he is an 'authority' among thieves. The lighthouse on his right forearm is a symbol of longing for a new life; he is 'waiting for freedom'. The sailing ship on the left shoulder means he is willing to attempt escape, see pages 84 and 187 for additional interpretations. The woman looking into the empty treasure chest is a variation on the tattoo 'I had everything, but now it's lost'. The pipe-smoking skeleton is a version of the tattoo *Memento Mori* ('Remember that you will die'). The manacles on the wrists denote sentences of at least five years each; if the manacles are broken it means that the prisoner escaped.

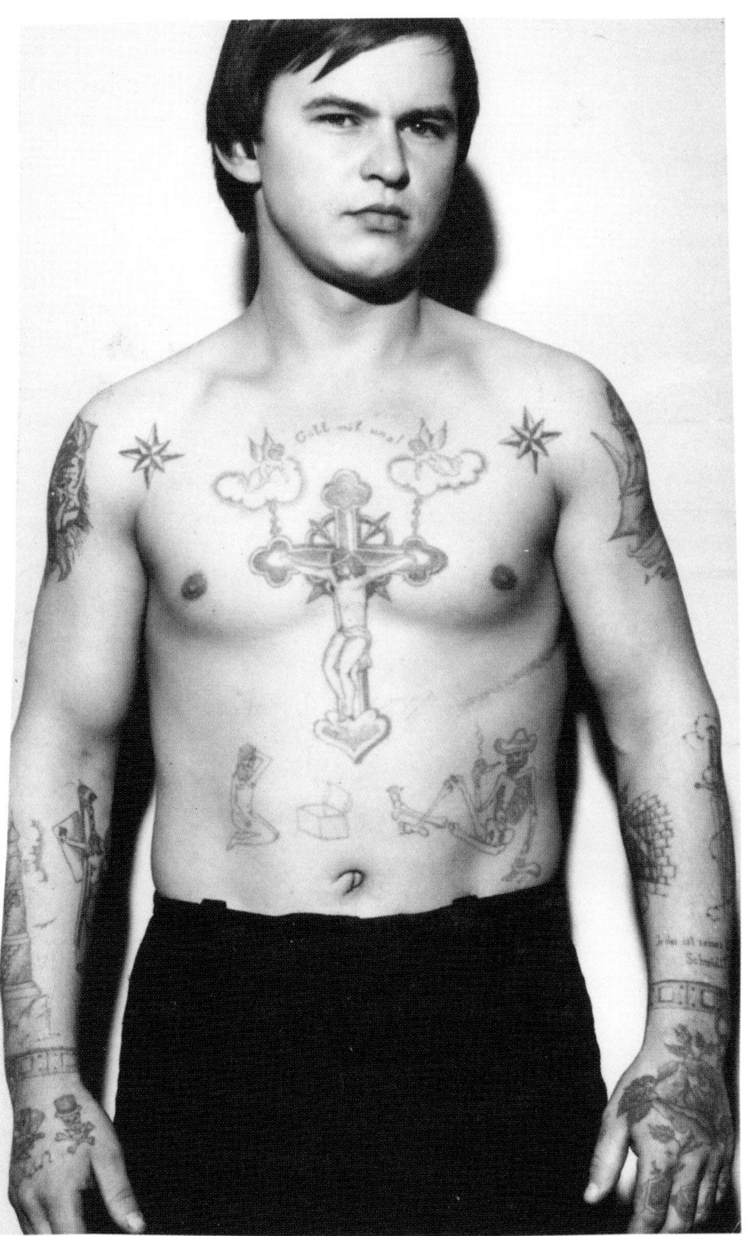

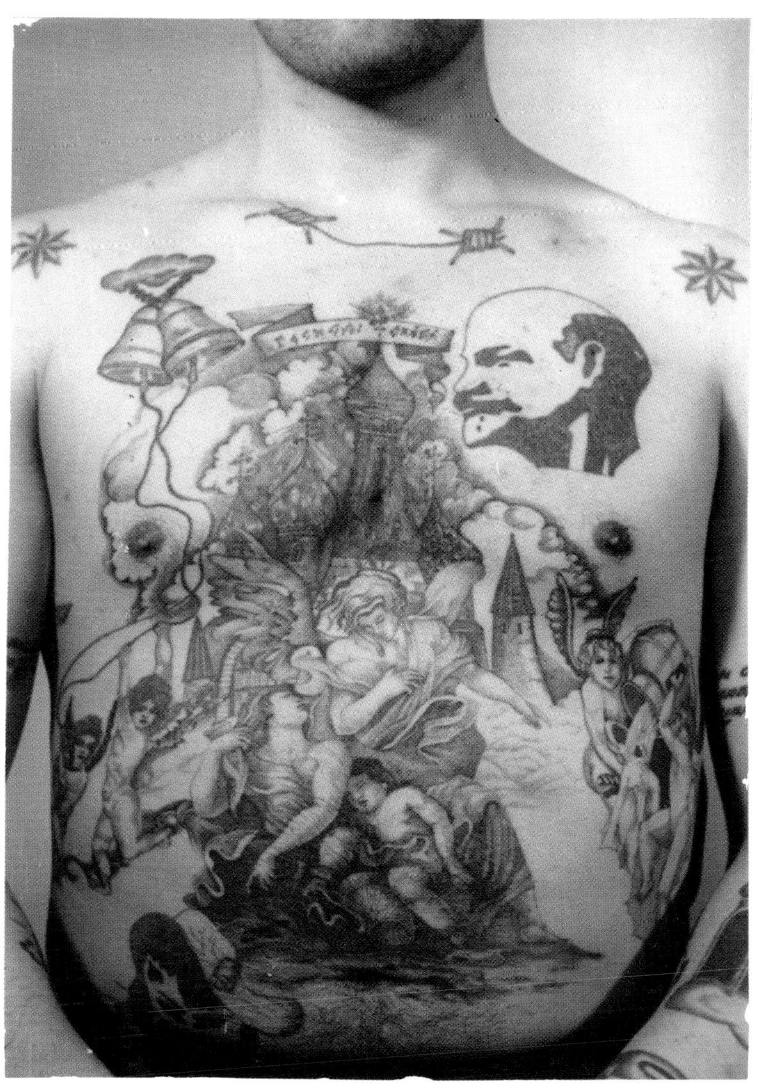

Text on the chest reads **'God save me'**.

Lenin is held by many criminals to be the chief *pakhan* (boss) of the Communist Party. The letters *BOP*, which are sometimes tattooed under his image, carry a double meaning. The acronym stands for 'Leader of the October Revolution' but also spells the Russian word *VOR* (thief).

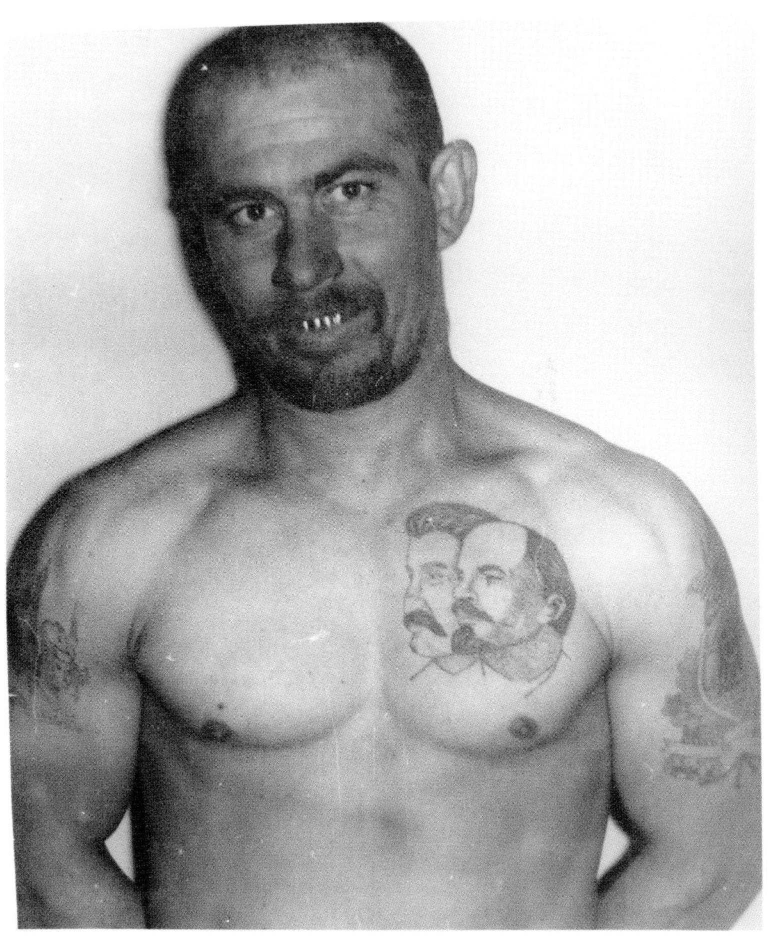

Often tattoos with portraits of Lenin and Stalin are intended to show patriotic feelings. However, some prisoners had portraits of Lenin and Stalin tattooed on their chest for 'protection', as it was commonly believed that the guards were forbidden to shoot at an image of their great leaders.

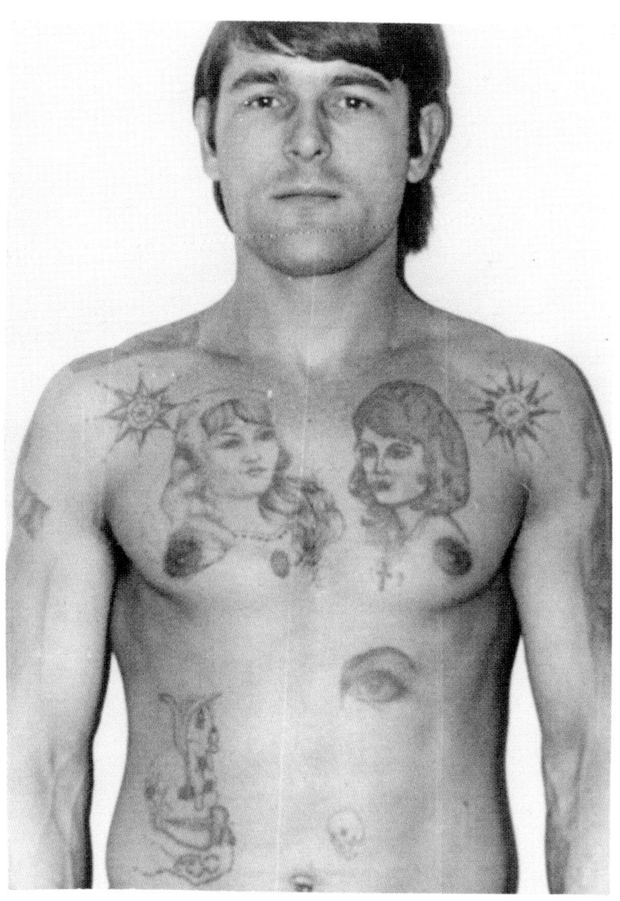

Eight-pointed stars are the emblem of an 'authoritative' thief, one who is loyal to the thieves' traditions (often these are supplemented by epaulettes on the shoulders also denoting rank, see page 95). There are many variations of 'thieves' stars'. Lines placed between the points of the star mean that the bearer has been enlisted into the forces but deserted to follow a criminal life; known as 'gunners', their tattoo literally means 'I despise the army'. The face of a woman who is wearing a necklace conveys 'I turned seventeen in the zone'.

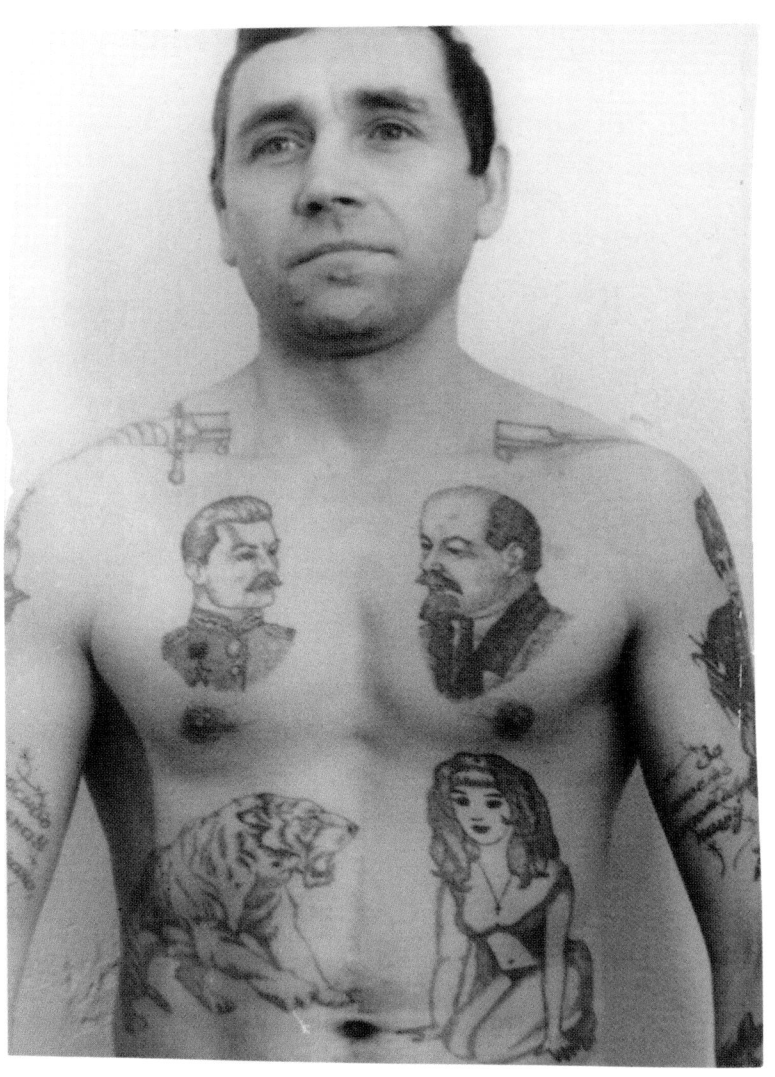

Text on the arm reads **'Thank you Dear Motherland for my ruined youth'**.

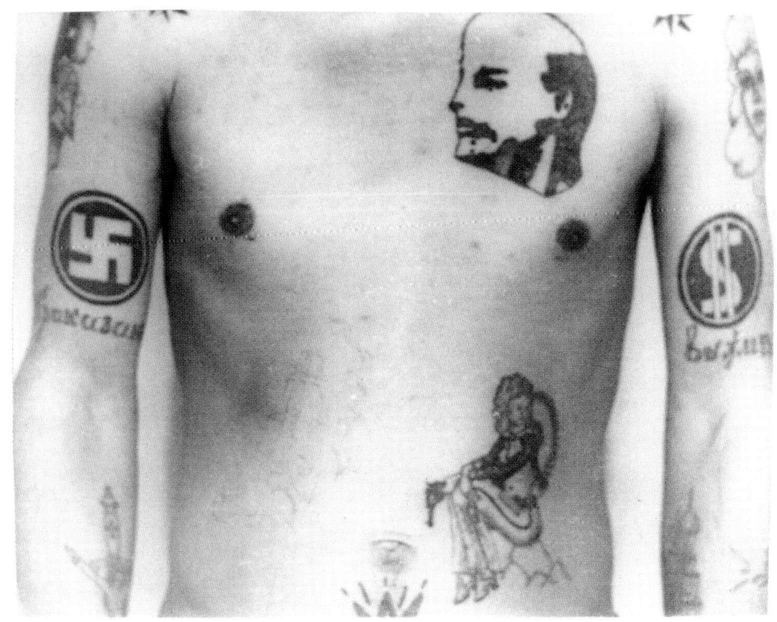

above: Text under the swastika reads **'Punished'**, text under the dollar sign reads **'Survived'**.

The swastika and Nazi symbols may mean that the owner has fascist sympathies, though they are more usually made as a protest and display of aggression towards the prison or camp administration. During the Soviet period the authorities often removed these tattoos by force either surgically or by using an etching method. Portraits of Lenin or Stalin were left untouched. The girl with a gun means 'I'm a bandit'. This tattoo demonstrates hostility towards the authorities and shows that the bearer is capable of cruel and aggressive behaviour.

right: Text across the chest reads **'He who is not with me is against me'**.

A tattoo of a mermaid can indicate a sentence for rape of a minor, or child molestation. In prison jargon the nickname for a person who commits this type of crime is *amurik* meaning 'cupid', *lohmatii* 'shaggy', or a *universal* 'all rounder'. They are 'lowered' in status by being forcibly sodomised by other prisoners, sometimes in groups.

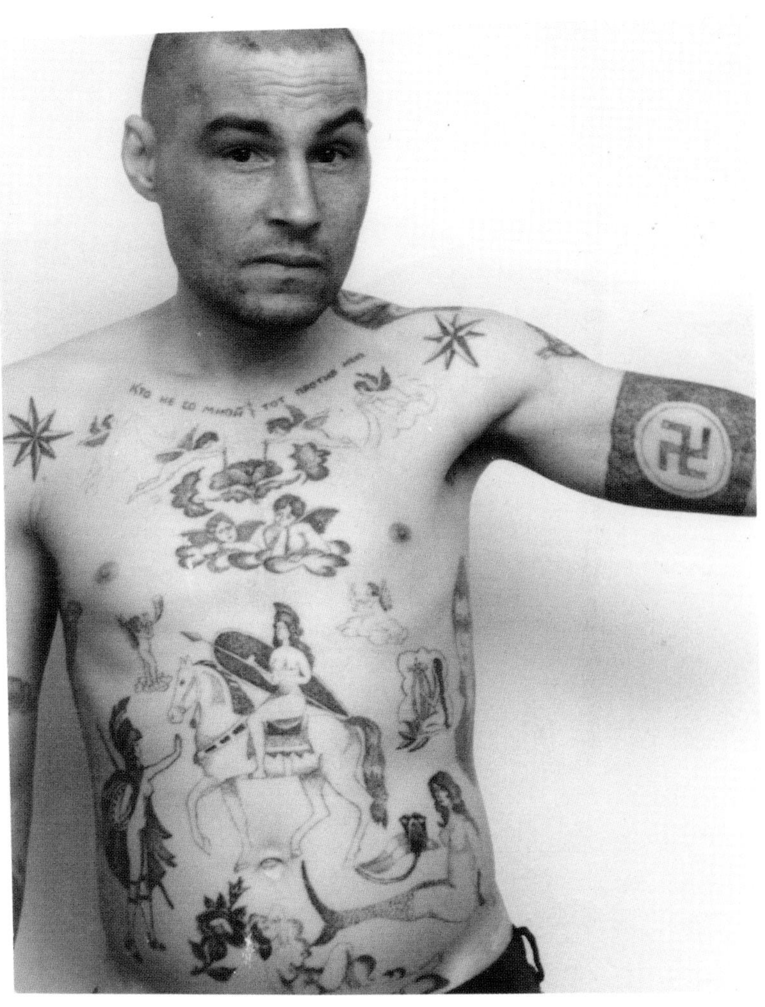

'There were regular criminals among the children in the camp and they exercised control over all the others. They forced the younger inmates to perform "services" for them. Those who refused were beaten. The older boys often mishandled the younger ones and sexually assaulted them. The "tutors" – that is the guardians – wandered about the place in a drunken state instead of trying to put a stop to the abuses of the thugs. On the contrary, the thugs were appointed as brigade leaders and told to push the others to fulfil their work quotas.'
Inmate, Oryol City Children's Camp, 1980.
Avraham Shifrin, *Prisons and Concentration Camps of the Soviet Union* (1980)

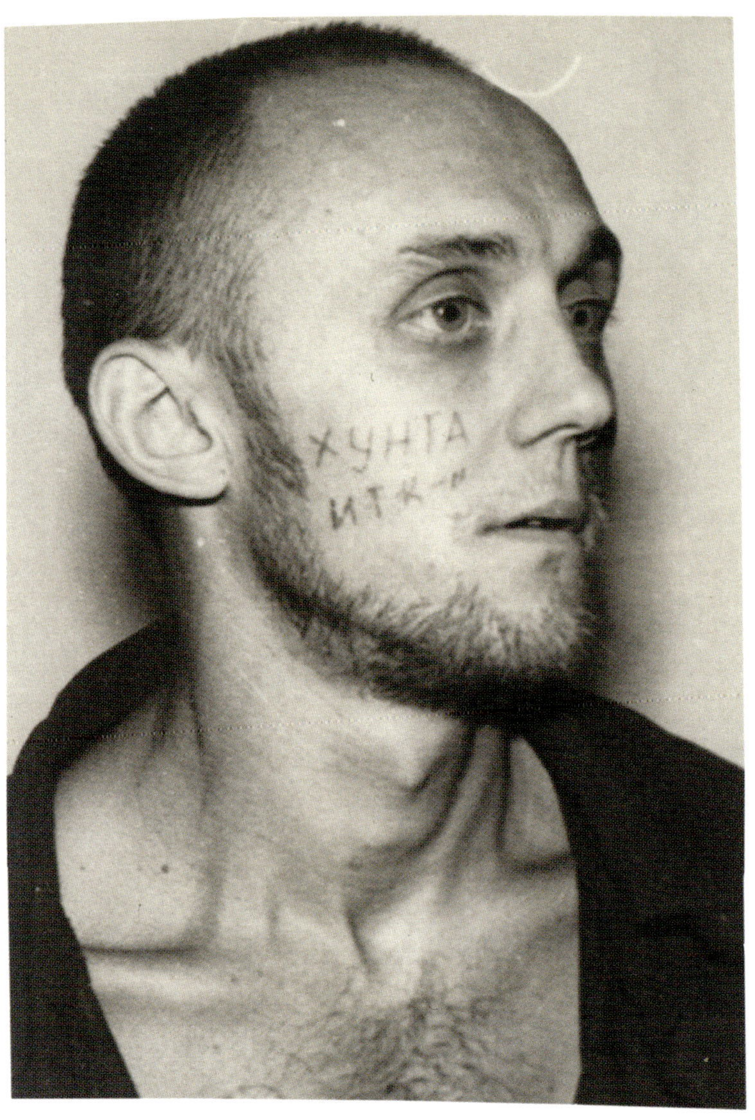

ХУНГА
ИТКИ

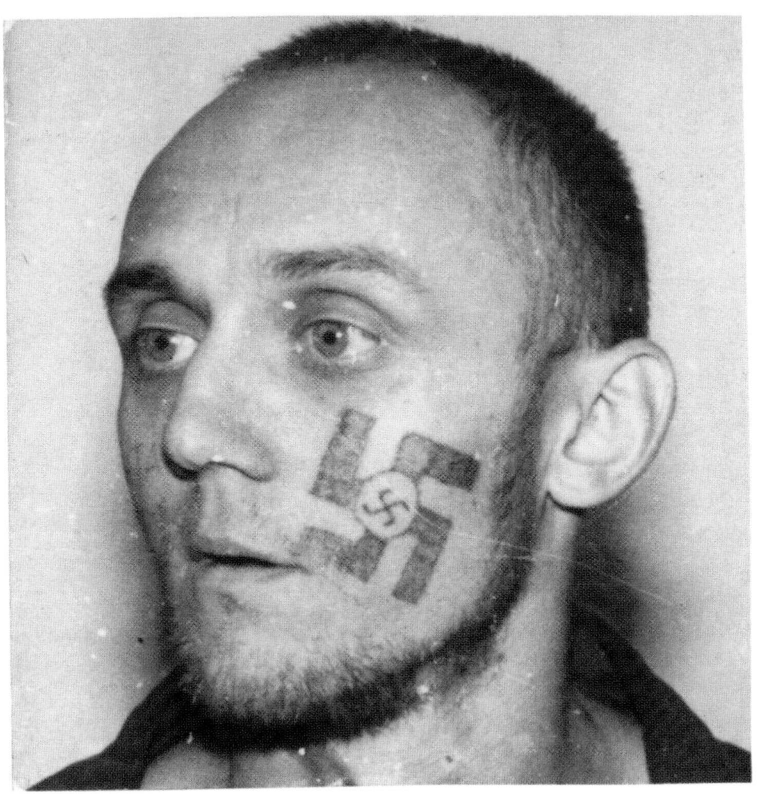

Text on the face reads '**JUNTA ITK–11**'.

This prisoner has been forcibly tattooed with the derogatory term for a faction (usually military) on one cheek and a swastika on the other cheek. It is thought that he had sided with the authorities against his fellow inmates in the zone. This type of tattoo would have dire consequences for the bearer, making him an 'untouchable' who is consequently repressed and violated by other convicts. Any inmate who works with the authorities against the thieves is called a *kozel* (goat), see also page 213. They often apply for transfer in an attempt to escape retribution (being forcibly tattooed, raped or murdered) by other inmates. In the zone the suit of diamonds is also known as the *kumovskaya mast* (chummy suit), and is similarly forcibly tattooed on to a *stukach* (stool pigeon), depriving him of status and marking him out as a target.

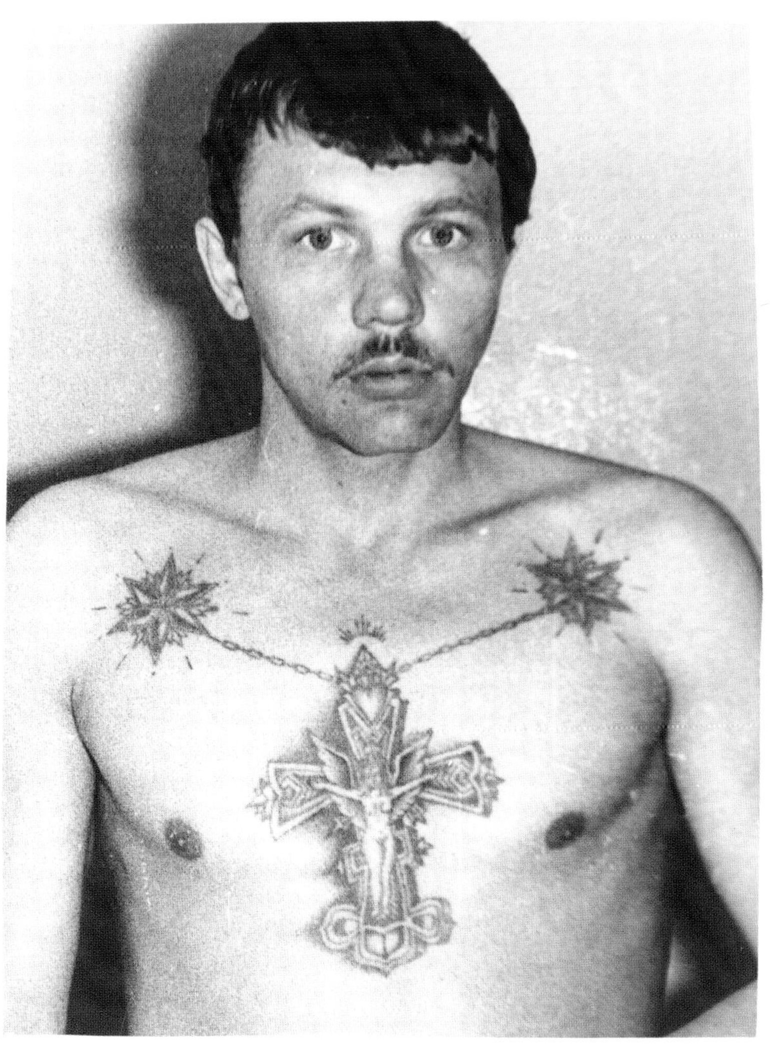

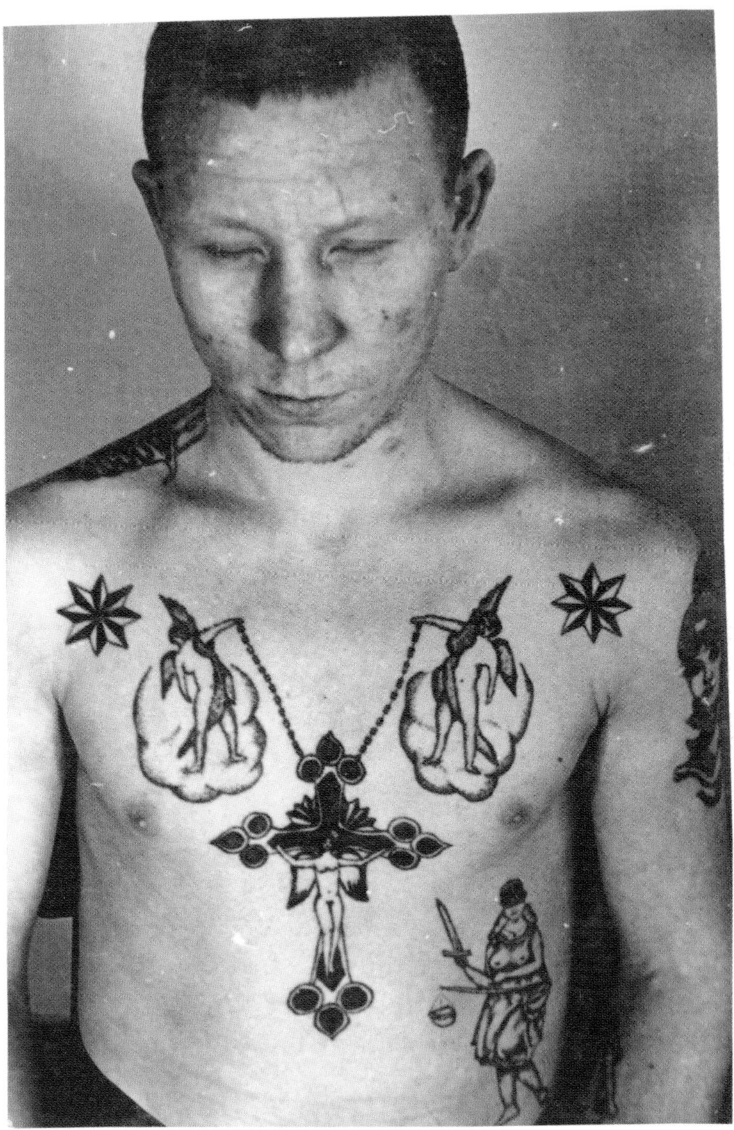

The thieve's stars on this inmate mark him as a criminal 'authority'. A cross with an angel on each side (either on the chest or the back) shows he is a 'butcher', a 'heavyweight' or a 'chopper': someone who has been convicted of murder and is serving their sentence in a special regime labour camp.

Text above the cross reads **'O Lord, Save and Protect your servant Viktor'**, text beneath reads **'God do not judge me by my deeds but by your mercy'**. Text above the waist reads **'I fuck poverty and misfortune'**.

The skull and crossbones show that the prisoner is serving a life term. The single eight-pointed star denotes that he is a 'semi-authority' among thieves. The girl 'catching' her dress with a fishing line on his left forearm is a tattoo worn by hooligans and rapists, see also pages 99 and 217. The snake coiled around human remains (positioned on the middle third of each arm) is a variation on an old thieves' tattoo. The snake is a symbol of temptation; here the snake's head has been replaced by that of a woman: the temptress. Tattooed on the right side of the stomach is a version of *Judith* (1504) as painted by Giorgione: this is intended as a symbol of a scheming, seductive woman who betrays a noble man, see also page 109.

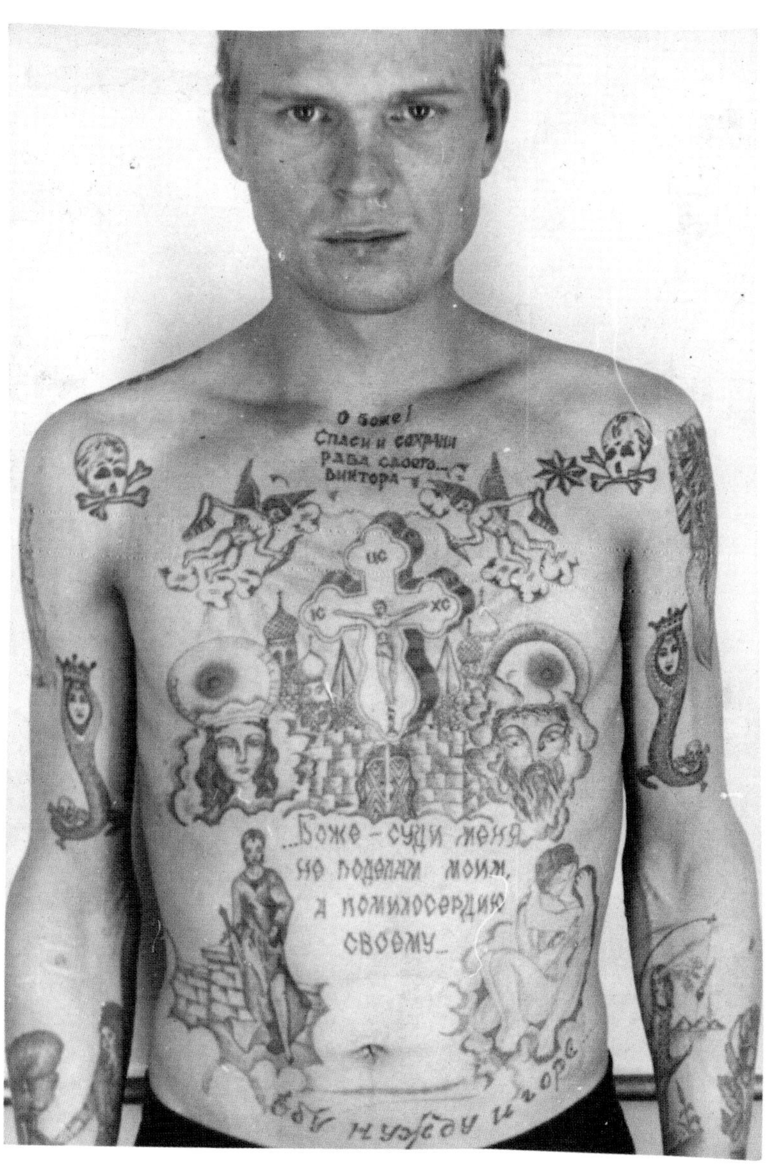
О Боже!
Спаси и сохрани
раба своего...
Виктора...

...Боже - суди меня
но делам моим,
а помилосердию
своему...

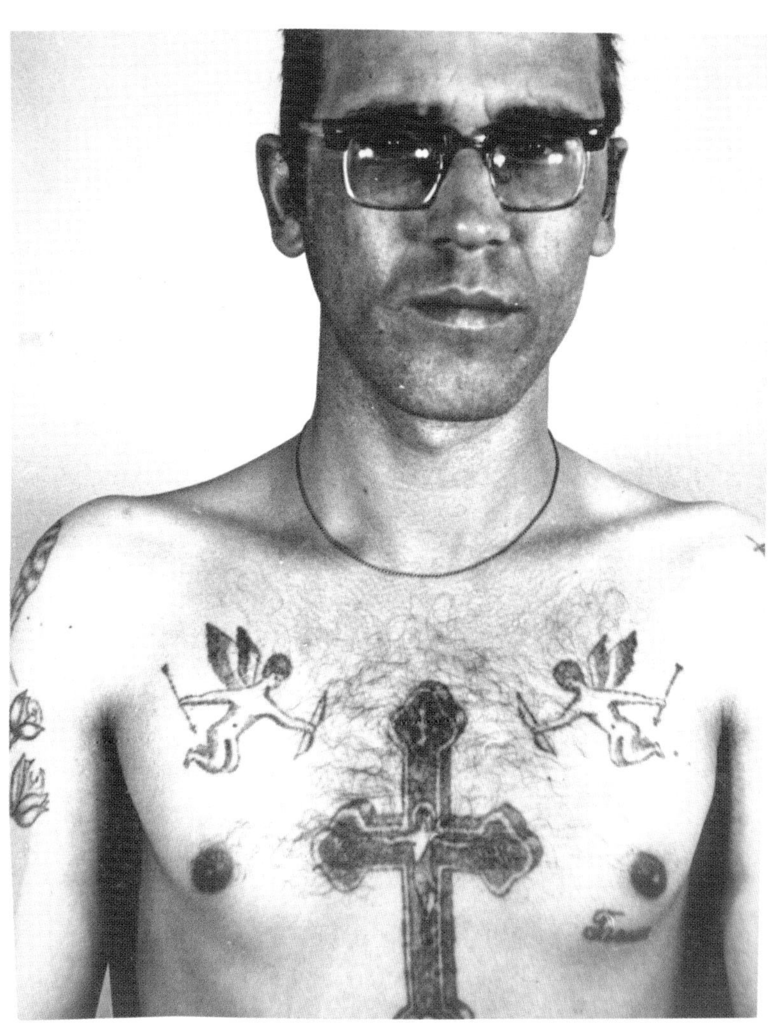

Text on the chest reads **'Galina'** (a woman's name).

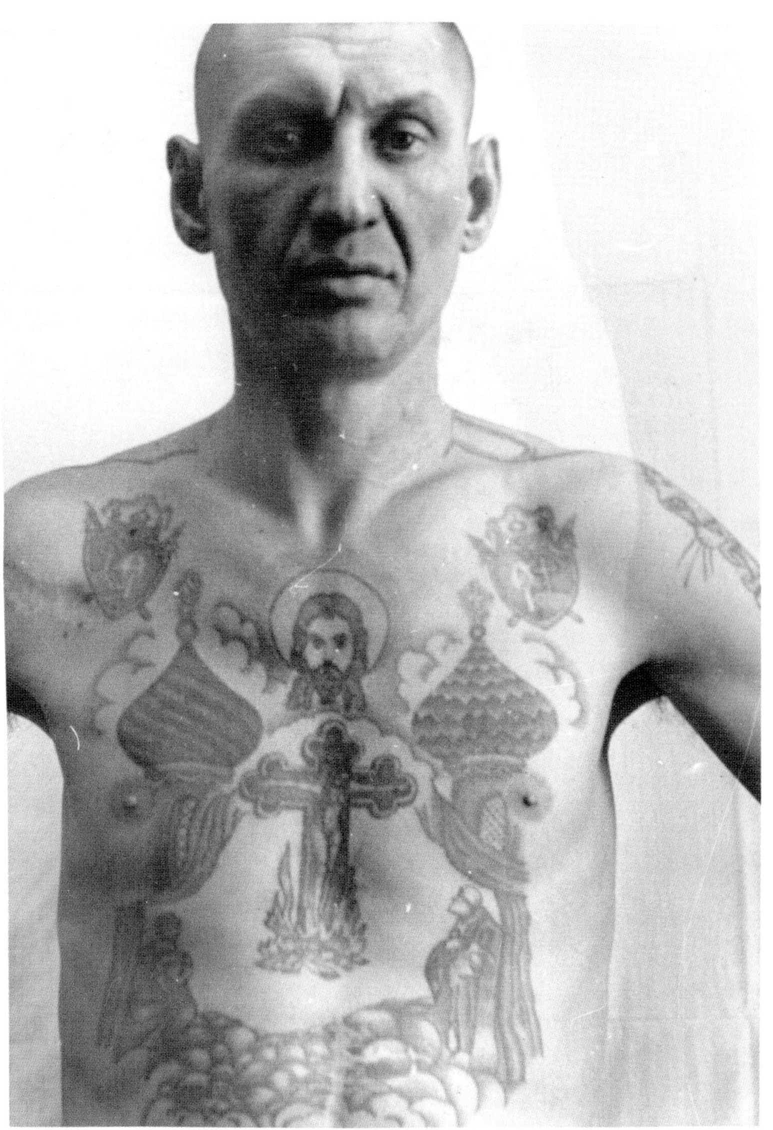

The mound with a cross on each shoulder stands for 'Death to activists' and shows that the convict took revenge against the authorities. A woman being burnt at a crucifix signifies that the bearer was pushed to murder a woman in revenge for her infidelity.

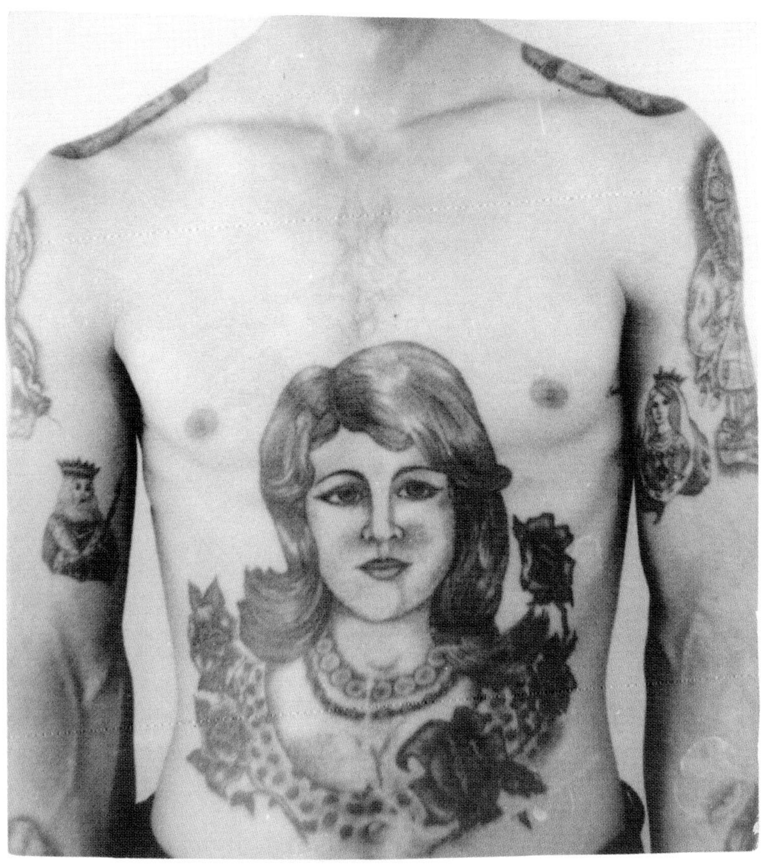

Criminals often carry memorial tattoos to a *biksa** who they love 'in freedom' (outside the prison). These might be tattooed on the chest or arm, sometimes alongside an image of the inmate behind prison bars.

* The term *biksa* (slut) refers to a sexually available girl. Although she may sell her services, she is respected by the criminals and must not be regarded as a common prostitute. The *biksa* box has been used in hospitals for over a century. At night nurses would sexually service male doctors, who accepted this as one of the perks of their job. On the way to their encounter, along the hospital's corridors or between its buildings, the nurses would carry the *biksa* (containing medical supplies) which served as an alibi if they were stopped. Over time the name has transferred from the box, to the 'active' nurses, to conventional 'active' girls.

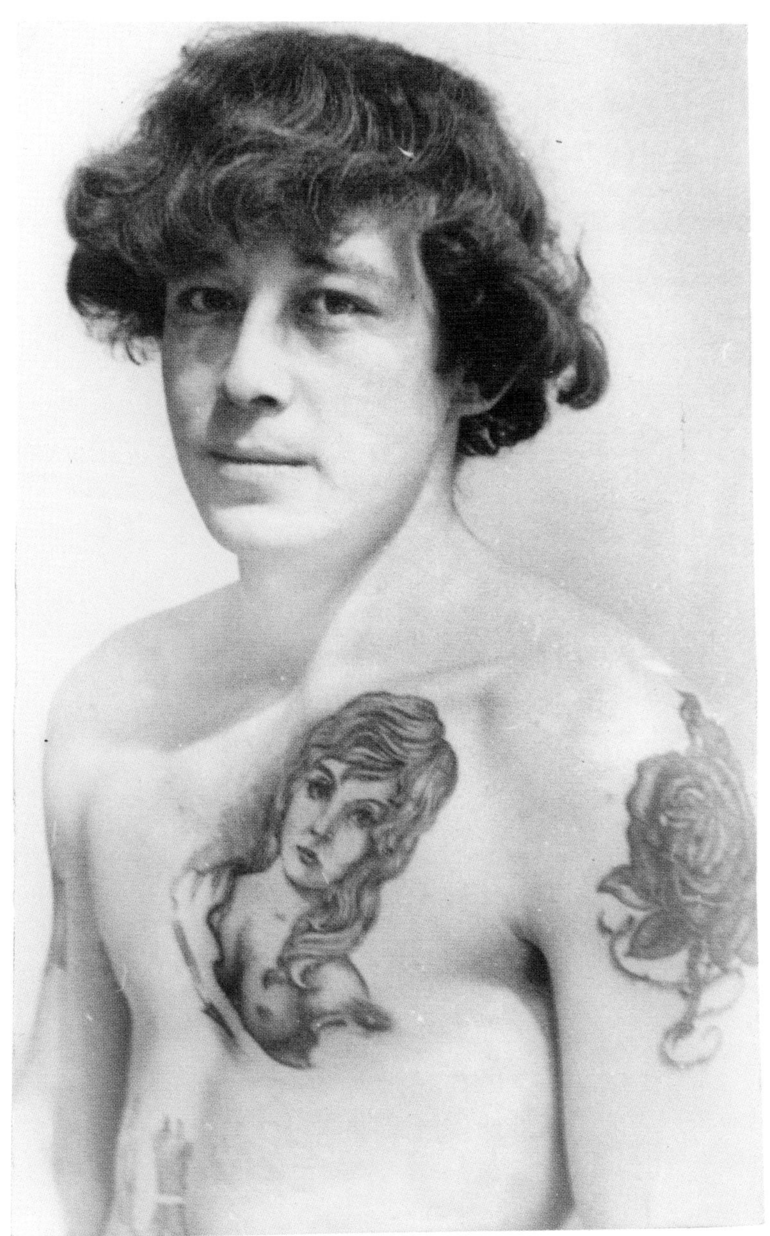

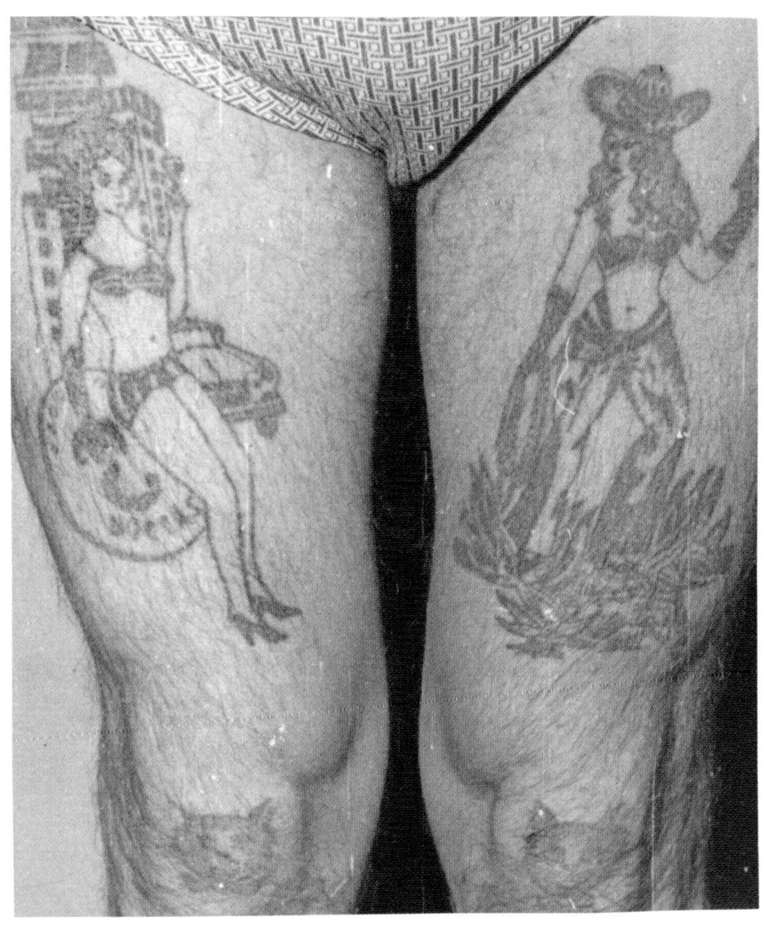

above: On the bearer's right leg is an Americanised variation of a tattoo meaning 'Don't love money – it will ruin you, don't love women – they will deceive you, but love freedom!' (In the traditional version the woman sits on a one kopek coin and the background is a Russian Othodox church.)

right: Text on the leg reads **'Silence and Peace. The convoy** [the escort which leads prisoners to work at locations outside the camp and guards them there] **is not needed here'**.

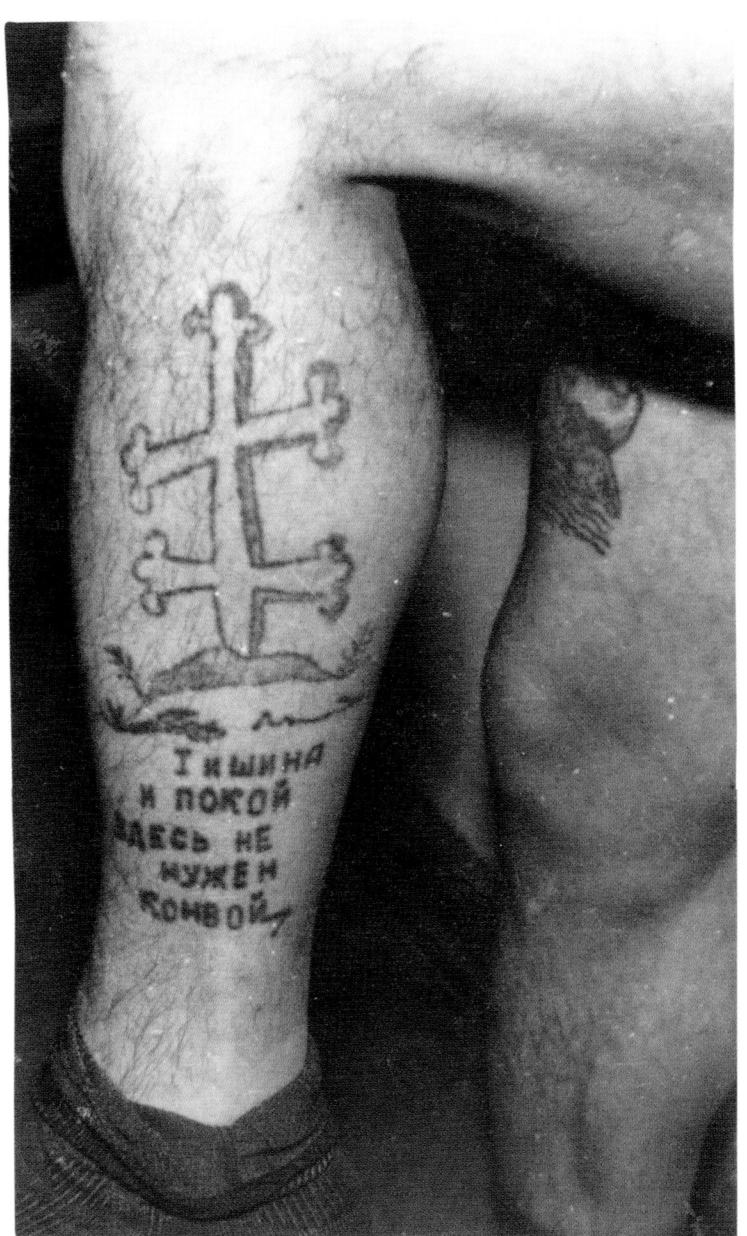
Тишина
и покой
здесь не
нужен
конвой

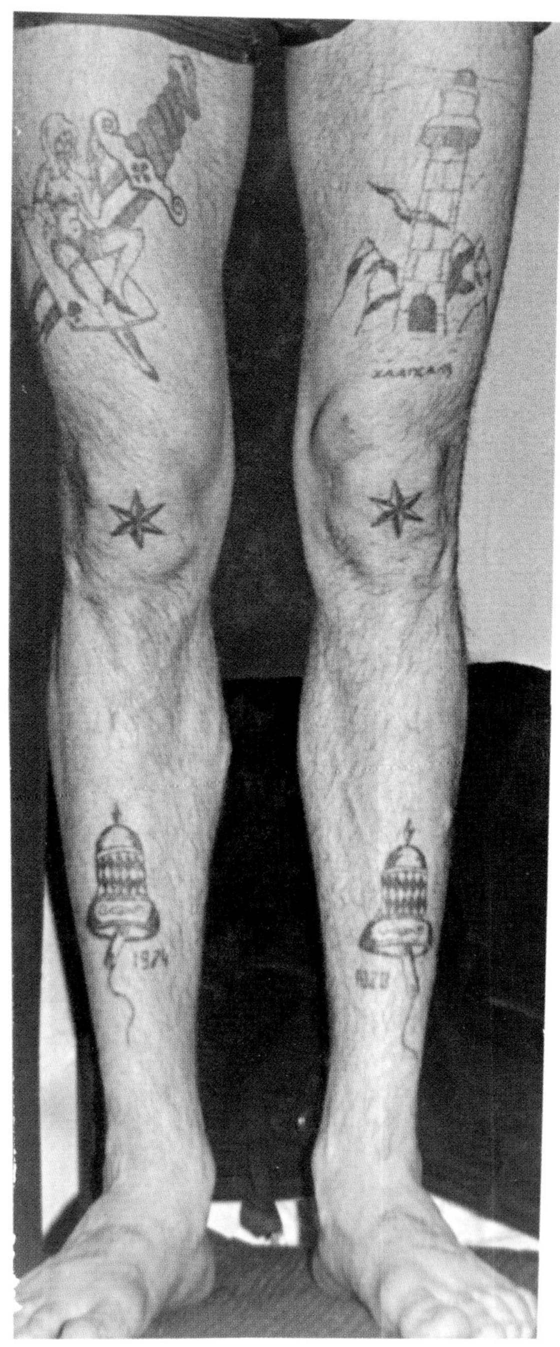

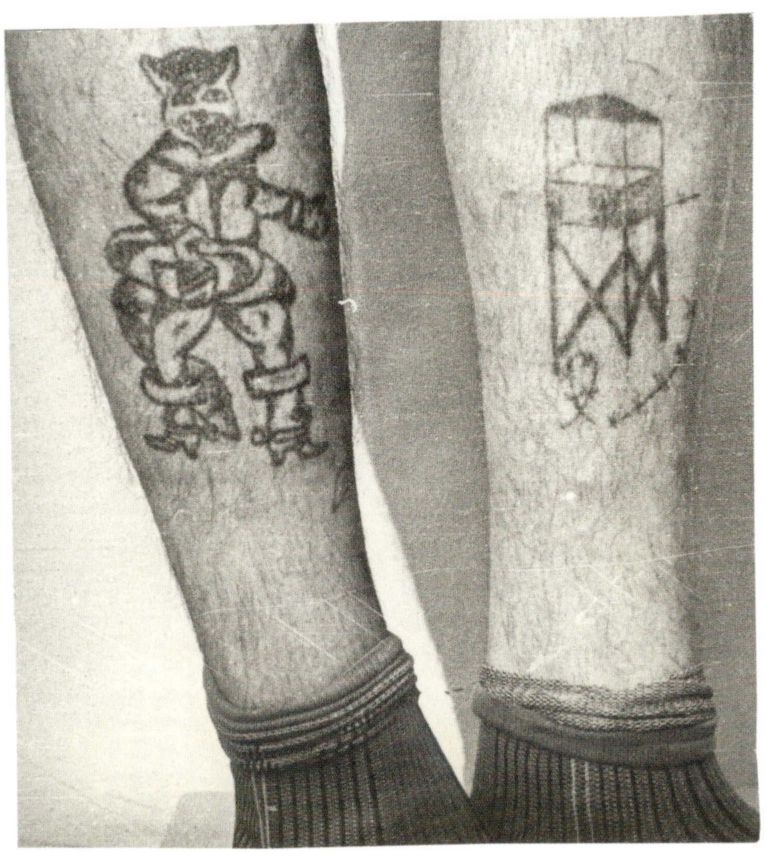

above: The image of a cat wearing boots (or of a rabbit with a sack over its shoulder) means that the bearer has previously broken out of a corrective labour institution, or that they are intending to.

left: The text on the leg reads **'Haapsalu'** (a seaside resort in Estonia).

The dagger is a symbol of a hooligan, known as *baklani*. The bells on the shins show that the bearer served his sentence in full 'to the bell', in this case from 1974 to 1978. Stars tattooed on to the knees mean 'I will not kneel before the police'.

On his right leg is the acronym '**SLON: *S malih Let Odni Neschastya***' (Only Misfortunes from an Early Age). Text under this reads '**Here is what** [is killing us]'. Text at the top of the left leg reads '**Few roads have been walked**'. Text by the knee reads '**Love**'. Text on the shin reads '**It** [the leg] **walks around the zone**'.

The acronym 'SLON' (literally 'elephant' in Russian) has been interpreted by Aleksandr Solzhenitsyn as *Solvetskie Lagerya Osobovo Haznacheniya* (Solovetsky Camps of Special Assignment). The Solovetsky Camps were prison camps situated on the Solovetsky Islands in the White Sea, where both criminal and political prisoners were sent. Solzhenitsyn suggests only this single meaning, but criminals have invented many other possible interpretations including: *Stalinskih Lagerei Ocobovo Hazhacheniya* (Stalin Camps of Special Assignment); *Smert Legavim Ot Nozha* (Death to cops from knives); *S toboi Lubimaya Odnoi Naveki* (With you, my favourite one, forever); *Smert Legavim, Oni Ne spasutsya* (Death to cops, they will not be saved); *Suki Lubyat Octrii Nozh* (Bitches love a sharp knife); *Suki Lubyat Odnu Naschastya* (Bitches love only the administration); *Serdtse Lubit Odnu Haveki* (The heart loves only one forever); *Slava Leninizmu, On Nepobedim* (Glory to Leninism, he is invincible); *Slava Leninu, Otesu Hashemu* (Glory to Lenin, our father); and *S malih Let Idni Neschastya* (Only Misfortunes from an Early Age). The classic version was documented by Solzhenitsyn, and then the others appeared, mostly as swearword combinations from criminals. Authoritative criminals consider tattoos on the legs to be of low rank.

The theatre masks on the right leg represent happiness (before prison) and sadness (after prison). The dagger, cards and money underneath are a variation of the popular tattoo 'These are the things that destroy us'.

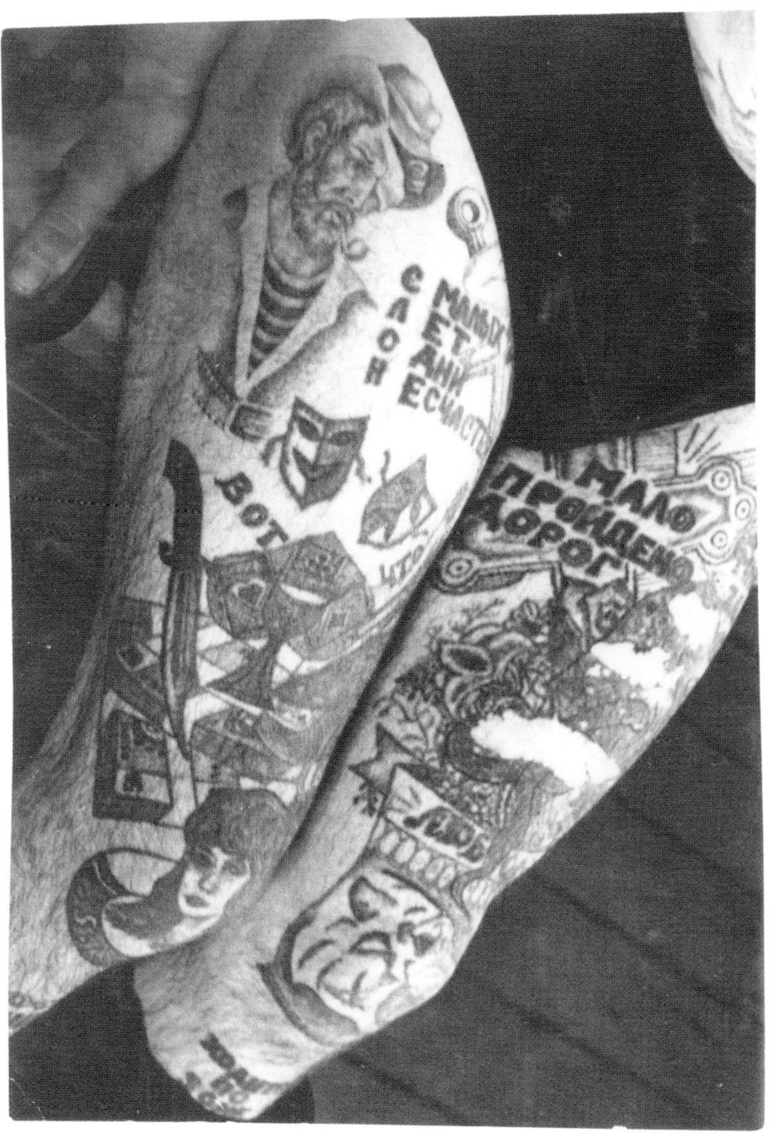

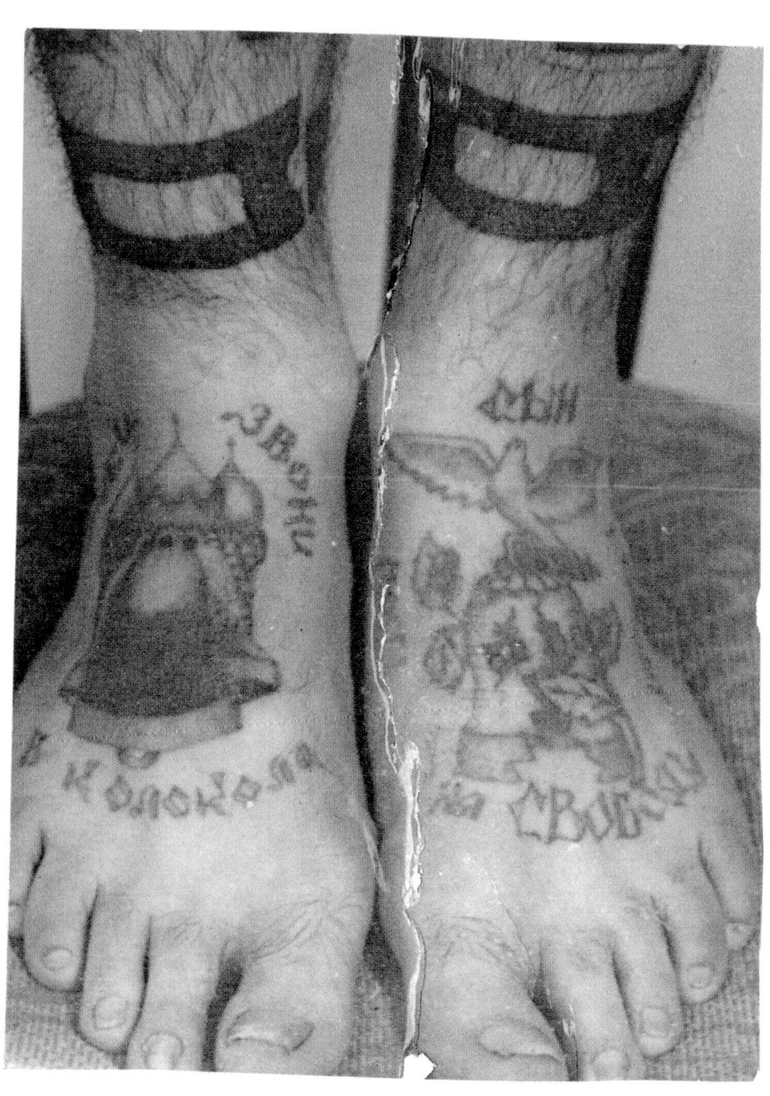

Text on the feet reads **'Ring the bells / Your son is free'**.

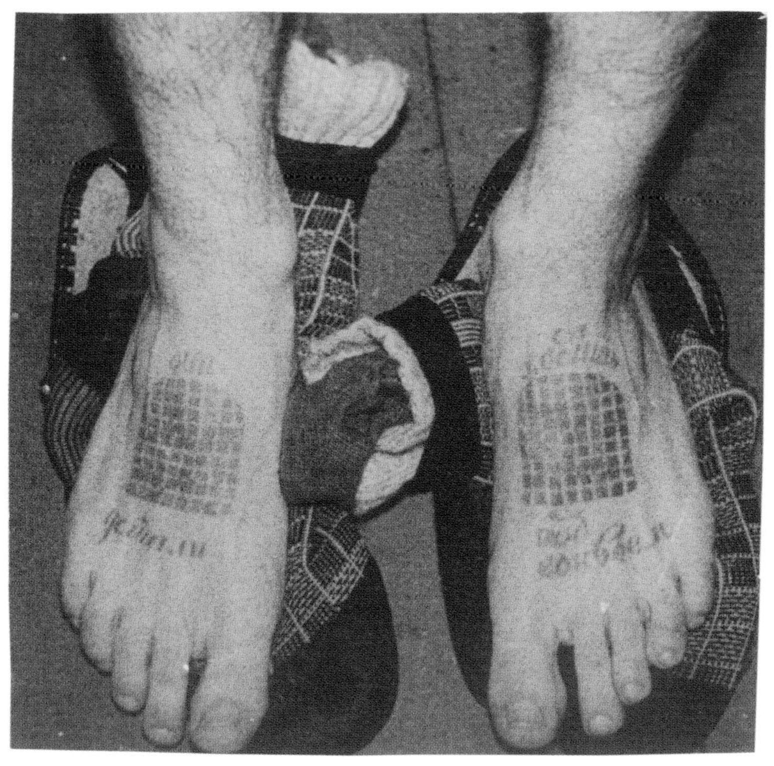

Text on the feet reads **'They are tired / From walking under convoy'**.

Feet are often used for humorous tattoos. For example, saying 'We've walked a long way together' or texts displaying the bearer's dominant position in the family like 'Wash them, wife'.

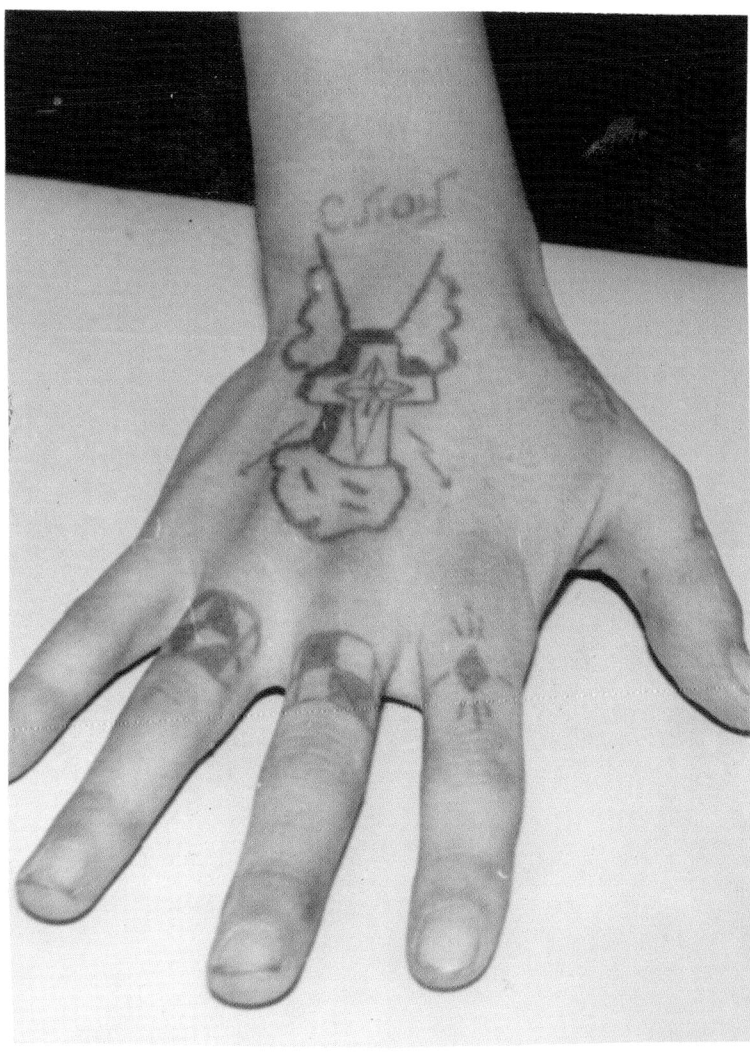

On the wrist is the acronym **'SLON'**, see page 141. A cross with wings means 'Freedom to the juvenile delinquent', 'Free me'. On the index finger: a *poezdushnik*, a thief who operates on suburban trains. A dark diamond indicates he is armed and may resort to violent acts. If unshaded, the thief prefers to steal from sleeping or drunken passengers. Lines above and below show years served. Middle finger: a 'chess ring' of four squares, convicted under article 144, for theft of personal property. Third finger: 'I took the thieves' path', the bearer was convicted of theft.

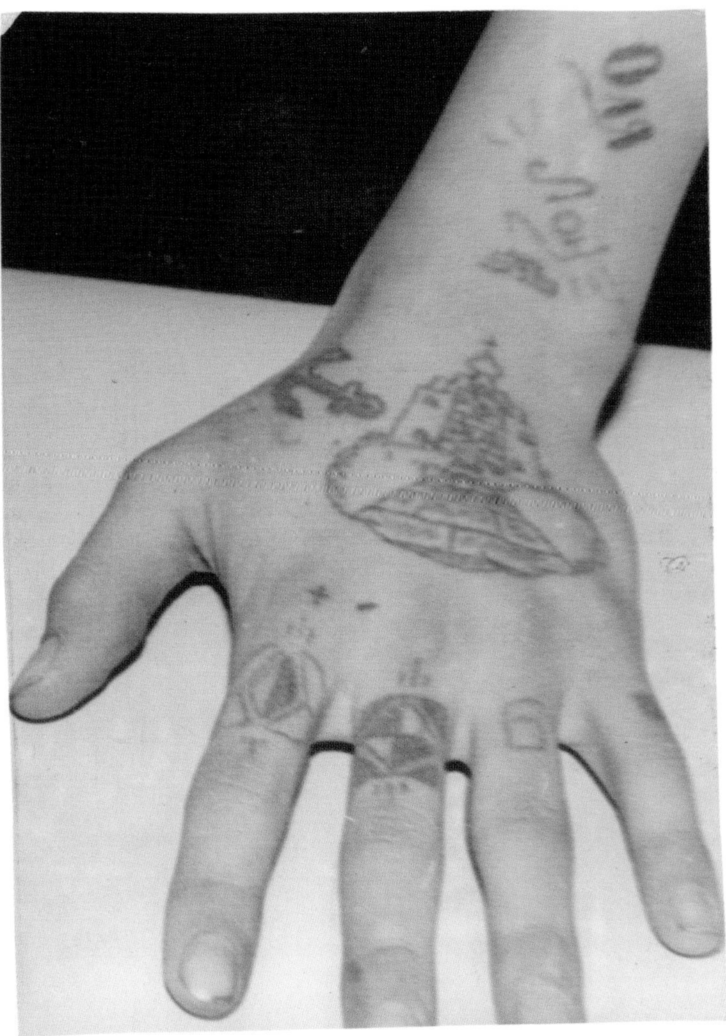

Text on the wrist reads **'Olya'** (name) and **'LON'**, which stands for *Lubit Odnu Naveki* (one love forever). The anchor symbolises a life of freedom. The marks on the knuckle indicate two prison sentences. The ring on the index finger means 'Recidivist thief'. Middle finger: 'Forever with thieves' the bearer has a criminal record. Third finger: **'6'** the lowest card in the Russian thirty-six card deck. This indicates the bearer is a *shesterka* (literally a 'sixer'), an underling or minion who runs errands for the criminal 'authorities', see also page 21.

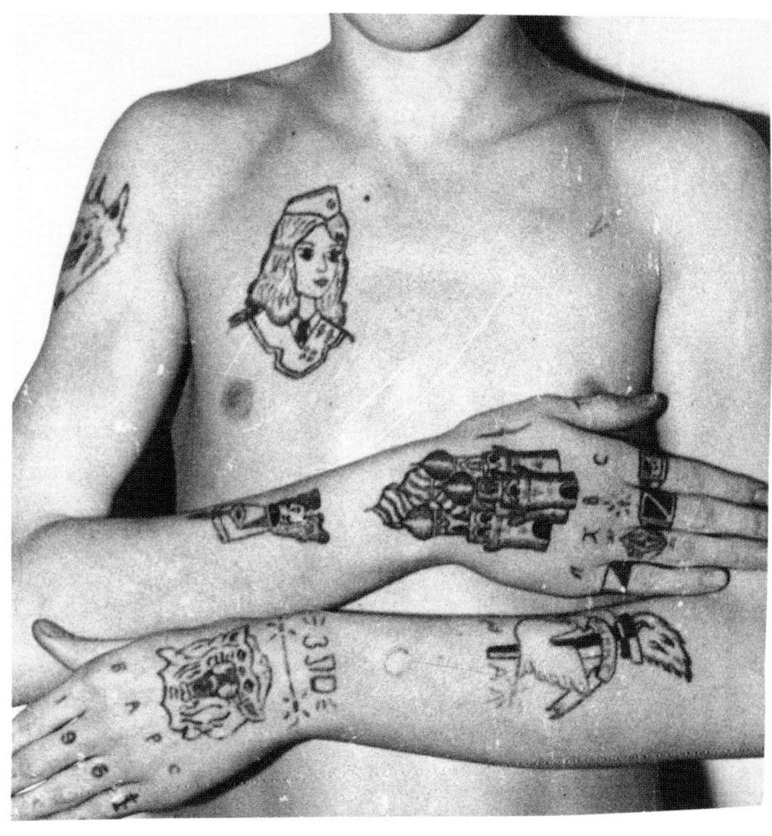

Text on the left wrist reads **'ZLO'** (Russian for 'evil') interpreted variously as *Zek Lubit Otdihat* (Zeks love to relax); *Zavet Lubimovo Otesa* (Testament to my loving father); *Za vse Legavim Otomshu* (I'll have revenge on all the cops). Text on the left hand is the acronym **'BARS'** (Russian for 'snow leopard') meaning *Bey Aktiv, Rezh Suk* (Beat up activists, kill the bitches). On the fingers **'196†'** (date of birth). The last number has been replaced with a Russian Orthodox cross, common practice when the bearer wants to appear older than his real age. The ring on the forefinger of the right hand means 'I was transferred from a VTK [Educational Labour Colony] to an BTK [Corrective Labour Colony] when I came of age'; on the middle finger 'I was a juvenile thief in a VTK'; third finger *Otritsala* hostile to law-enforcement and 'bitches' [prisoners attempting to reform]; little finger 'half my life in prison' or 'inclined to reoffend'. Text across the knuckles reads **'LHVS'** *Legavim Huy Voram Soboda* (To trash cops the dick, to thieves freedom); if asked the meaning of this acronym by the authorities, the standard reply would be *Lublu Halvu Varene Sahkar* (I love halva, jam and sugar).

The girl in Nazi uniform tattooed on the chest does not necessarily represent a fascist viewpoint, but an attitude of antagonism towards the Soviet system.

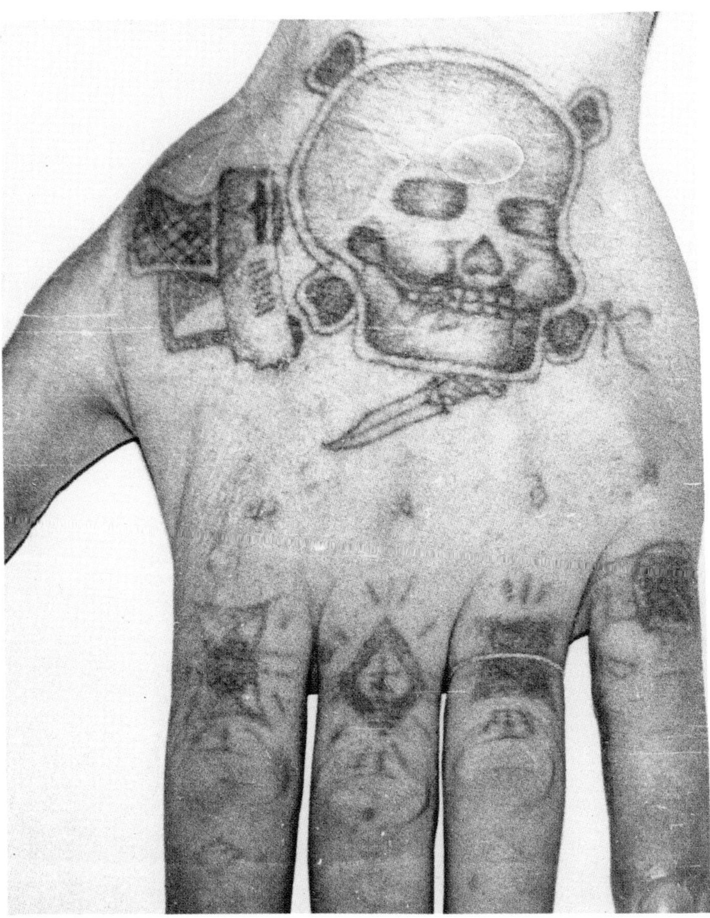

Text across the knuckles reads **'NADYA'** (a woman's name). Forefinger *Patsan* one of the most respected inmates of a VTK. Middle finger the 'thieves' cross' of a pickpocket. Third finger 'I served my time in full', 'From start to finish', 'Went without parole': the prisoner served his complete sentence with no remission for working with the system. Little finger 'The dark life': the bearer has repeatedly been sent to a punishment cell.*

The skull and crossbones, gun, knife and letter 'K'[iller] denote a murderer.

*There are three types of punishment cells: in the ShiZO *Shtrafnoi izolyator* prisoners are given a reduced food ration and confined to the cell (usually 6 x 7 ft) for fifteen days. They sleep on a board-covered concrete floor. These conditions contribute to the spread of tuberculosis. The DIZO *Distsiplinarnii izolyator* is a segregation cell, for violators of the colony rules. Mattresses are provided. The maximum term is ten days. The PKT *Pomeshchenie kamernogo tipa* is an internal colony prison for persistent violators of colony rules. Prisoners are allowed out of their cells to work. The maximum term in a PKT is limited to six months.

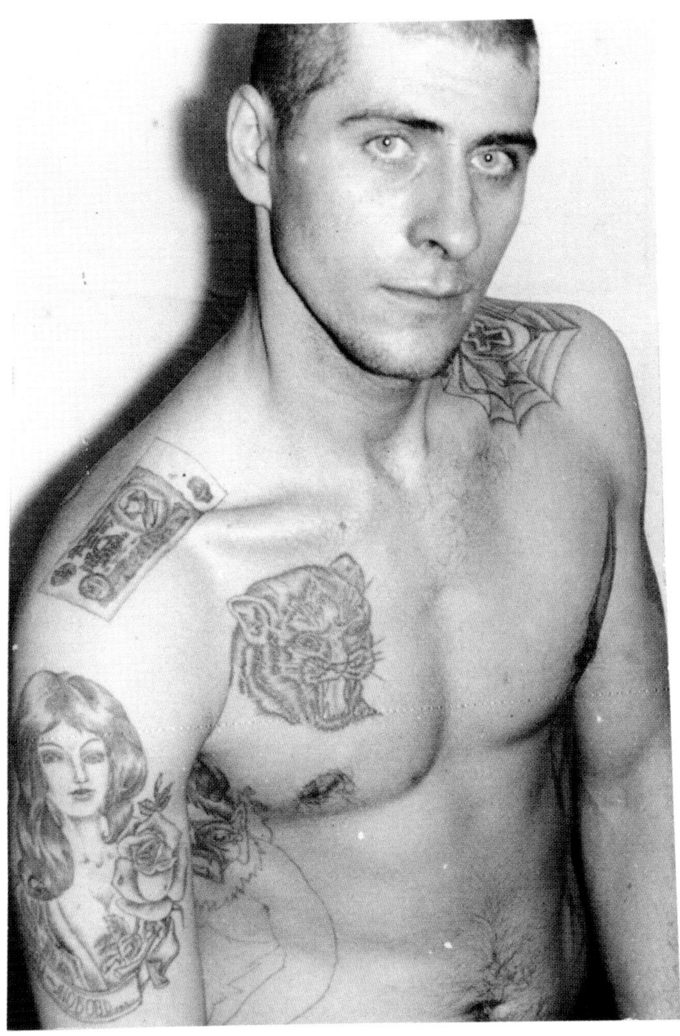

A spider in a web tattooed on the left side of the neck is a thieves' tattoo meaning that the bearer has been repeatedly punished for violating the rules of the penal colony. Punishment is usually carried out by placing the inmate in a 'pressing cell' where he is continually beaten and raped by 'pressers' (other inmates who are working with the administration to break the influence of the thieves and force them to renounce their ways). On the other shoulder is a ten rouble note. The sign of a counterfeiter, more generally it means that the bearer follows a criminal path.

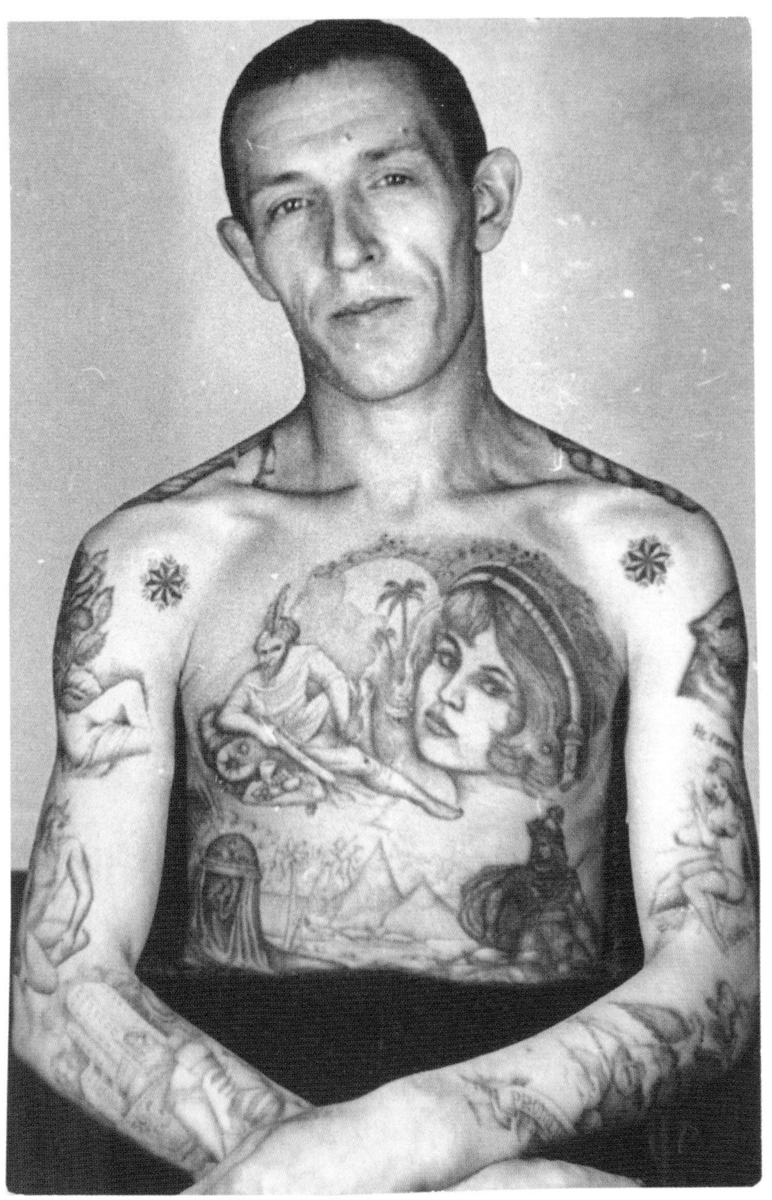

The double-headed eagle is a Russian state symbol that dates back to the 15th century and was used by Peter the Great. In 1993, after the fall of Communism, it replaced the hammer and sickle as the coat of arms of the Russian Federation. This photograph taken in the Soviet period shows this emblem tattooed as a bold symbol of power and rage against the USSR, see also page 215. It can also be interpreted as 'Russia for the Russians' or 'For a Russia without Yids, Wogs and Marxist-Leninists'. The Statue of Liberty implies a longing for freedom, while the dark character holding a gun denotes a readiness to commit violence and murder. The eyes on the chest signify 'I can see everything' and 'I am watching', the powerful tattoo of a criminal 'overseer'. The eight-pointed stars tattooed on the shoulders mark the bearer as an 'authoritative' thief.

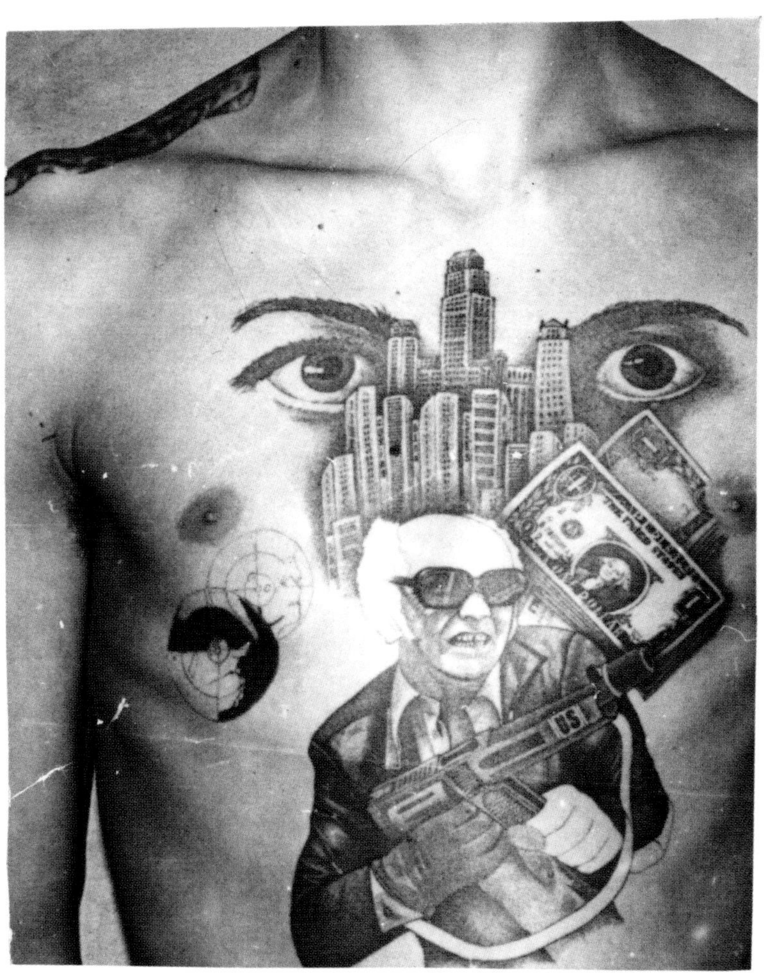

The character depicted in the tattoo is Hunchback, the brutal leader of the 'Black Cat Gang' from the Soviet era crime series *The Meeting Place Cannot Be Changed* (1979). In the story he ends up in prison. Here, by contrast, he fights back against Soviet authority. The letters 'US' on his submachine gun, alongside the skyscrapers and dollar bills, embody the ideological opponents of the Soviet Union and indicate a hatred of the government. The eyes signify that 'I am watching over you' (the other inmates in the prison or camp). The epaulette tattooed on the shoulder denotes the inmates 'rank' among the criminal caste.

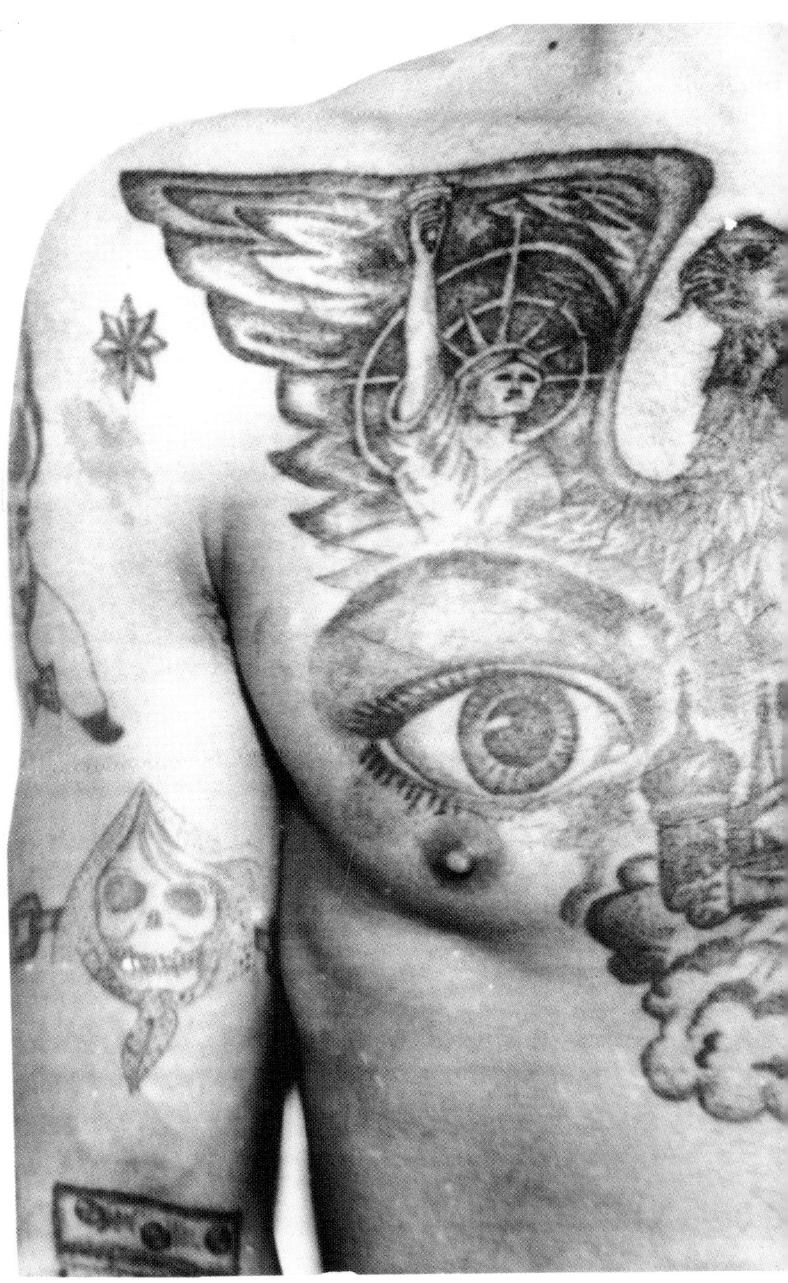

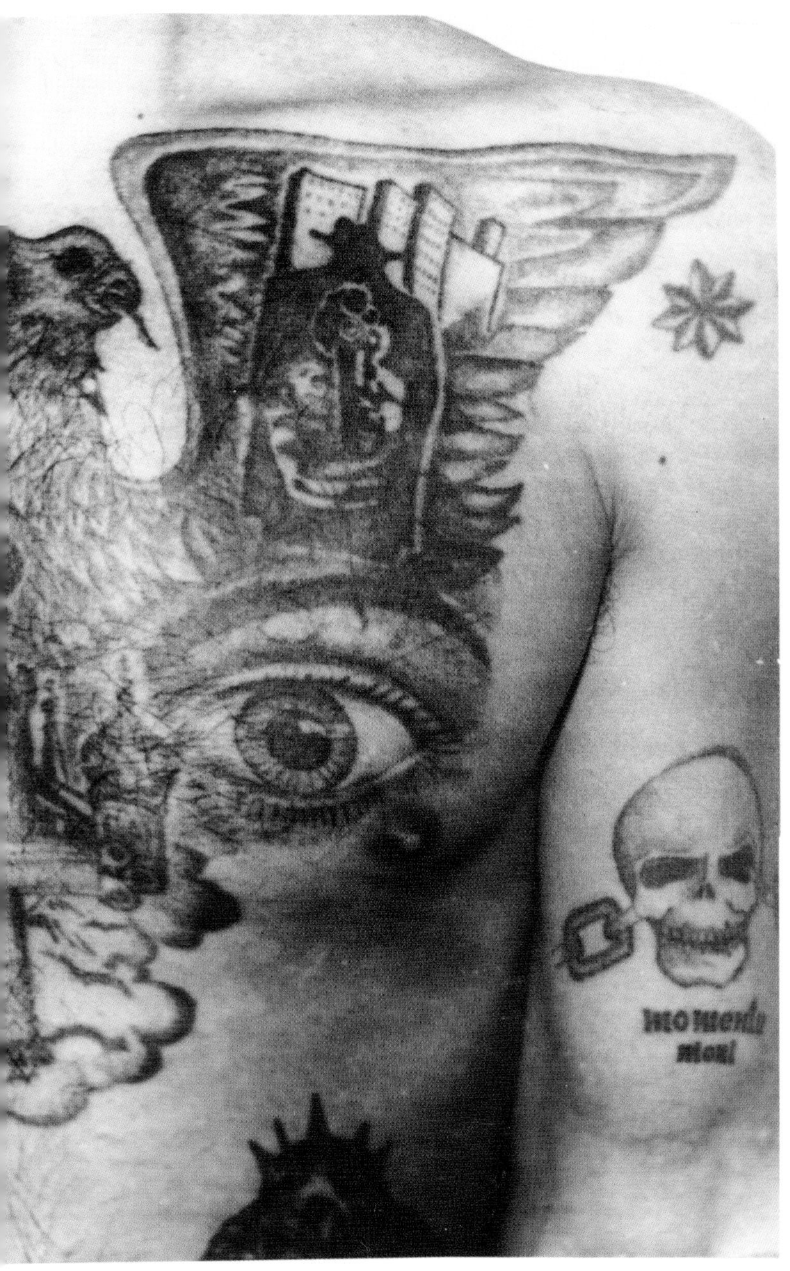
momento
mori

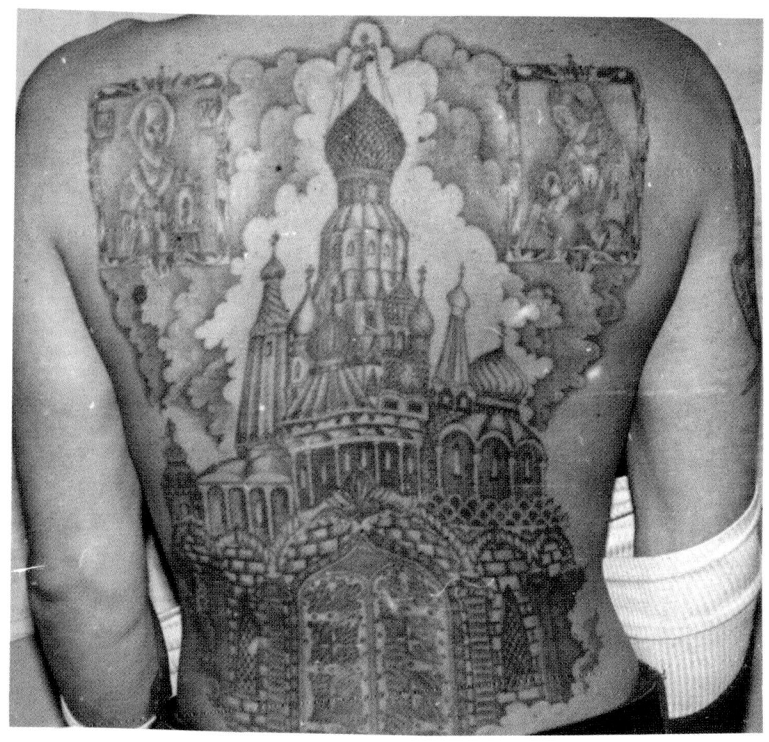

The abundance of religious subjects can be easily explained. A truly religious person normally thinks a tattoo humbles the bearer and keeps his religious feelings away from desecration. However, in the context of the Soviet prison or camp system (the zone), tattooed images of crosses, churches, bell towers, saints and monasteries have absolutely nothing to do with religious beliefs. They stem from the desire to show oneself as an outcast, as someone who has been misunderstood and is doomed to suffer. In the zone, a church or monastery is interpreted as the unambiguous sign of the caste of thieves.

By contrast an ordinary citizen who practises religion is committing a crime punishable under Soviet law. The guilty are arrested and incarcerated alongside ordinary criminals. The regime believes that political and religious prisoners are ideologically more dangerous than the criminal element, who generally receive better treatment as an acknowledgment of their 'professional' status.

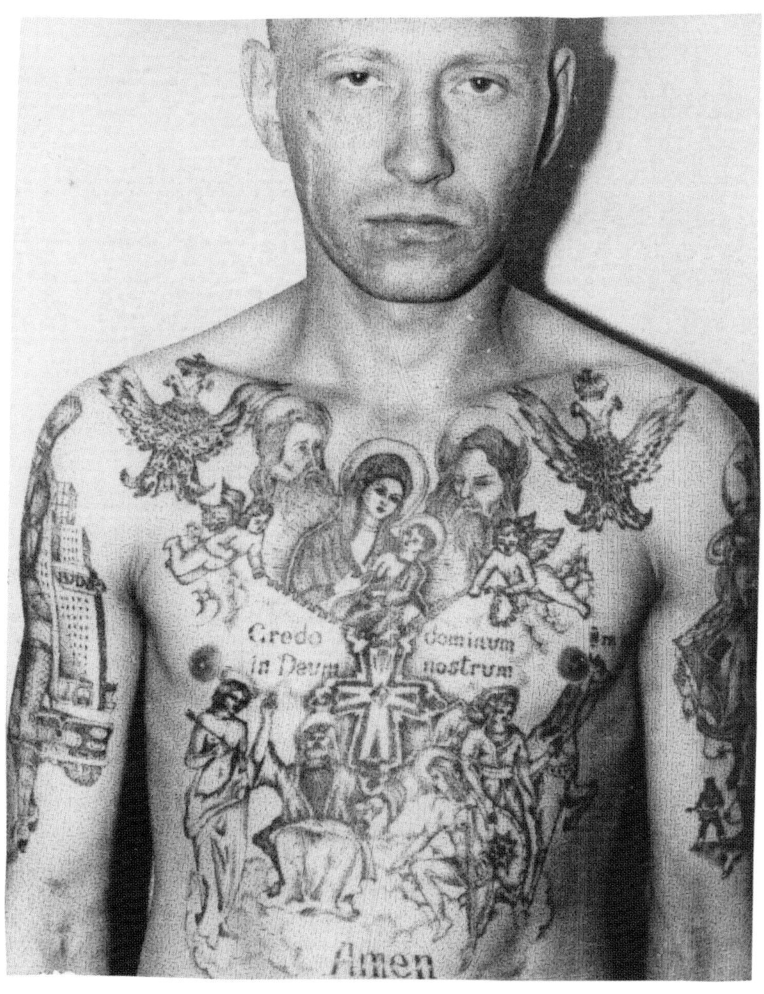

Text on the chest is the Latin prayer *Credo in deum dominum nostrum* meaning **'I believe in our Lord'**. Text underneath reads **'Amen'**.

The Russian double-headed eagles on this inmate's shoulders are a pre-Revolutionary emblem and represent aggression towards the Soviet regime and an intolerance of non-Russians. *Shramovanie* (scarring), in this instance on the face, but also on the body, can also carry significant meaning in the criminal world. Like tattoos they can be viewed as *raspisnii* ('decorations' in criminal slang) which contain the story of the thief's life.

A woman being attacked by a lion means that the bearer of the tattoo was imprisoned for rape. The eyes on the stomach denote a homosexual, see also pages 69, 177 and 179.

There was a case of a prisoner named Alexandr who was sent to prison for hooliganism at the age of nineteen. This particular general regime colony was ruled by *blatniie*, see footnote on page 66 – authorities who had moved there from a colony for juvenile offenders when they had come of age. It was the *blatniie* who would organise the *propiska* (registration) for newcomers. *Propiska* is a kind of test on the knowledge of prison rules and the unwritten code. One of the inmates jumped on Alexandr, saddled him and ordered him to ride around the *khata* (cell), and kept asking 'What station is it?' The person 'being registered' had to reply 'prison', otherwise everyone would ride him. He was asked different questions and every incorrect answer brought a blow to the neck. In the end the authority known by the nickname Krita brushed Alexandr with a broom over his face, thus labelling him as a *chukhan*, meaning 'untouchable'.

Another newcomer was asked a question: 'Petya, do you like waffles?' Petya did not know that a 'waffle' meant 'penis' in the prison jargon, so he replied 'I do'. In the zone an ignorance of jargon and other prison rules is no excuse. He was subjected to oral rape by the 'authorities'.

A typical example of how a law-enforcement officer would react to the complaint of an inmate who had been raped by a group comes from Tabulga (Chistoozyorny District, Novosibirsk Region). He replies calmly, 'Don't worry. No man in my colony has ever got pregnant, and you won't either!'

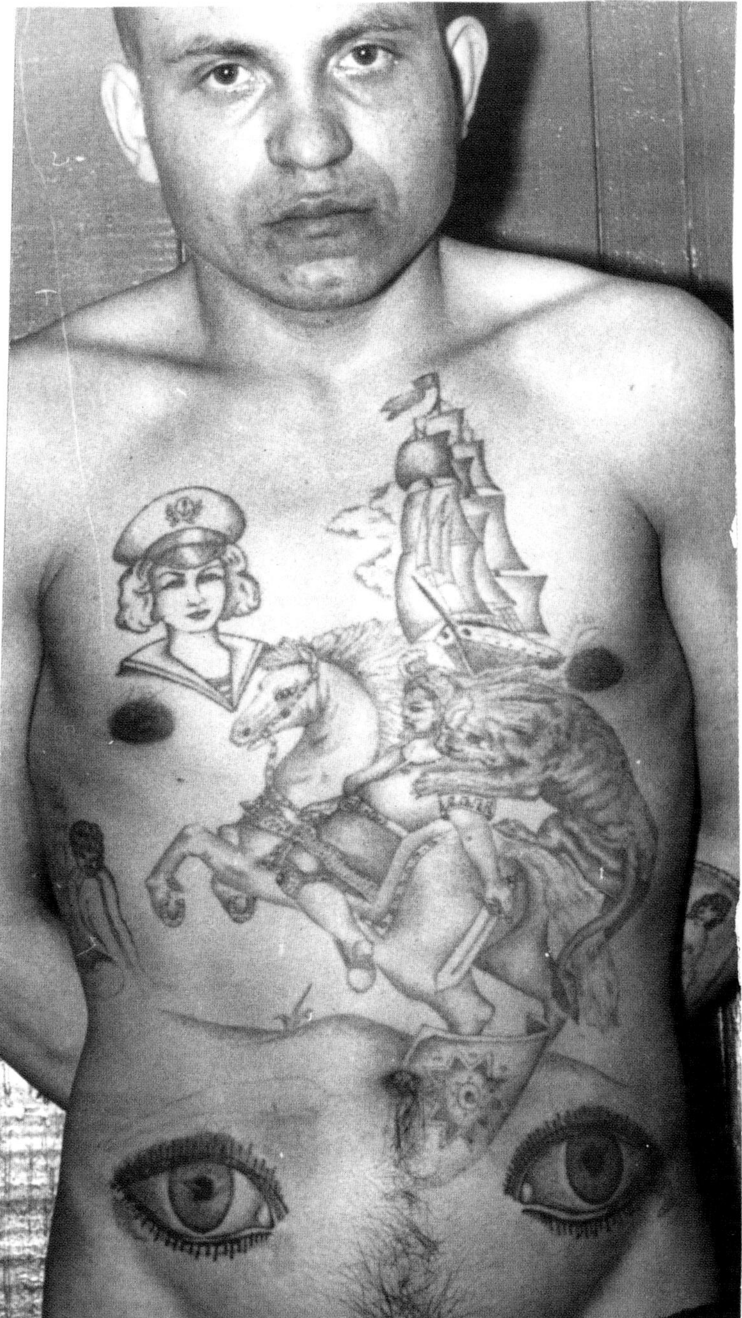

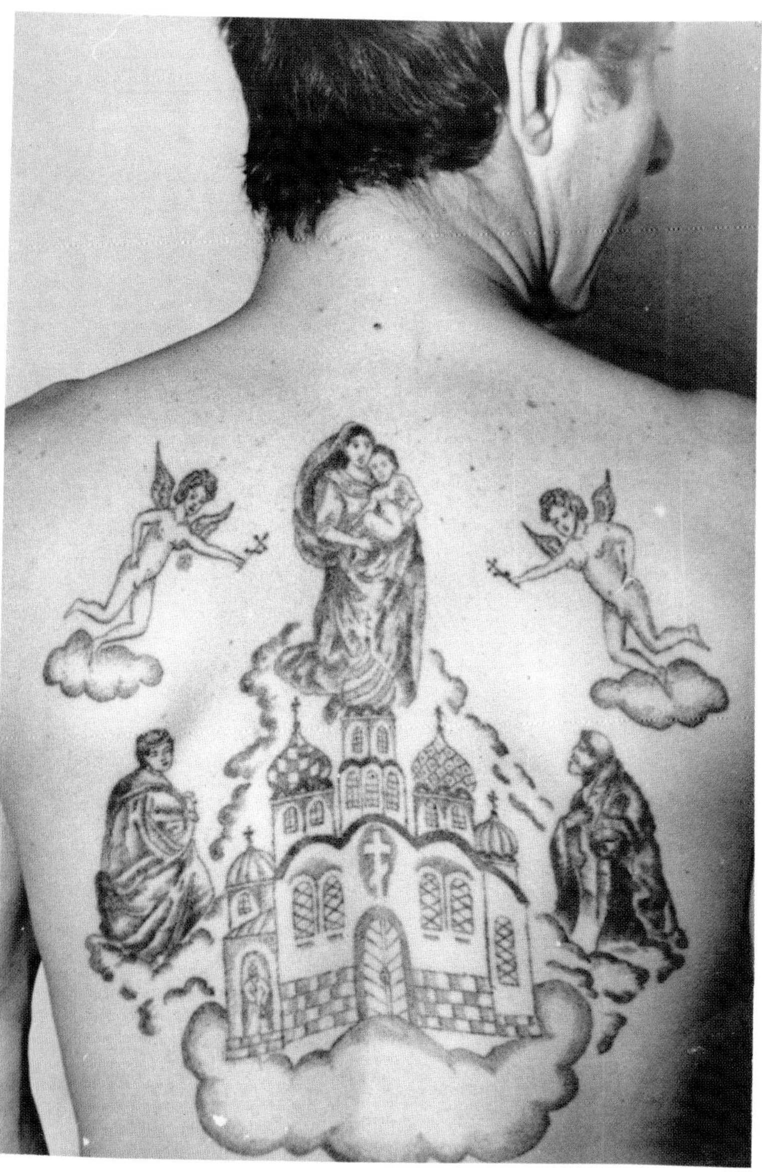

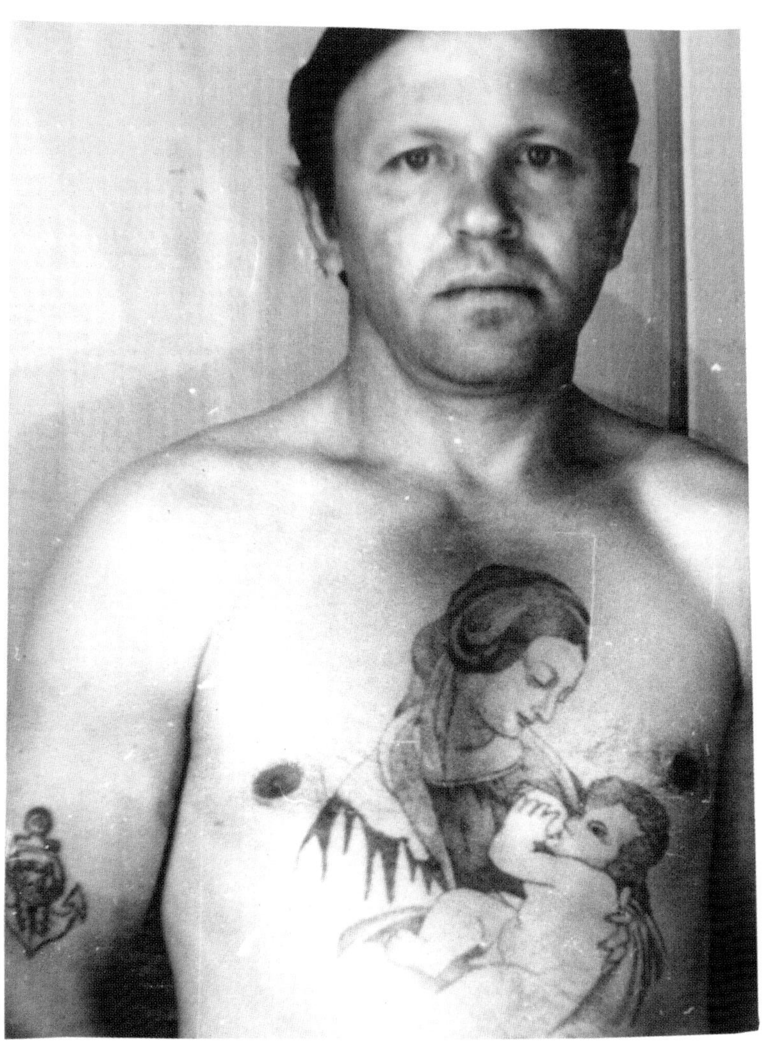

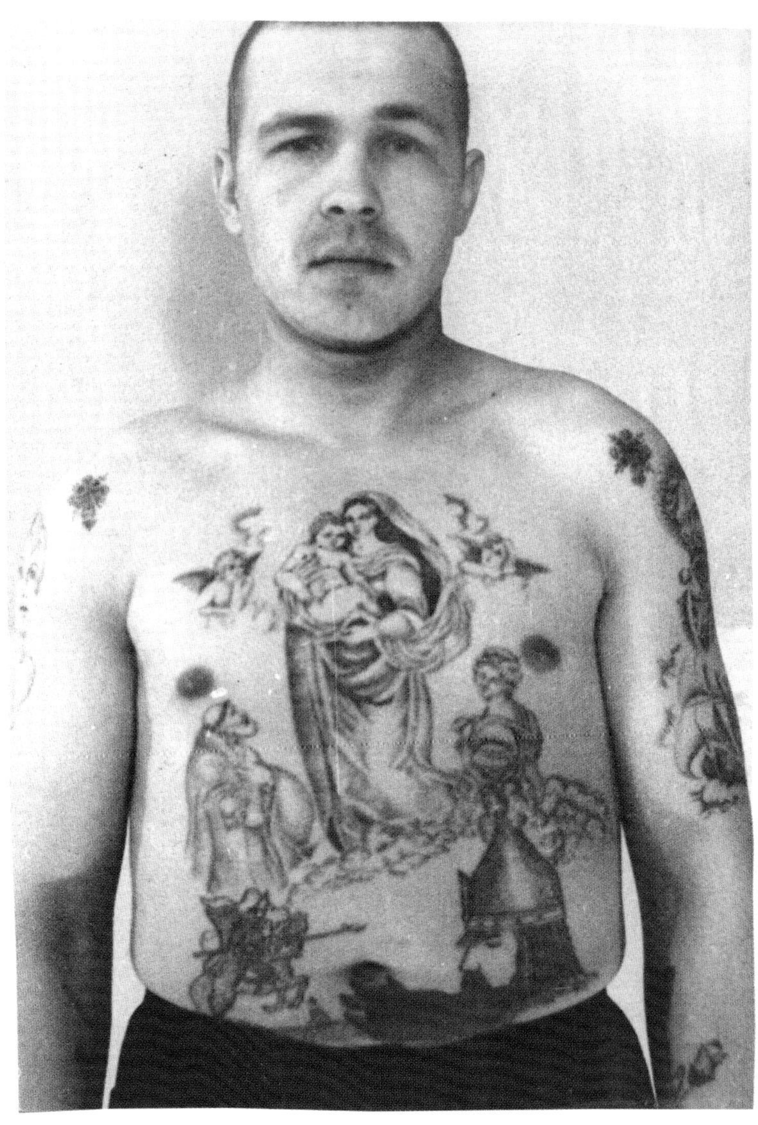

The portrait of a woman on the shoulder is known as the 'Prison Passport' and signifies that the bearer celebrated his seventeenth birthday in prison (indicated by the woman wearing a cross on a chain).

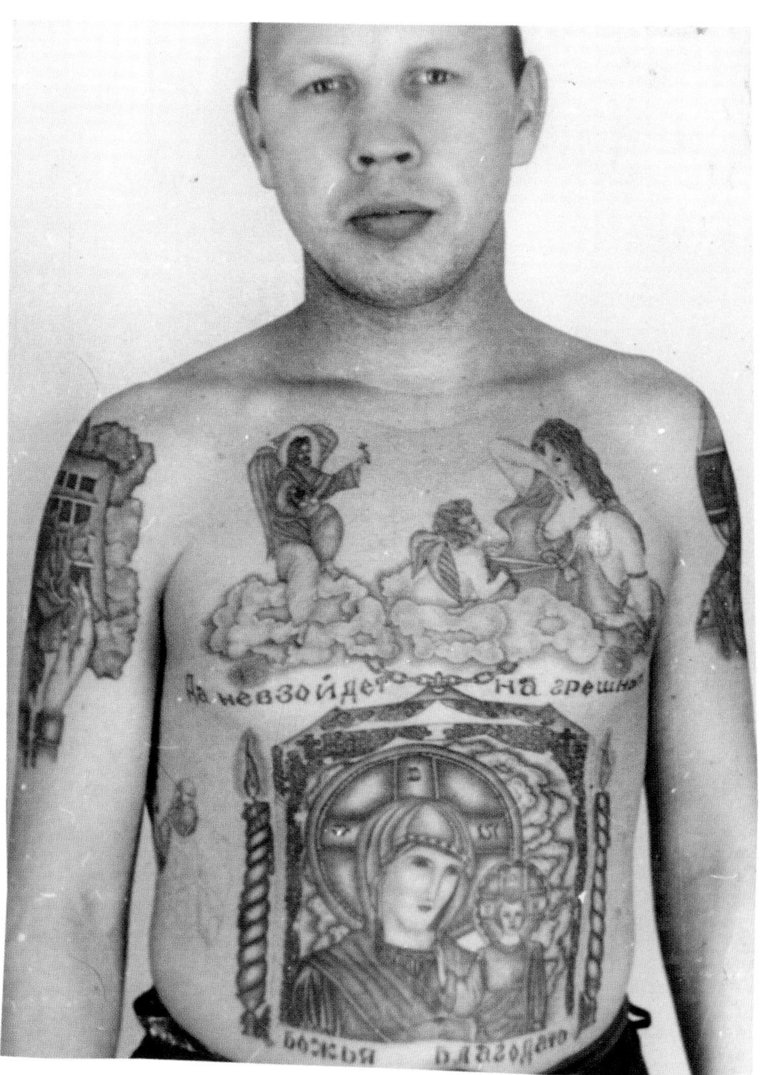

Text across the chest reads **'God's blessing may not come upon the sinner'**.

The shackled hands tattooed on this inmate's shoulder gently hold a rose (from which a leaf is falling) up to a cell window. This means he turned eighteen in the VTK (Educational Labour Colony).

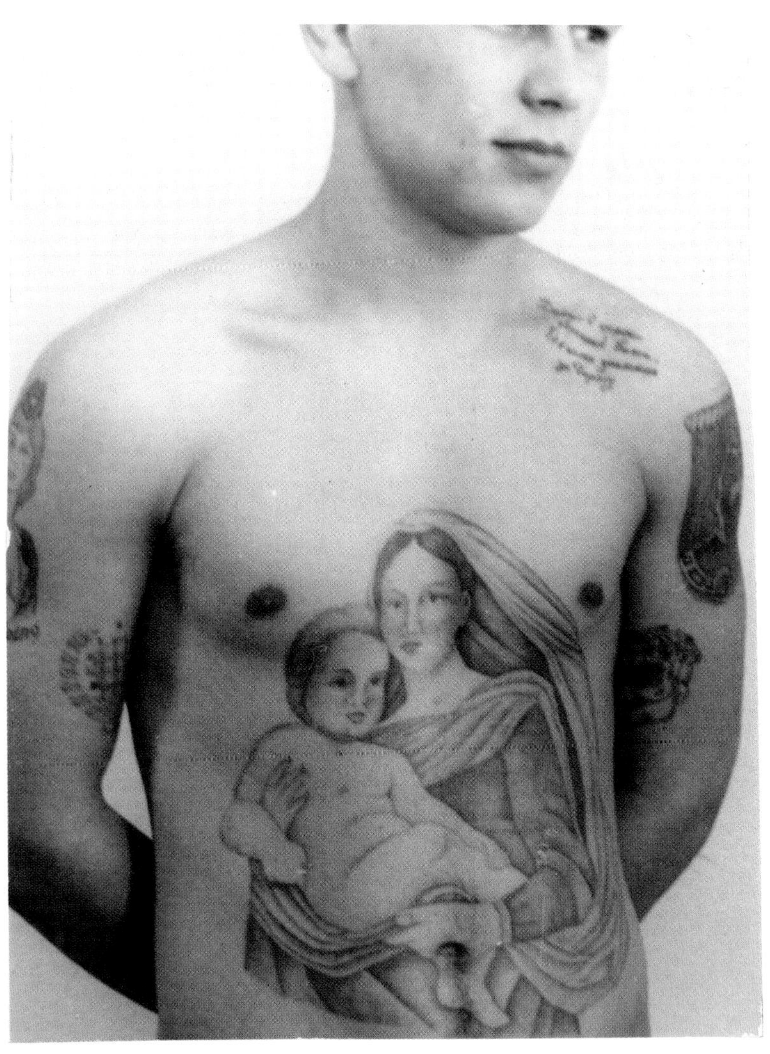

Text on the shoulder reads **'Give me a return ticket to my youth, I paid for it a long time ago'**.

As well as being frequently used as a talisman, the Madonna and Child indicates imprisonment from an early age. On the right arm is a derivative Soviet coat of arms containing the gridded bars of a prison cell and an anti-Communist text. These tattoos show that this criminal is an open opponent of the Communist Party who is frustrated with the length of his sentence.

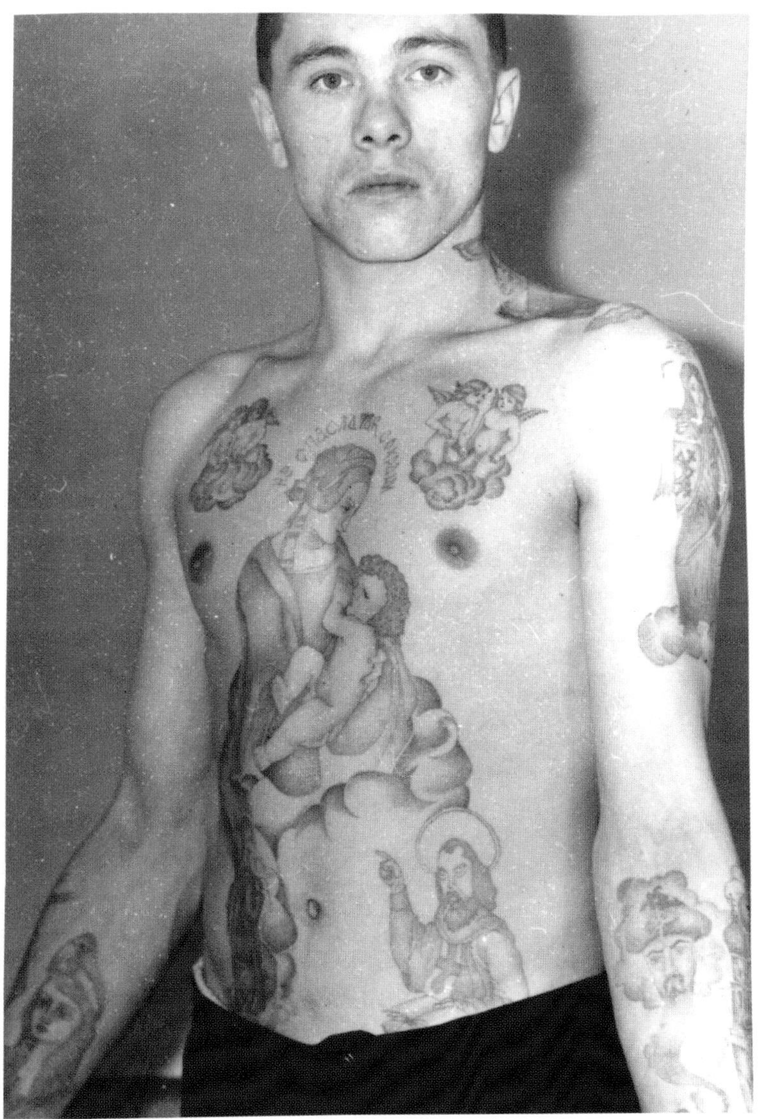

Text over the Madonna reads **'Since you didn't save me, protect me'**.

The genie on the left forearm is the symbol of a drug addict. The woman in Nazi uniform on the right forearm is a sign that the bearer is prone to violence and rage and that he has an antisocial, anti-Soviet attitude.

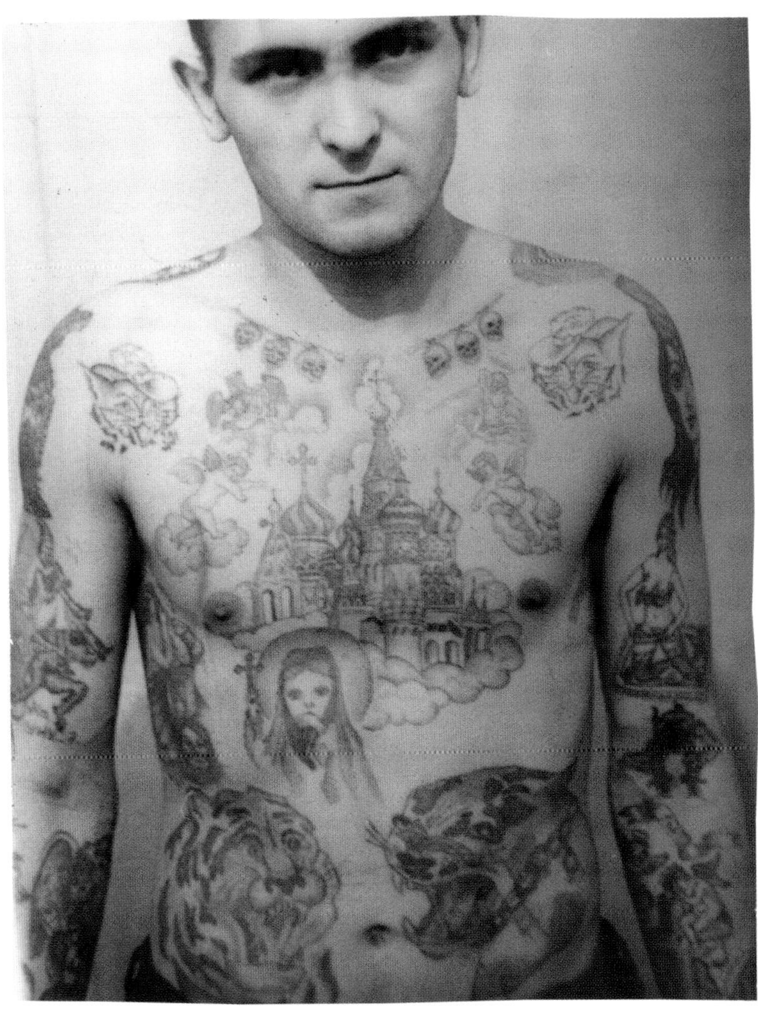

On the right arm: a devil carrying a man on his back is the sign of a drug addict. Text underneath reads **'To the moon'**.

The cats wearing hats tattooed on the shoulders indicate a burglar who prefers to operate alone at night, breaking into premises with bad security or no security at all. He uses skeleton keys and avoids any noise and violence (indicated by a bow tie). This tattoo may also be applied to the back of the hand. The tiger and leopard are signs of aggression.

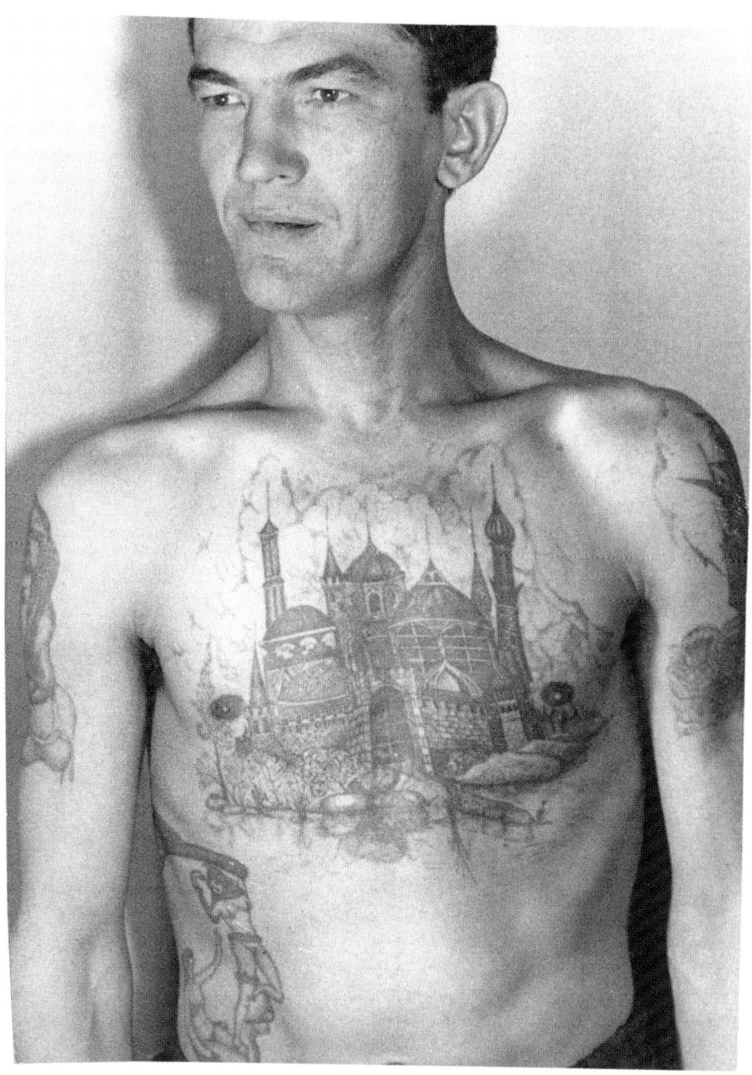

A tattoo of a multi-domed monastery surrounded by a wall can be worn by a *medvezhatnik* (a 'bear hunter' in Russian, the jargon name for a safecracker). A criminal with these skills is considered to be prison aristocracy, among the elite of the thieves' world. The number of domes can refer to the number of convictions and length of custodial sentence. On the side of the stomach a naked woman with a snake entwining her body is a sign of cruelty or guile.

Text on the neck reads **'If you haven't seen grief, love me'**. Latin text across the collarbones reads *Vivere memento* **'Remember to live'** and *Memento Mori* **'Remember that you must die'**. Latin text on the shoulder reads *Dum Spiro Spero* **'While I breathe, I hope'**. German text on the chest reads *Gott mit uns* **'God with us'**. Text above the church reads **'Save and protect your servant'**. Latin text under the church reads *Pereant qui ante nos nostra dixerunt* **'May they perish who have expressed our bright ideas before us'**. On the arm reads **'Save and protect your slave'**, **'Everything that we lose is not ours'**. Latin text underneath reads *In vino veritas* **'In wine** [there is] **truth'**.

A spider means the prisoner is following the criminal path. A spider in a web means that the zone is woven into everything and that the bearer is the boss of this situation. If the spider is climbing up the web then the bearer of the tattoo is fully committed to a life of crime; if it is climbing down then the wearer is attempting to break free of his criminal lifestyle. The syringe tattooed on the inmate's ribcage indicates that he is a drug addict. Inmates who are addicted to drugs will often cover the insides of their arms with dark tattoos in an attempt to conceal their needle marks.

The first specialised colony for substance users opened in the Omsk region in 1965, twenty kilometres from Omsk. Although it was a special institution, inmates would still manage to obtain drugs. There are hundreds of methods: hidden in paper, fabric, fruit, vegetables, fish or eggs, for instance. One twenty-nine year-old man from Armenia, with many tattoos, was a chronic drug user. He was sent to the punitive confinement unit for breaking the rules – persistently trying to use stimulating agents including toothpaste, washing-up liquid, shoe polish, lotions, perfume, hemorrhoid suppositories. There he started suffering withdrawal symptoms, shivering and twitching, literally banging his head against the walls; he tore up the veins on his arms with his teeth and drank his own blood. After undergoing withdrawal, he was questioned by the guards and they noticed he had no fingernails. He explained that he had torn them out and smoked them to ease withdrawal symptoms. He'd done the same with his toenails. At the end of the interview he added with a sly and somewhat proud smile: 'Necessity is the mother of invention'.

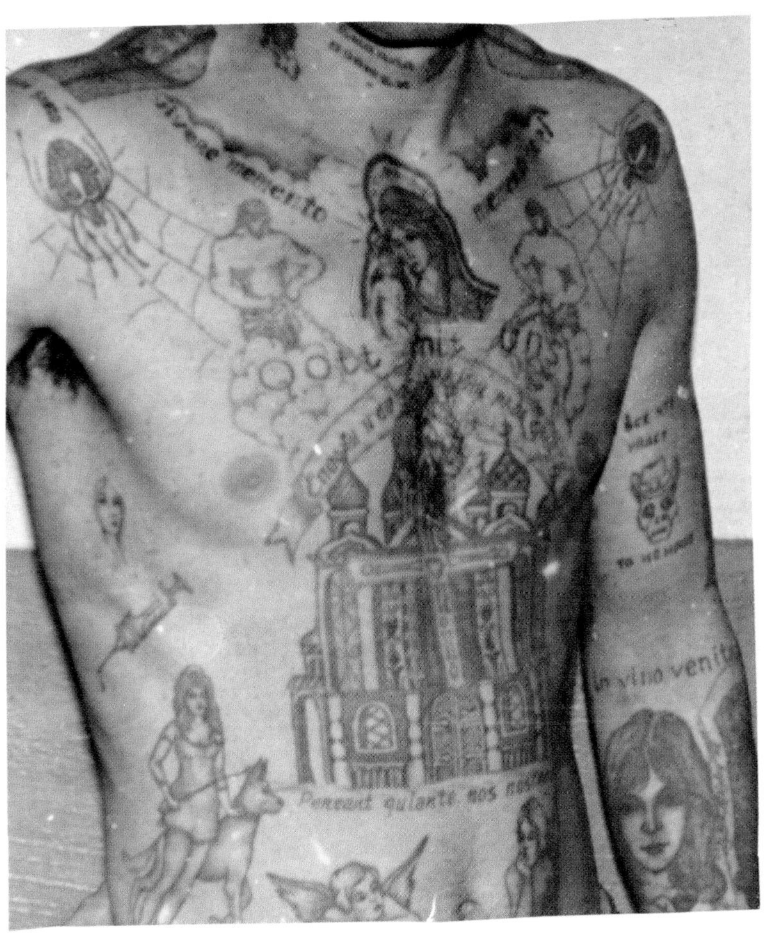

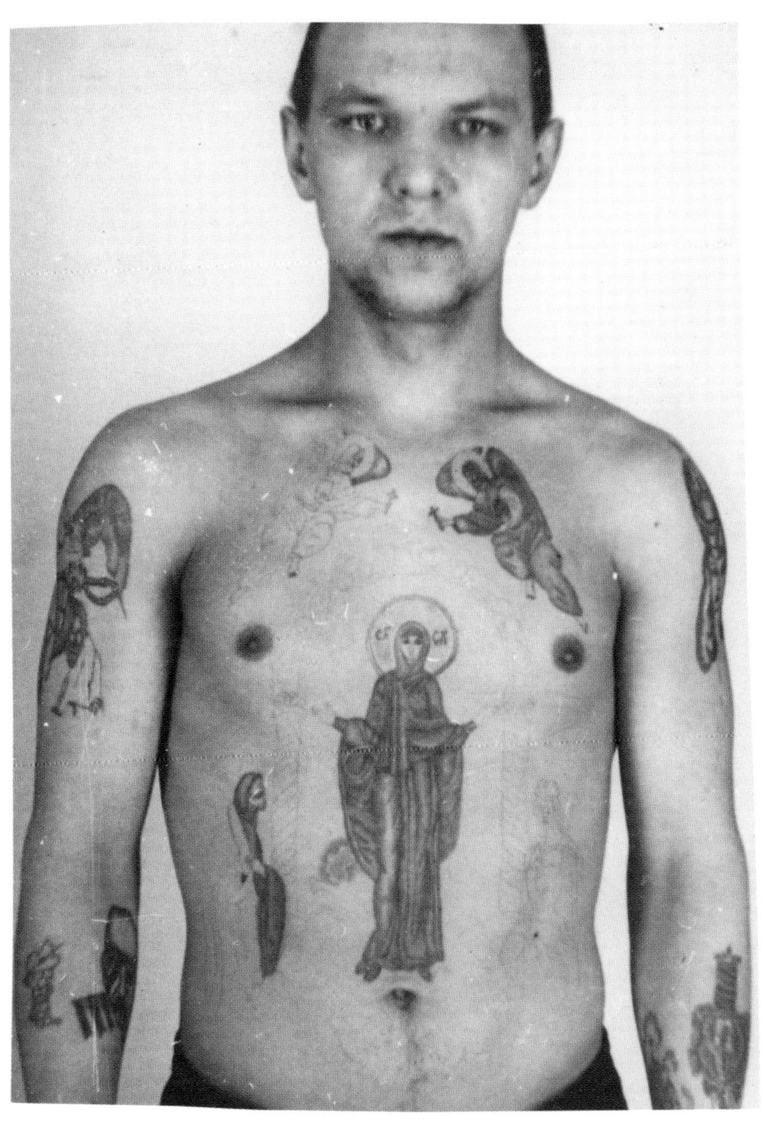

Text in the halo reads **'SP'** and **'SH'**, acronyms meaning **'Save and Protect'**.

The unfinished religious tattoos on this inmate are a work in progress.

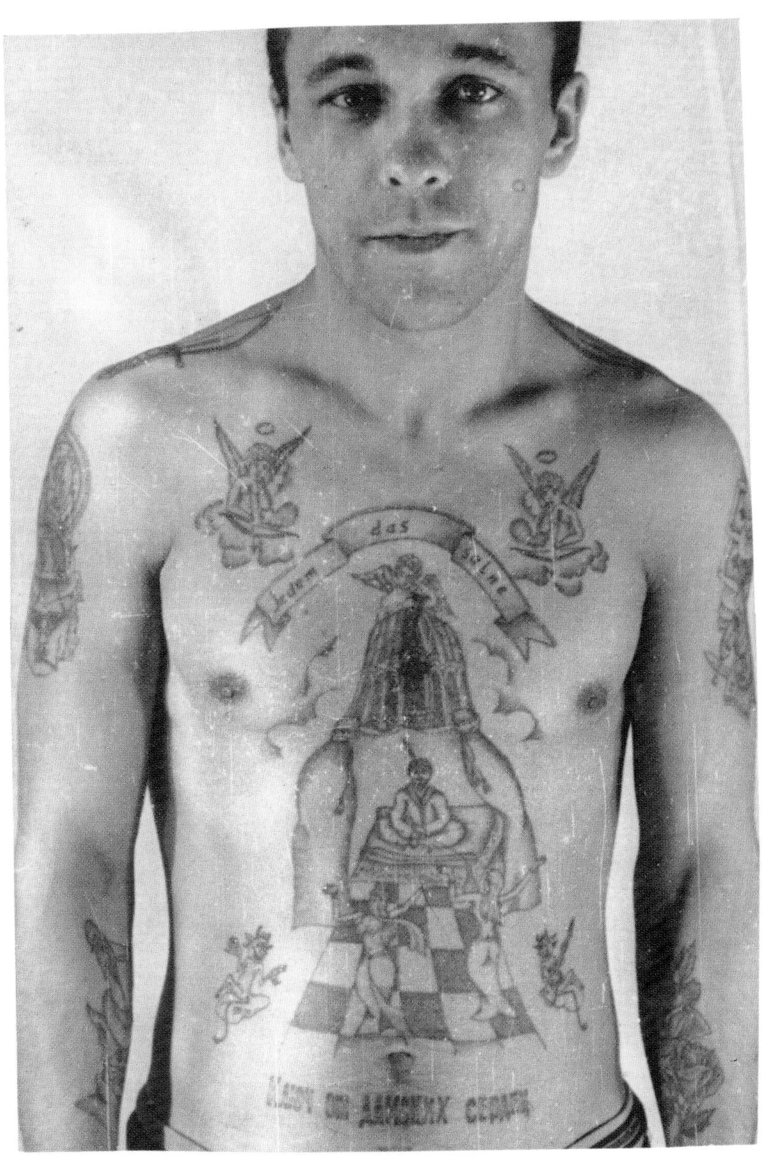

German text across the chest reads *Jedem das Seine* **'To each his own'**. Text above the waist reads **'The key to a woman's heart'**.

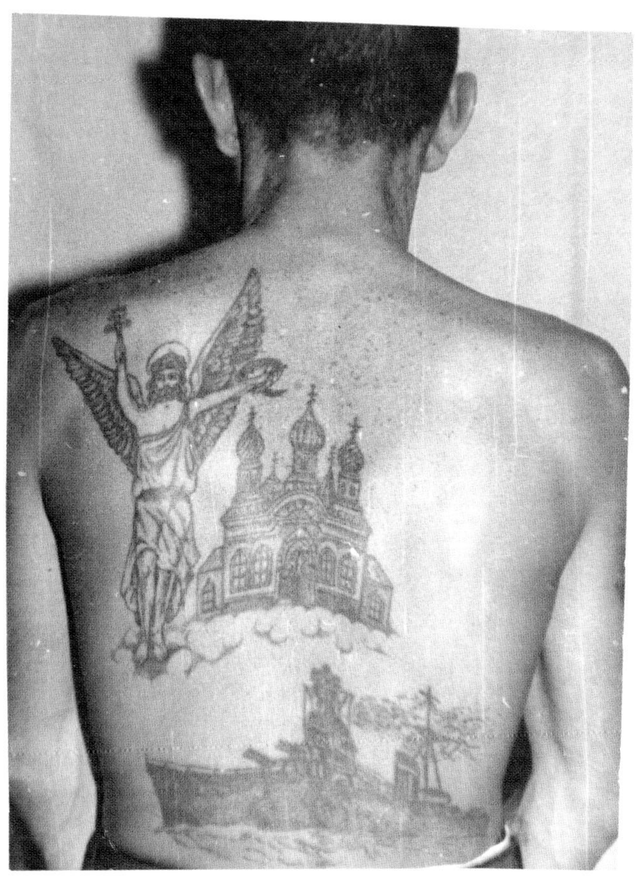

right: The tattoos on this inmate mimic those of higher-ranking criminals and indicate he has adopted a thieves' mentality. However, he does not wear the 'thieves' stars', he is not a *vor v zakone* (thief-in-law) and therefore holds no real power among this caste.

As soon as normal inmates enter the mass population of the 'zone' (either a prison or a camp), they realise that the thieves are in charge. They copy both their tattoos and mannerisms in an attempt to elevate their status. For self-protection they need to show themselves to be exceptional, experienced, brave and seasoned men. In addition to fear, respect and the obedience of friends, their tattoos are intended to demonstrate a desire for self-assertion and the conquest of authority in the criminal environment.

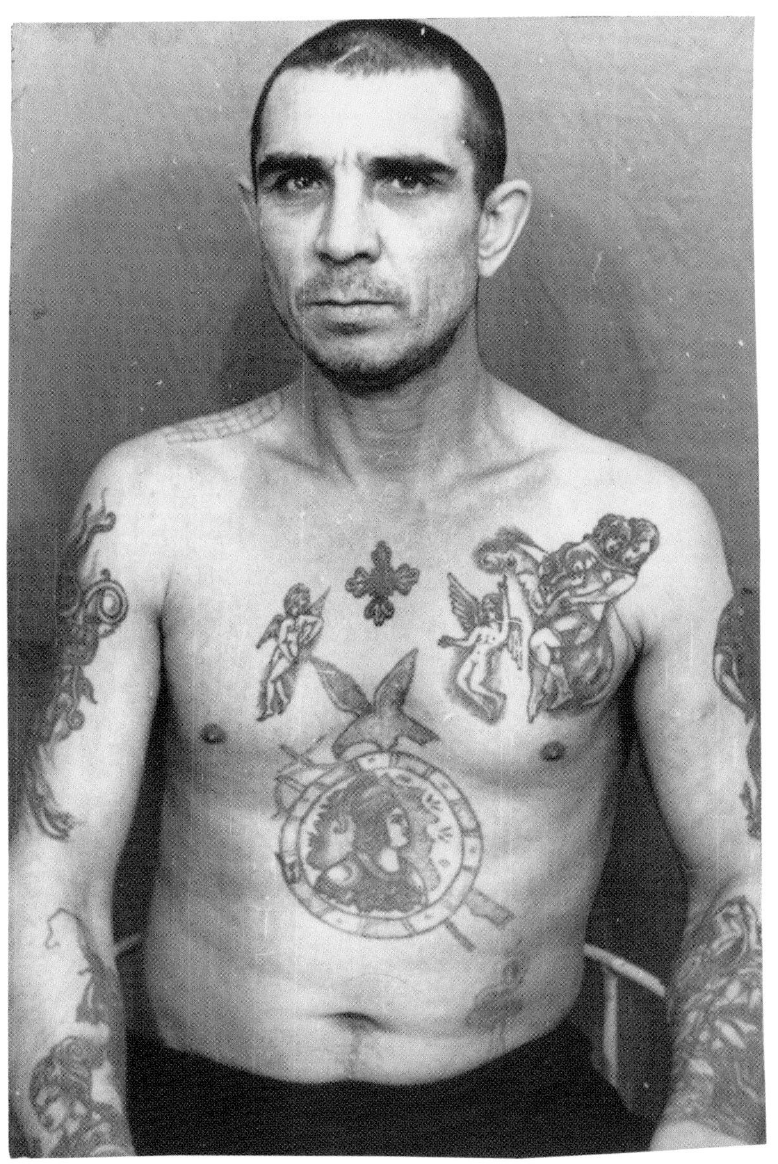

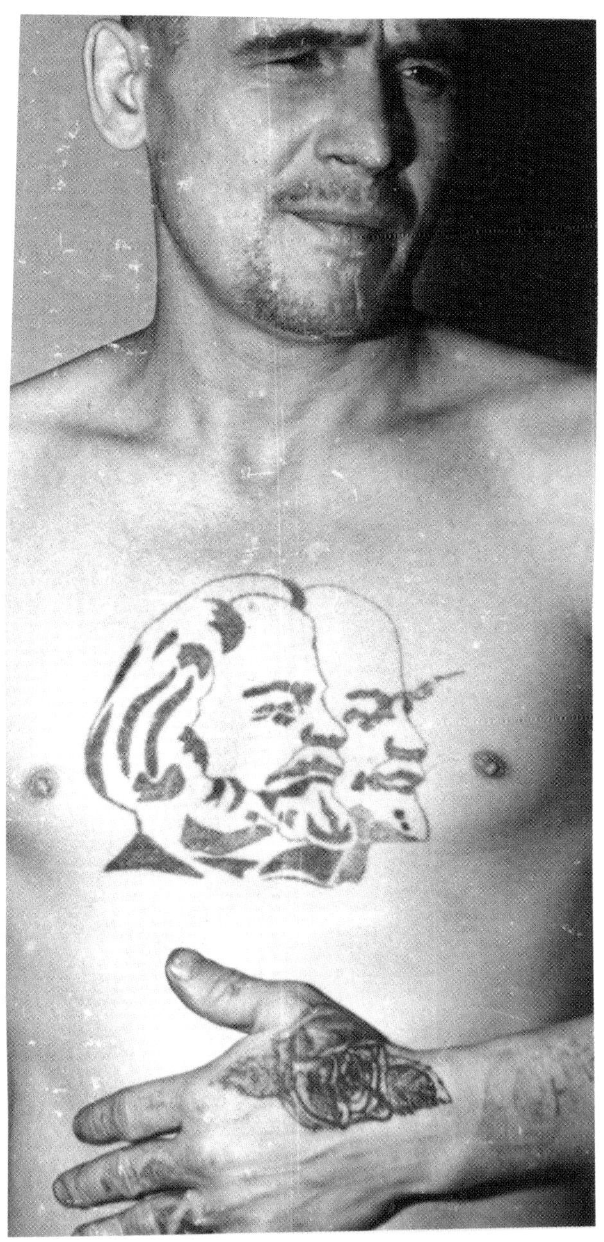

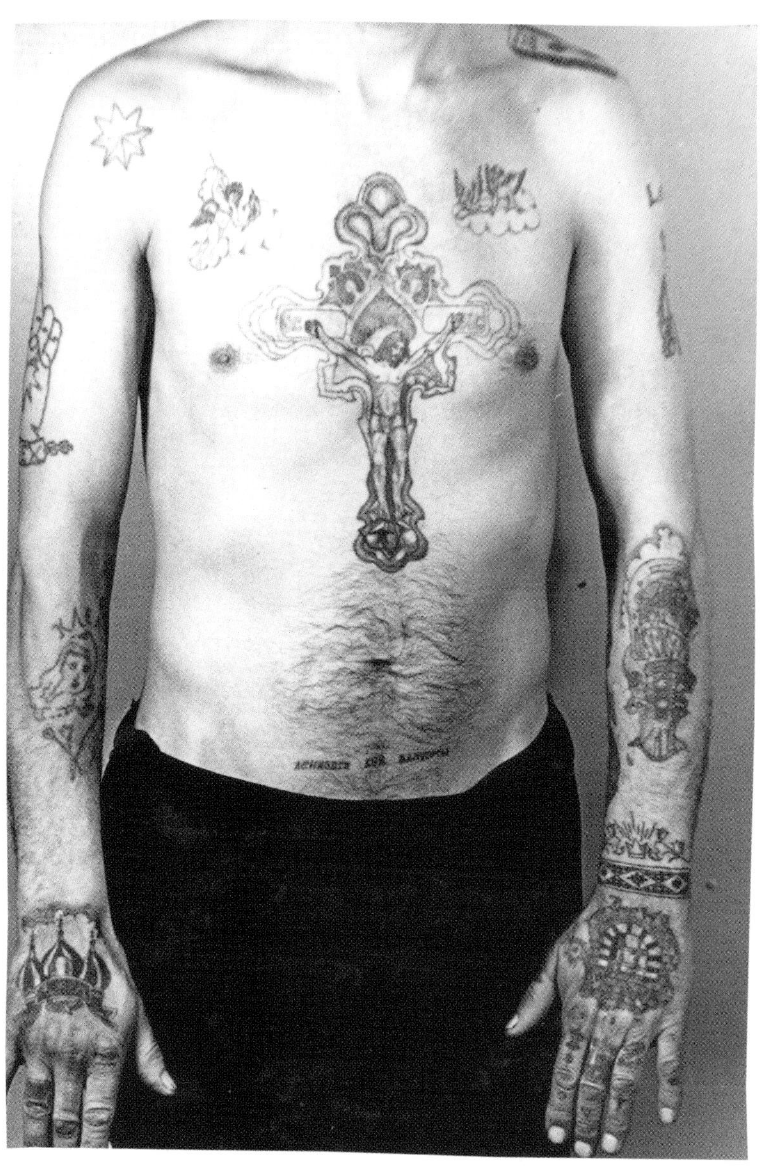

Text above the waist reads **'Lazy cock…'**. Text on the arm reads **'KLEN'** meaning *Klyanus Lyubit Eyo Navek* **'I swear to love her forever'**.

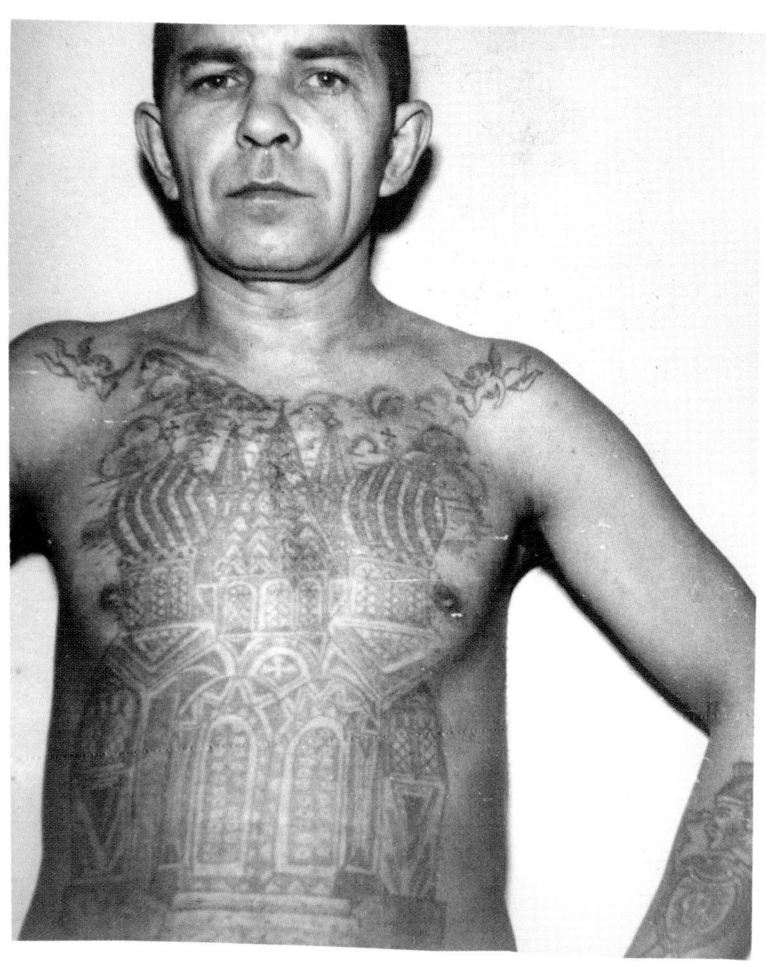

'Tens of thousands of people have been beaten to death by thieves. Hundreds of thousands of people who have been in the camps are permanently seduced by the ideology of these criminals and have ceased to be people. Something criminal has entered into their souls forever. Thieves and their morality have left an indelible mark on the soul of each.'
Varlam Shalamov, *The Red Cross* (1958)

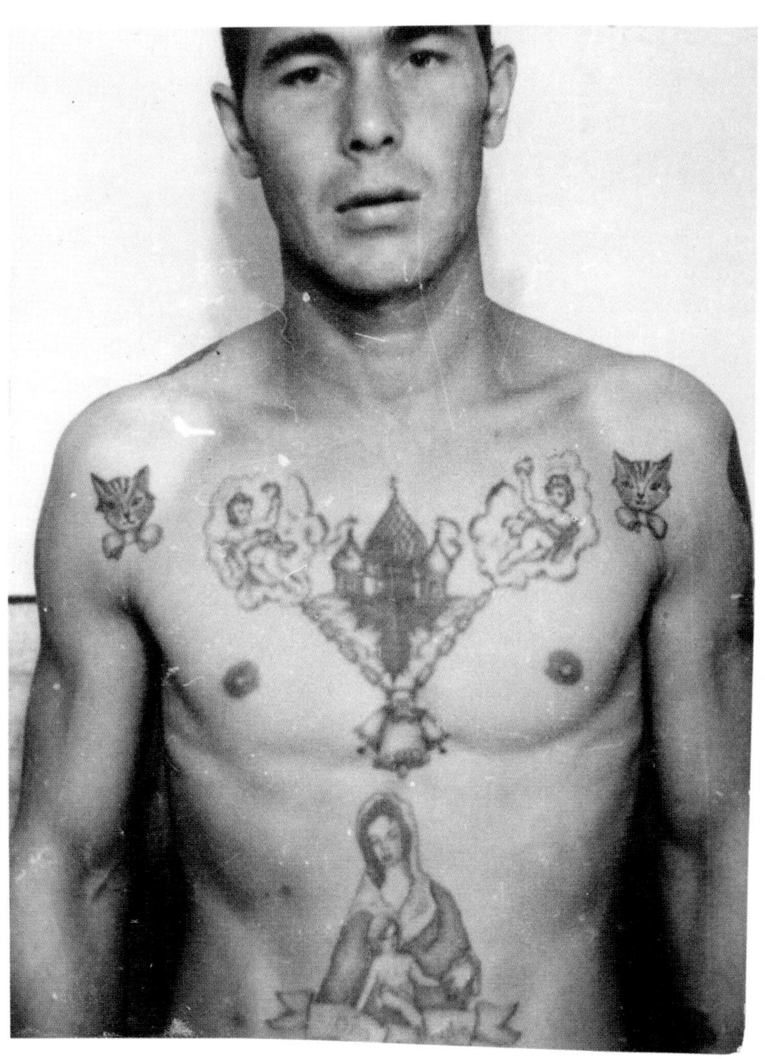

Cat heads tattooed on both sides of the chest show that the wearer is cunning, an able cheat, and can gain the victim's trust easily. The abbreviation *KOT* (literally 'cat' in Russian) stands for 'native prison resident', see also page 187.

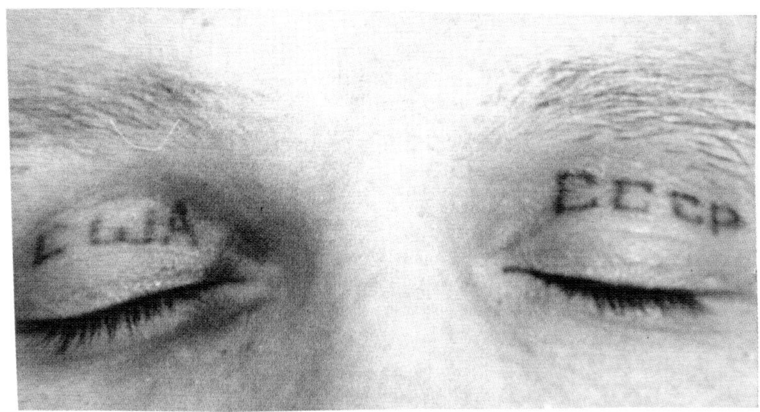

above: Text across the eyelids reads **'USA / USSR'**.

right: On the stomach a woman on the telephone (that leads to his penis) asks: **'Hello, are you up?'**. Tattooed on the tip of the penis is the State Quality Mark of the USSR. Text across the feet reads **'They are tired / But there is no fucking way you will catch them'**.

An image of a church with domes on the thigh (or forearm) represents criminals who have stolen from churches (usually gold candlesticks or other such furnishings), as well as criminals who have stolen money from parishioners in the church during the service.

The eagle carrying a skull pierced by a knife is the sign of a high-ranking travelling criminal who has committed murder and is prone to violence.

Above each knee a hand is tattooed giving the *kukish* or *fig* (an obscene gesture in Slavic countries) towards each other.

A leaf tattooed on the legs is the sign of an individual thief who has strayed from the caste of thieves, the so-called 'Polish thief'. In some colonies 'Polish thieves' are considered to be traitors, thieves that 'went bitch'. Following the strict tradition of the 'thieves' code', a *vor v zakone* mustn't work but can only live on 'professional' income which he has made as a thief, and must avoid committing other crimes. (When tattooed on the hands, a fallen leaf can mean the wearer lost parents at a young age, had no shelter, was 'torn away from life').

Tattooed on the feet are the Hare and Wolf characters from the cartoon *Nu, Pogodi!* (*Well, Just You Wait!* [1969–2006]) see also pages 75, 77 and 204.

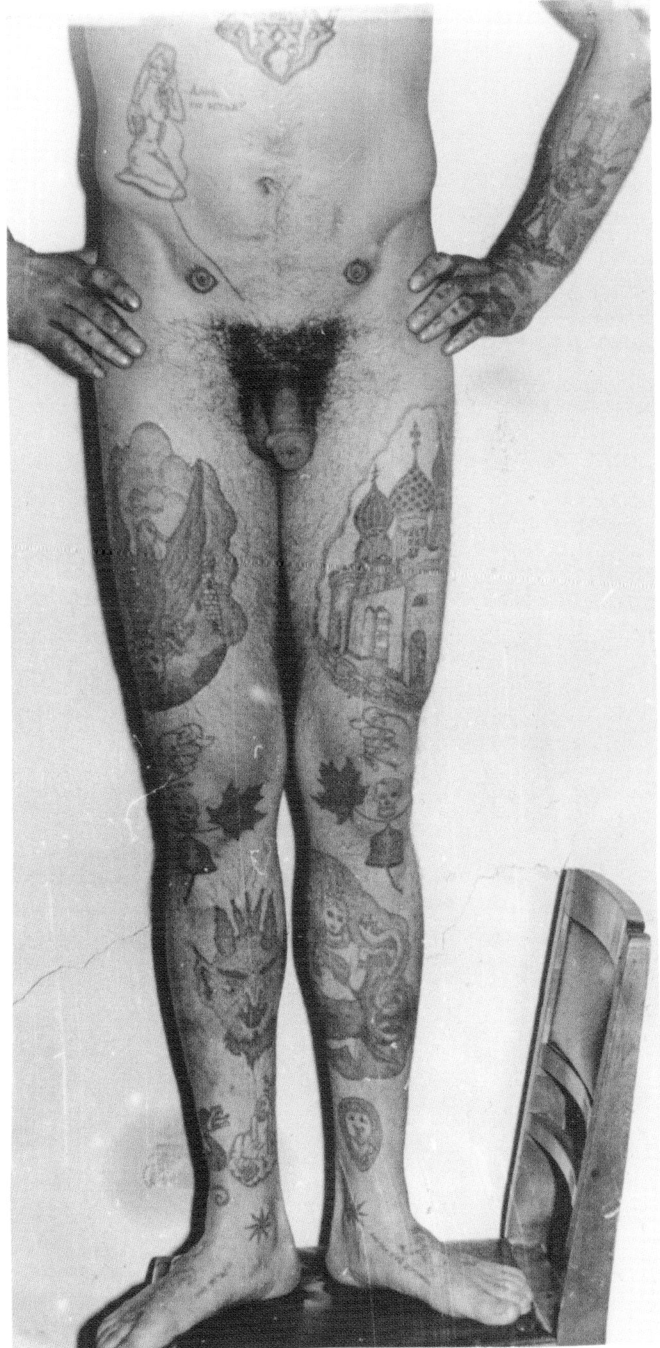

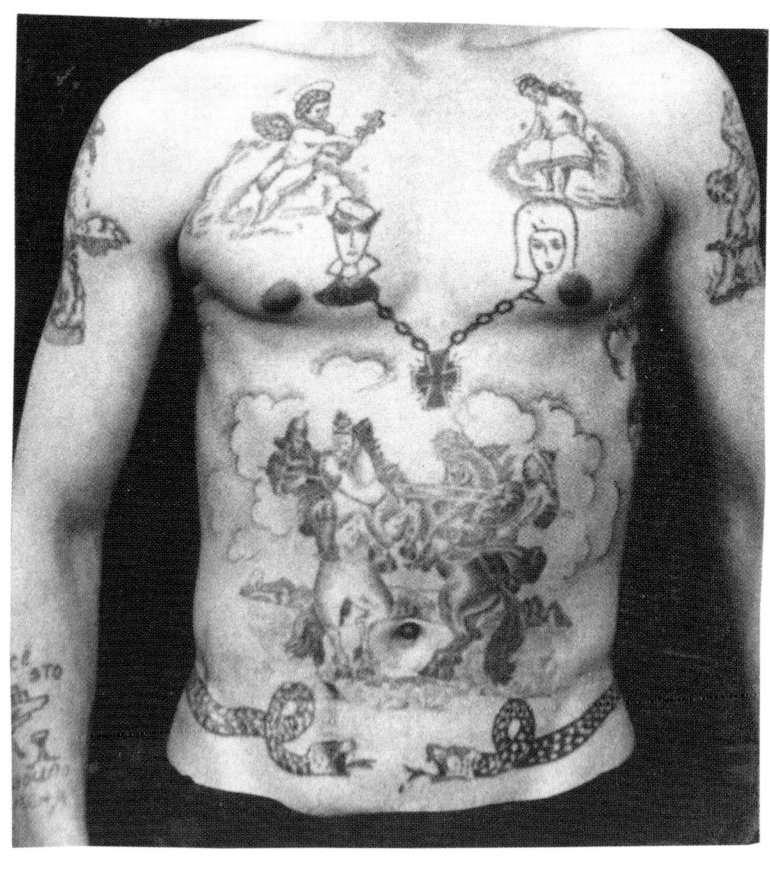

Text on the arm reads **'All this killed me'**, a variation on the tattoo 'This is what's killing us'.

The snake 'belt' denotes the inmate is in the grip of drug addiction.

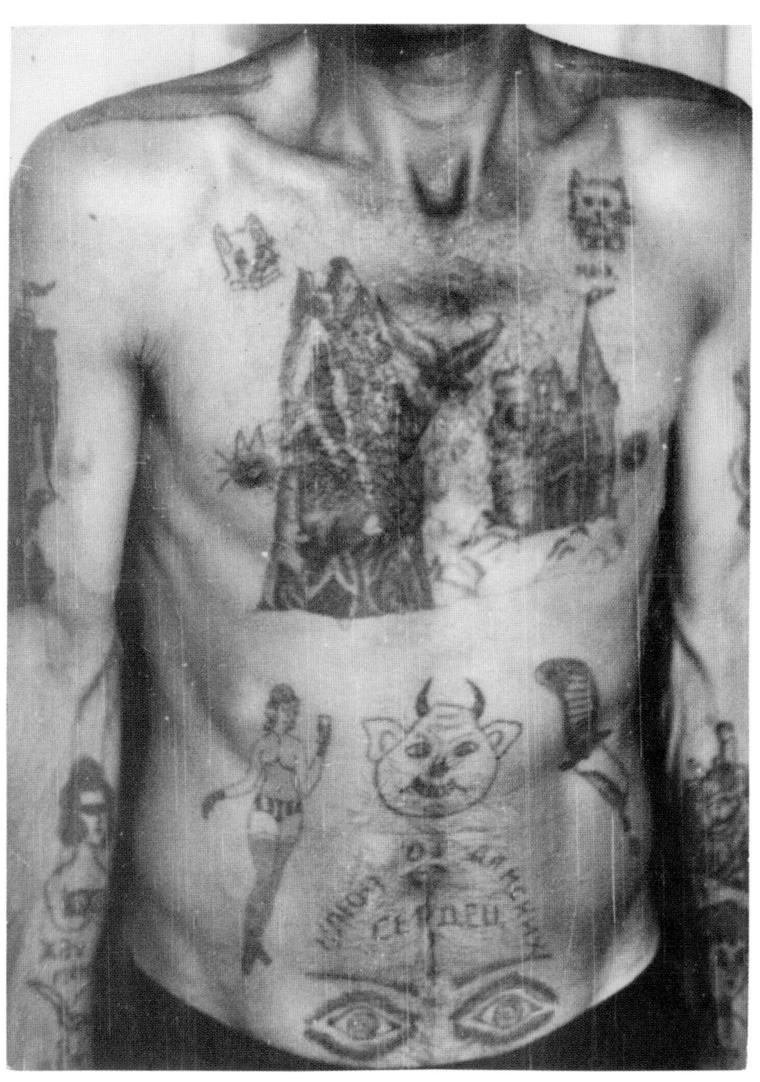

Text on the right wrist reads **'Wait for me'**. Text around the navel reads **'The key to a woman's heart'**.

A nipple has been tattooed to make a cat's face. The eyes above the waistline indicate a homosexual, see also pages 69, 156 and 177.

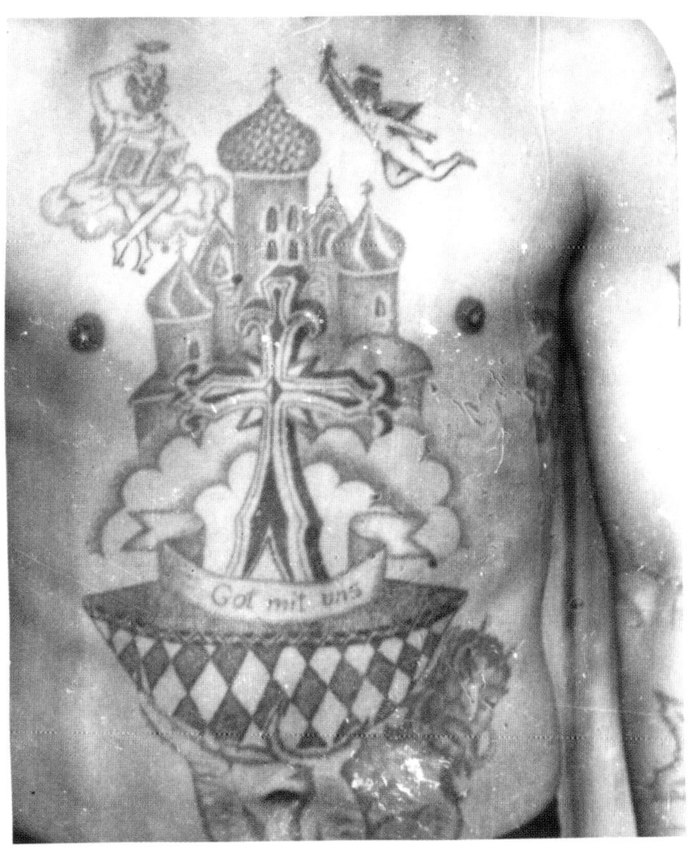

above: German text on the stomach reads *Gott mit uns* **'God with us'**, see also page 119.

The lack of work or any activities in the cell make detainees search for entertainment, and one of the possibilities is tattooing. It makes a change within the monotonous routine and draws the attention of all the inmates in a cell. Choosing a design, preparing tools, the actual process of tattooing, reaction of the person getting tattooed – all these activities cheer inmates up for a while and help to pass the tedious time. Drab existence, forced idleness and restriction on liberty of movement, often accompanied by depression, cause irritation and a yearning for entertainment.

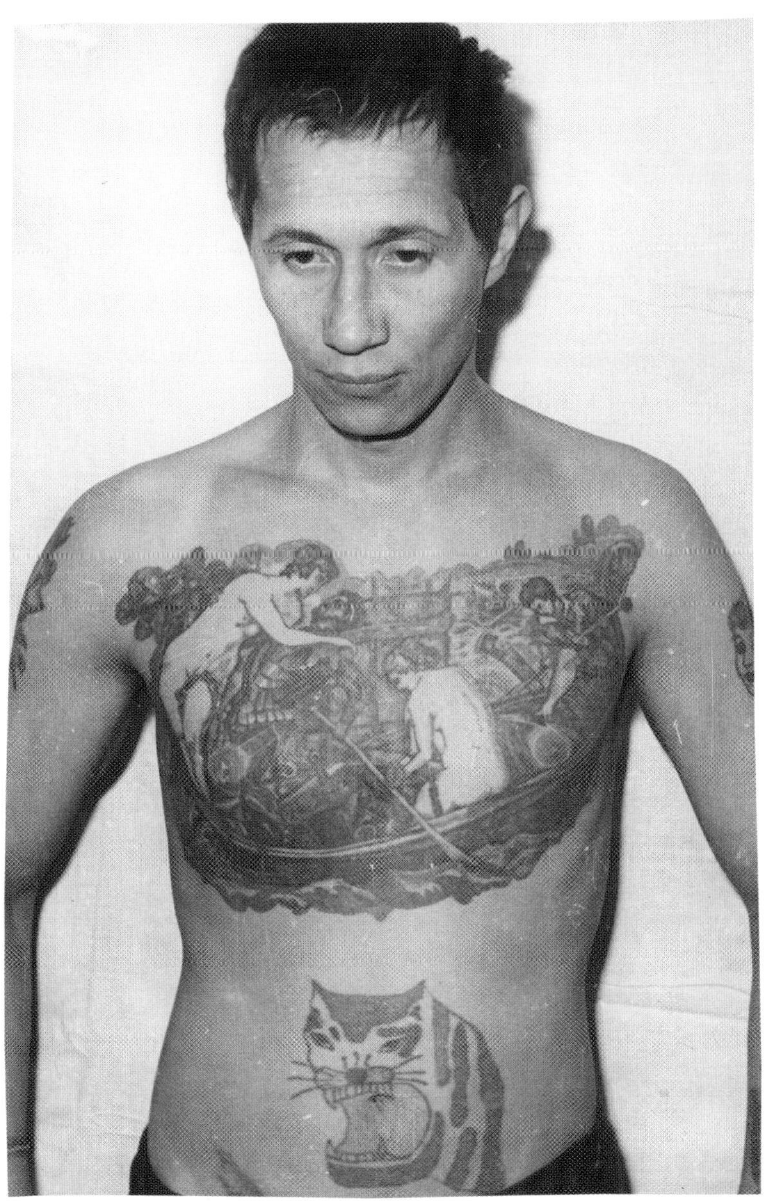

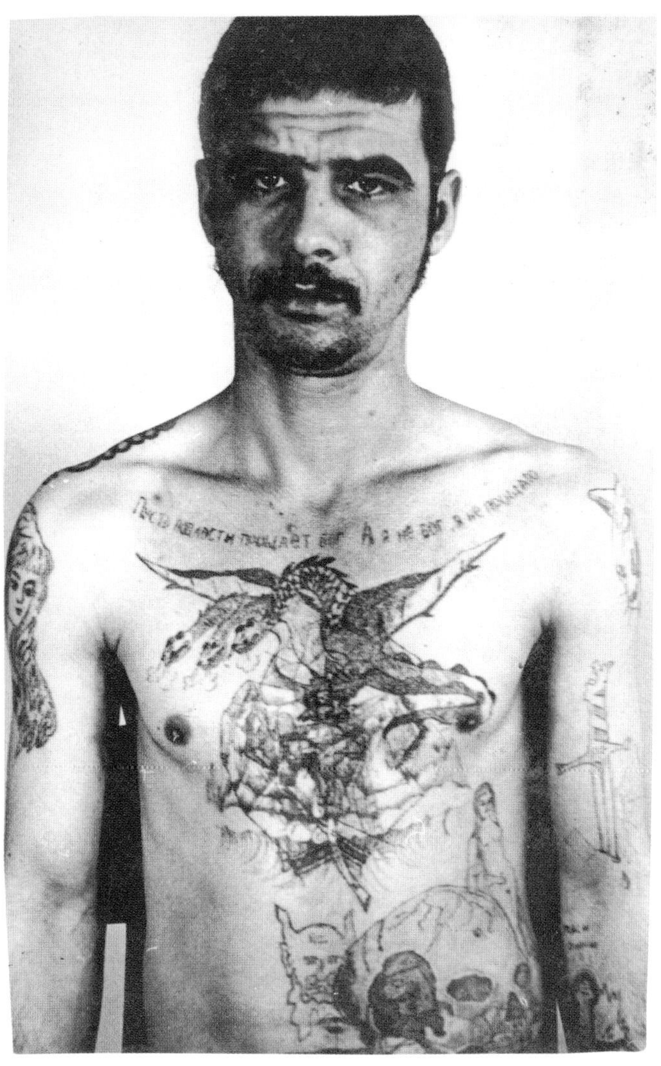

Text across the chest reads **'Let God forgive treachery. I'm not God, I don't forgive'**. Text on the arm reads **'Save and forgive'**.

The dragon tattooed on to the chest denotes a 'shark' – a person who has looted state or collective property, or embezzled large amounts of money. The shaft of a dagger embedded in the arm is the sign of an inmate who is especially aggressive and has a particularly negative attitude to the authorities. It is also applied to persons convicted of murder.

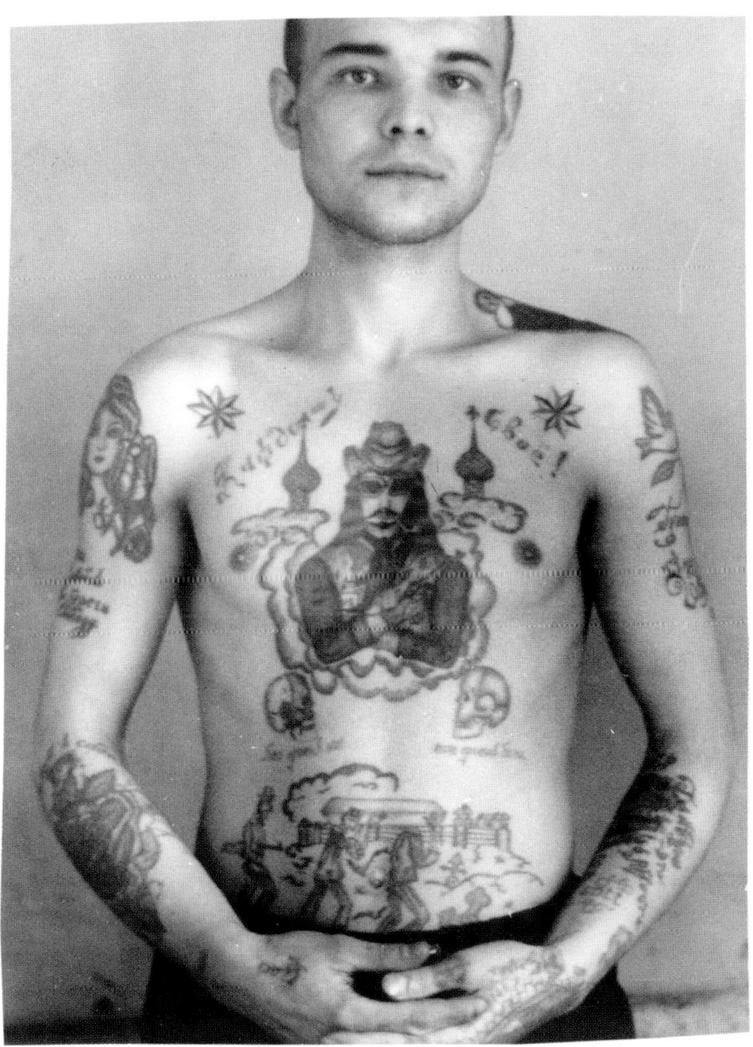

Text on the right arm reads **'Save love, keep freedom'**. Text on the left arm reads **'Sinner'**. Text across the chest reads **'To each his own'**. Text underneath the skulls reads **'God against everyone, everyone against God'**. Text on the wrist in German reads *Mein Gott* **'My God'**.

A cowboy with a gun shows this thief is prepared to take risks and is ready to exploit any opportunity. A dove carrying a twig (left shoulder) is a symbol of good tidings and deliverance from suffering.

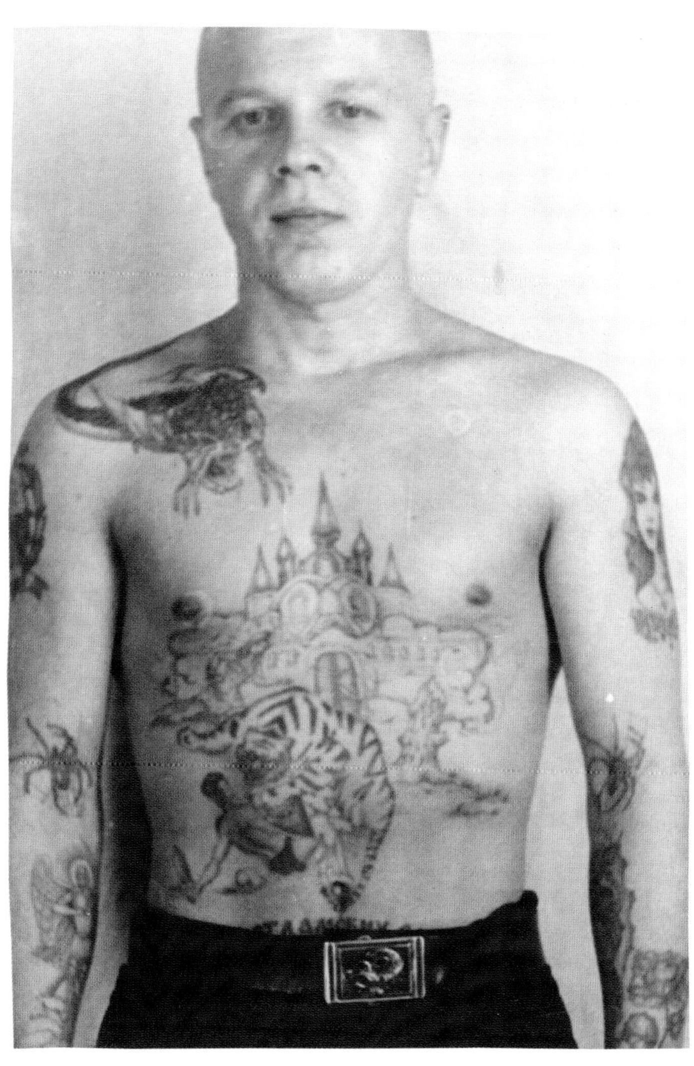

above: Text on the waist reads **'The key to a woman's heart'**.

right: The tattoo on the left forearm is known as the 'Heartbreaker' – a woman dressed in high boots and wearing a musketeer hat carries a sword that pierces a heart. On the right forearm the woman in front of a prison window with a dagger means 'Revenge for betrayal'. The church domes in the background show the sentence for this crime (in this case four years).

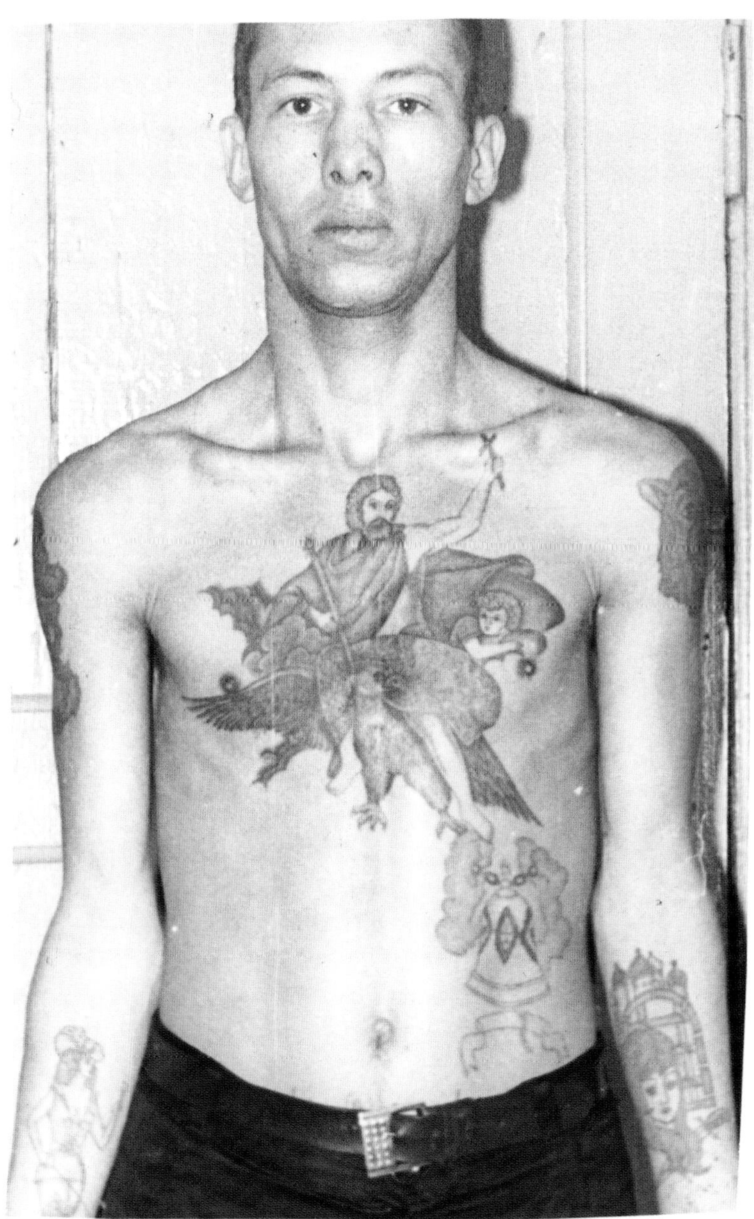

Text on the right wrist reads **'1975-1984 ITK'** *Ispravitelno Trudovaya Koloniya* (1975-1984 Correctional Labour Colony); the rose above the dates denotes the bearer spent his youth in prison. The acronym on the left wrist reads **'STV'** *Severnaya Gruppa Voisk* (Northern Army Group) applied during conscripted army service.

This thief is tattooed in the traditional fashion with a large image (usually a church or a cross) taking up the most important part of the body: the chest. This is intended to show a devotion to the thieves' traditions and stand as proof that his body is not tainted by betrayal, that he is 'clean' before his fellow thieves. The number of cupolas on the church signifies the number of convictions (in this case six).

The image of a cat's head with open eyes applied to the pectoral muscle, the scapular region or on the top third of the shoulder area signifies a residential burglar, who enters premises through a window or unlocked door. This tattoo is also applied to criminals who strangle their victim (usually rapists).

On the left leg a sailing ship with a white body, shaded sails and flags on the masts is the distinctive sign of a *gulnoy** – someone who has fled from custody, putting themselves in an illegal situation† to engage in criminal activity. Also a 'nomadic traveller', a migrant offender who travels to various cities to commit theft.

On the right leg is a genie emerging from a lantern. The sign of a drug addict, this can also mean that the bearer was convicted of a crime while under the influence of narcotics.

* Taken from the Russian verb *gulat,* to walk.

† Former convicts were not permitted to live in cities and were exiled to '101 km' – a generic term for the distance in kilometres any convict must keep from a large city after serving their sentence. Convicts caught outside their assigned dwelling area were detained. After three consecutive detentions the convict would be imprisoned for violating the residence law.

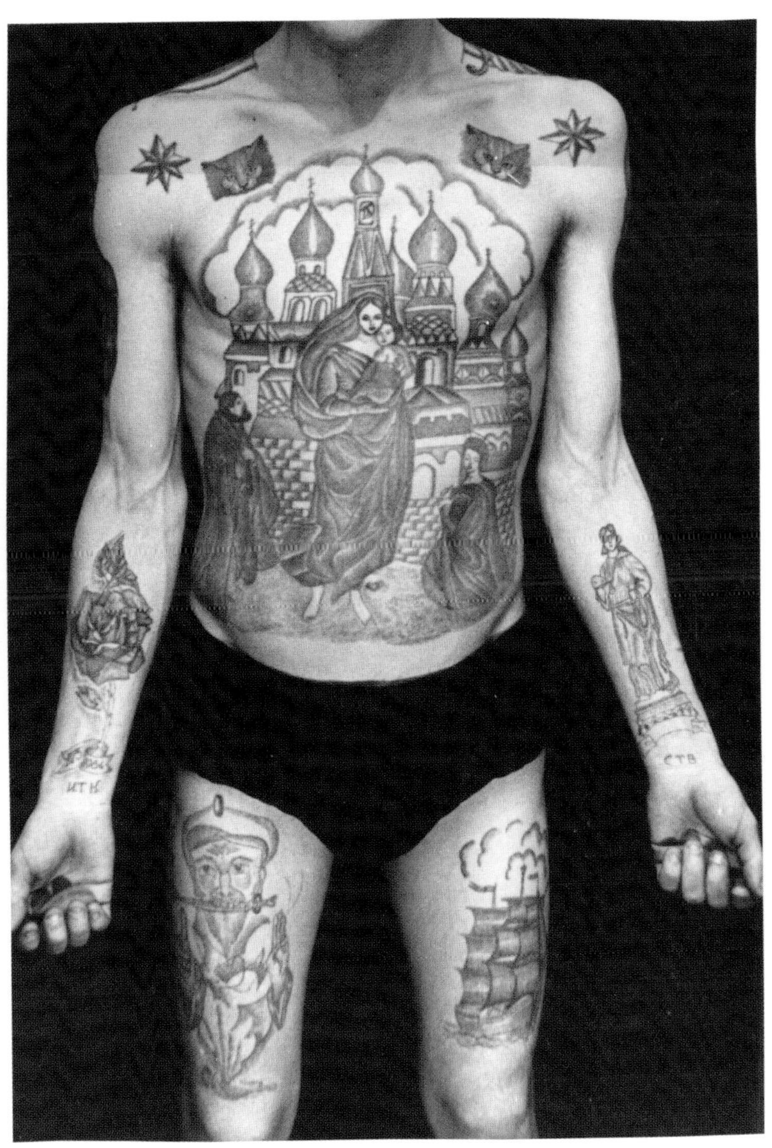

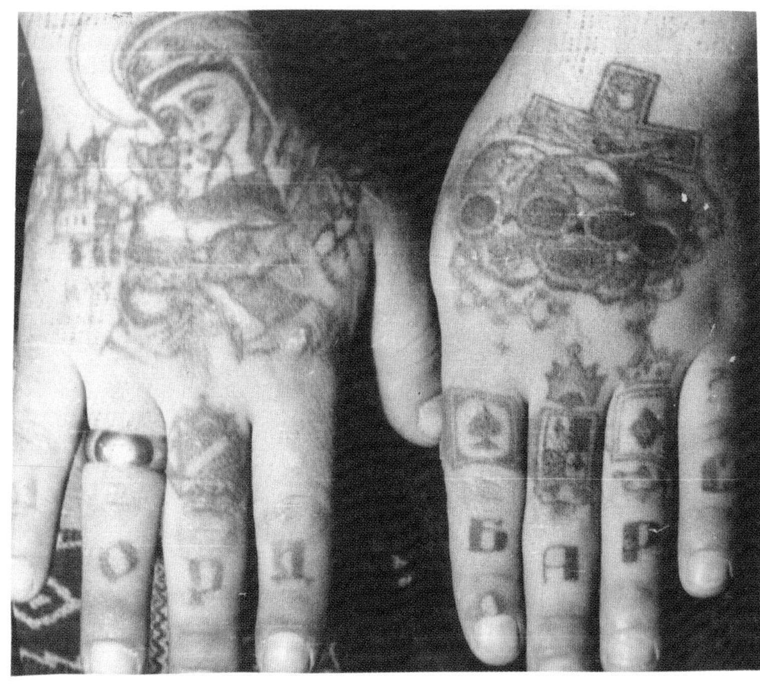

above: The left-hand middle finger 'I've passed through the zone'; right-hand forefinger '*baklan*' or '*patsan*' a prisoner sentenced for a misdemeanour, who holds the same views as the *otritsaly* (those who refuse to submit to prison rules); middle finger 'an authority', a high-ranking thief; third finger '*patsan*', a 'lad', a young authoritative thief, the most privileged inmate of the VTK (Educational Labour Colony). Text across the fingers of the left hand forms the acronym **'LORD'**, which has several interpretations including: *Legavym Otomstyat Rodnye Deti* (Coppers Beware, Our Children will Avenge Us), or *Lubi Otets, Rodnihx Detei* (Father, Love Your Children), *Lagernie Orli Raduot Druzei* (Camp Eagles Make Happy Friends). Text across the right hand reads **'BARS'** (Russian for snow leopard) interpreted as *Bey Aktiv, Rezh Suk* (Beat up activists, kill the bitches).

right: Text on the arm reads **'I have fully paid for the journey. I shall not forget my dear mother'**. Text on the wrist is a list of correctional labour colonies **'ITK-2, ITK-12, ITK-16, ATLYAN, MDVK, GDVK'**. On the hand it says **'Hello** [thieves]'.

Hinges are commonly tattooed on to the interor of the elbow joints – an example of prison humour.

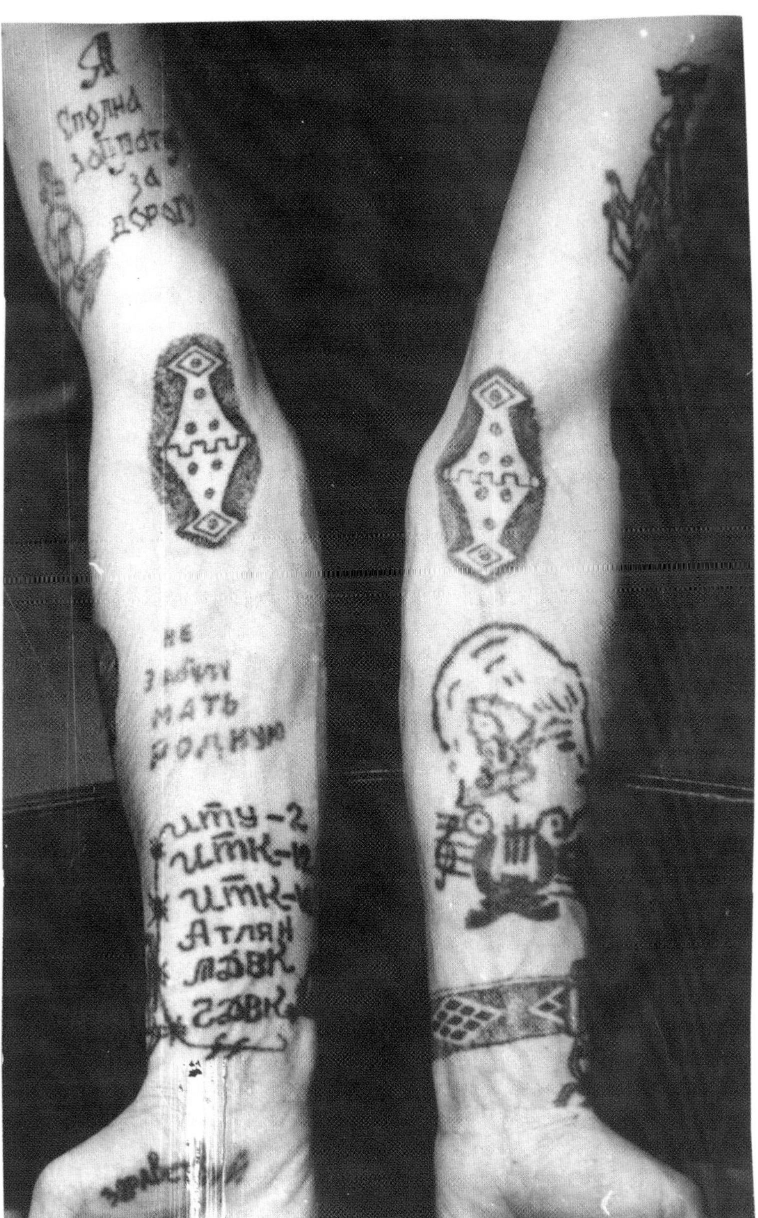
Я
сполна
заплатил
за
дорогу
не
забуду
мать
родную
ИТУ-2
ИТК-13
ИТК-4
Ялта
ЛВВК
22ВК

The acronym **'SOS'** variously stands for *Spasite Ot Syda* (Save me from judgment); *Spasayus Ot Suk* (I saved myself from the bitches)*; *Spasayus Ot Sifilisa* (Saved from syphilis); *Spasi, Otets, Syna* (Save me, father, your son); *Suki Otnyali Svobodu* (Bitches robbed my freedom). Text across the hand is the name **'Tanya'** and above the rising sun reads **'Quiet Love'**. Crosses on the knuckles: trips to the zone; each cross represents a sentence served. Typically these tattoos are made by house-burglars, or 'tiger-beetles' as they are referred to in the criminal environment. These tattoos are intended to show other inmates that the bearer is incapable of duplicity, that he will not cooperate with the administration. Index finger: worn by negative elements in prison and may also be a sign in memory of parents who died while the bearer served time in prison. Middle finger: 'I stayed in until the bell' worn by prisoners who served their sentence in full, without remission. Forcibly applied 'lowering' ring tattoos are often concealed using this design once the offender has left the zone. Third finger: the inverted spade is the sign of a 'cormorant', an inmate sentenced for hooliganism (an offence which is regarded with contempt by thieves and would lower the status of any thief convicted of it). Little finger: 'Woe to the vanquished', 'To live is to fight'. This ring denotes power, strength and aggressiveness. The bearer will not hesitate to become violent or commit murder. The domes and lines above each ring denote authority, convictions and years 'sitting' for each term.

Manacles on the wrists indicate a prison term of more than five years. The long rays of the sun stand for convictions (usually for pickpocketing), the shorter rays between them for imprisonment by a court.

* The 'bitch' caste developed following World War II. According to the 'thieves' code' (the 'laws' that are followed by all legitimate thieves), none of their number are allowed to take up arms and fight in the military on behalf of the authorities. In the thieves' world this is considered shameful treason. During the war this situation became impossible: many thieves were rounded up and forced to fight against the Nazis in penal units. After the war, when the thief combatants returned, far from being hailed as heroes, they were ostracised by their fellow thieves who took advantage of their 'legitimate' position and declared the collaborating thieves to be *suki* (bitches). This meant that they were lowered, and would have to work like any ordinary *muzhik* (peasant), with the 'thieves-in-law' living off their labour. But the bitches were a large and powerful force, and would not accept this role. They decided to form their own criminal elite, offering their help to the camp officials to keep the legitimate thieves under control. The authorities accepted the offer of the 'bitch caste' and the wars between the 'thieves' and 'bitches' erupted. These brutal battles resulted in many deaths; the administration was forced to divide the camps into 'local zones'. Separated by a fence, these distinct areas were designed to keep the warring factions apart and reduce incidents of massive disorder.

Thieves and bitches came from the same background and spoke the same slang. If a bitch found himself in the thieves' zone he would attempt to pass himself off as a 'legitimate thief' in order to survive. Both sides were also tattooed in the same way, but for a time, small modifications led to the tattoos becoming a means of telling thief from bitch. An arrow was added to the image of a dagger piercing a heart (to signify revenge against the bitches). Similarly tattooed acronyms acquired new meanings that acted as a secret code, known only by the thieves. Despite these efforts eventually these ciphers became part of the general prison lore and their strength as weapons against the bitches was lost.

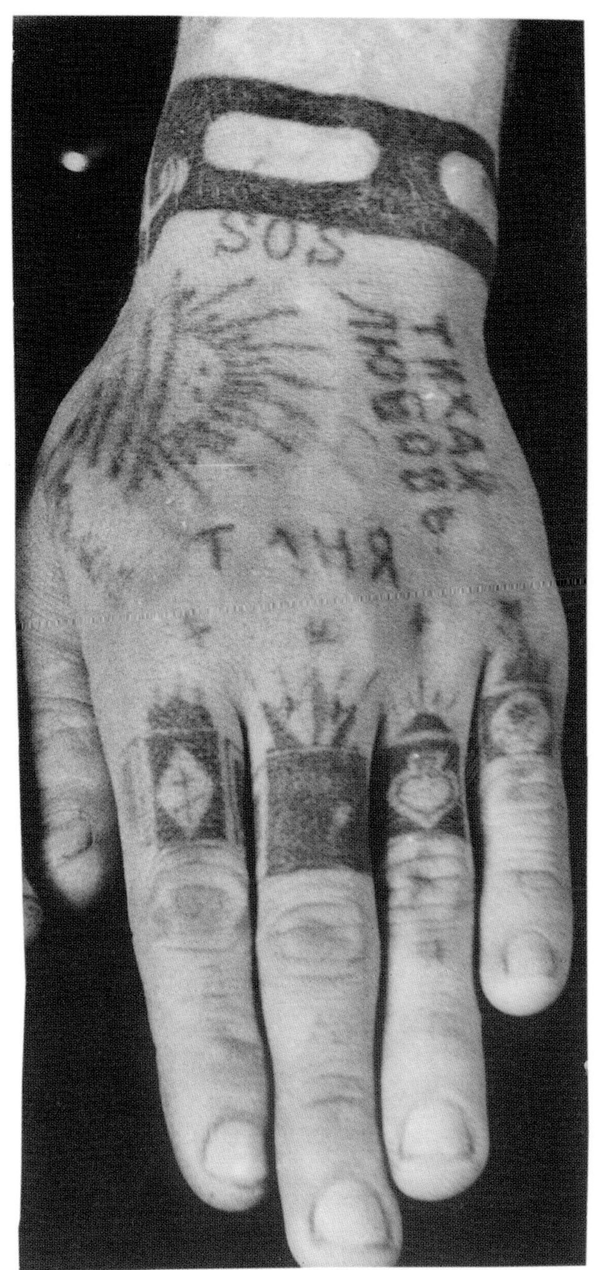

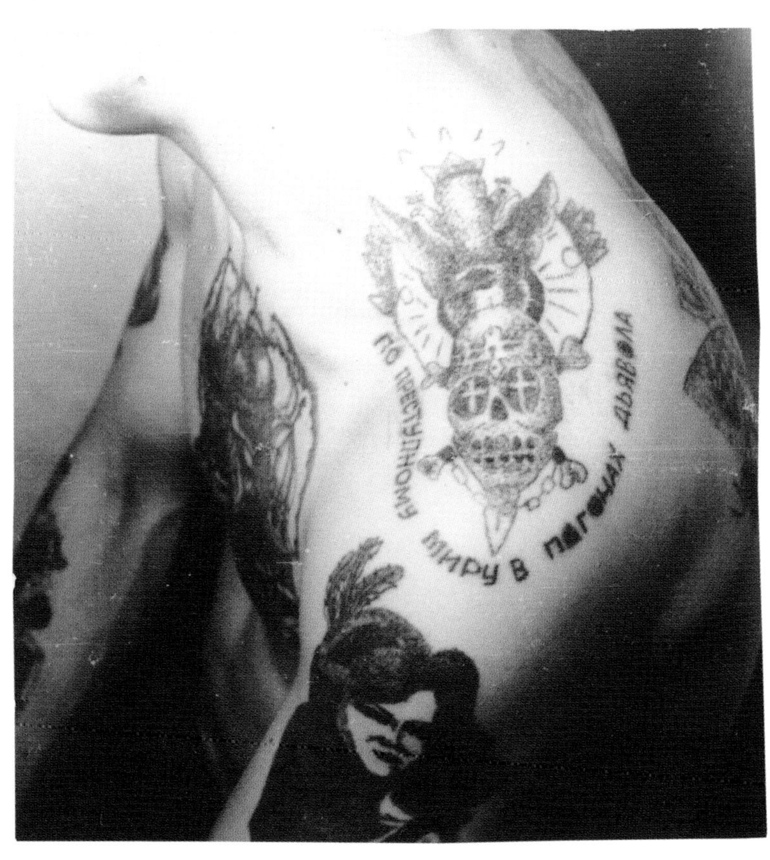

Text on the shoulder reads **'Around the criminal world wearing the devil's epaulettes'**.

The depiction of a knife through the skull denotes a murderer; when worn as an epaulette it means that the bearer has murdered a policeman. The double-headed eagle on either side of the handle of the knife is a sign of Tzarist Russia. It can be interpreted as meaning both 'Russia for the Russians' (an aggressive attitude towards ethnic minorities) and as a display of an antagonistic attitude towards the Communist authorities.

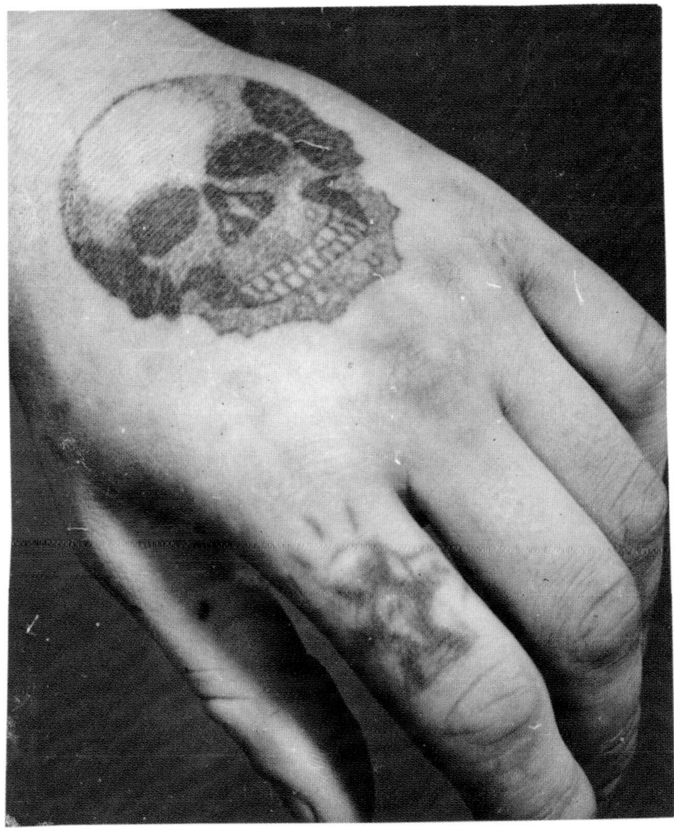

The skull is the symbol of a murderer. Thieves consider prisons their true home and accept that a large part of their life will be spent behind bars. A criminal cannot become a *vor* without being repeatedly imprisoned: 'Home for angels is heaven, home for a *vor* is prison'. For prisoners serving long or life sentences, the prospect of release is dim or non-existent. Some are completely institutionalised; they cannot imagine life 'in freedom' and in many cases they do not want it. Their only interest is to make the most of their existing situation, to gain power and status within the zone. Committing murders to order is a simple method of achieving this. Following the abolition of the death sentence for murder (repealed in 1947), the number of murders in prisons and camps escalated dramatically, practically working as a form of inmate population control for the administration. For the criminals, adding another ten years to a life sentence was of no consequence as they did not wish to be released anyway.

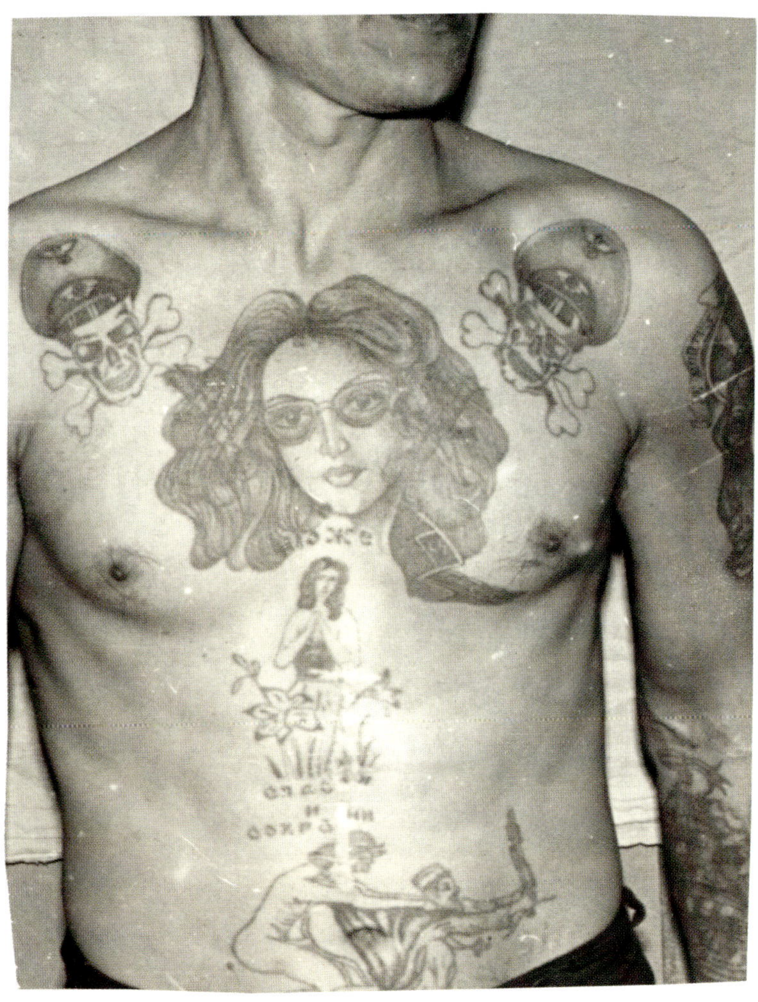

Text on the stomach reads **'God save and protect'**.

The pornographic tattoo on the stomach of this inmate shows a horned devil character with a stereotypical 'Jewish' nose sodomising a Russian Orthodox priest who holds a Russian Cross. This type of tattoo is typically forcibly applied, usually for losing at cards and being unable to pay the debt. The loser will also be made to pay the tattooist.

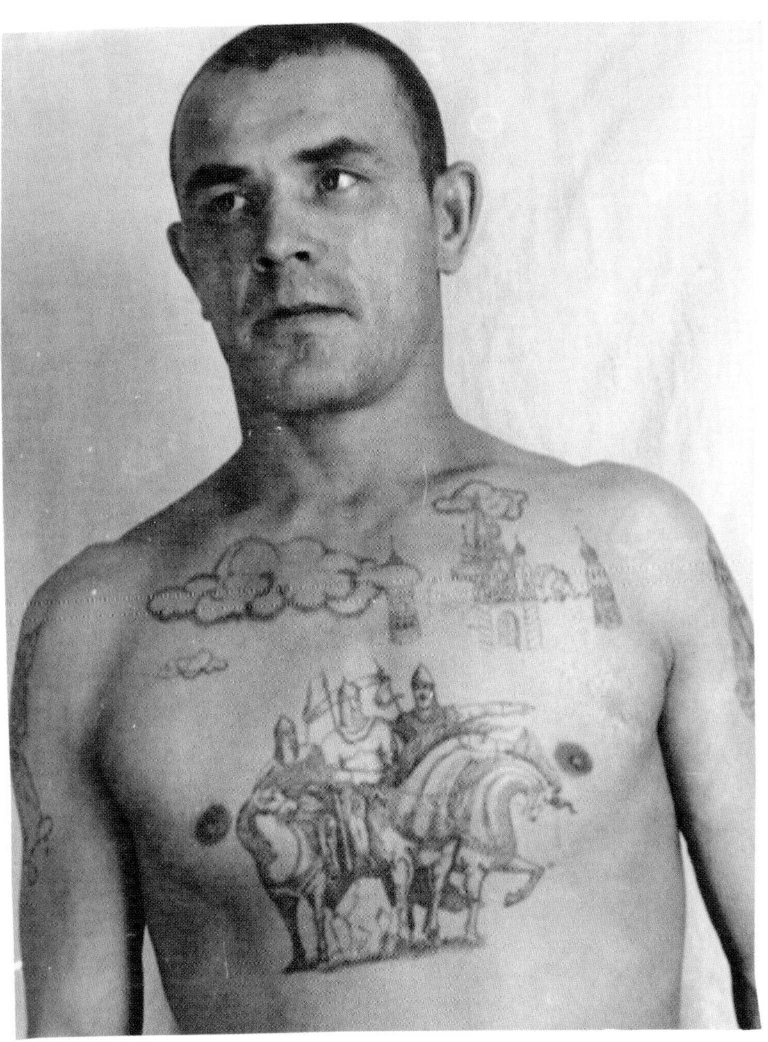

A chest tattoo depicting three bogatyrs. These were medieval warrior-knights who roamed the vast expanse of Kievan Rus', their adventures becoming legend. The most famous was Ilya Muromets who, alongside his compatriots Dobrynya Nikitich and Alyosha Popovich, became synonymous with the defence of their homeland, integrity, and both spiritual and physical power. This tattoo is based on the famous painting *Bogatyrs* (1898) by Viktor Vasnetsov. As well as meaning 'Keep Russia for the Russians', it displays both warrior power and aggression towards the authorities.

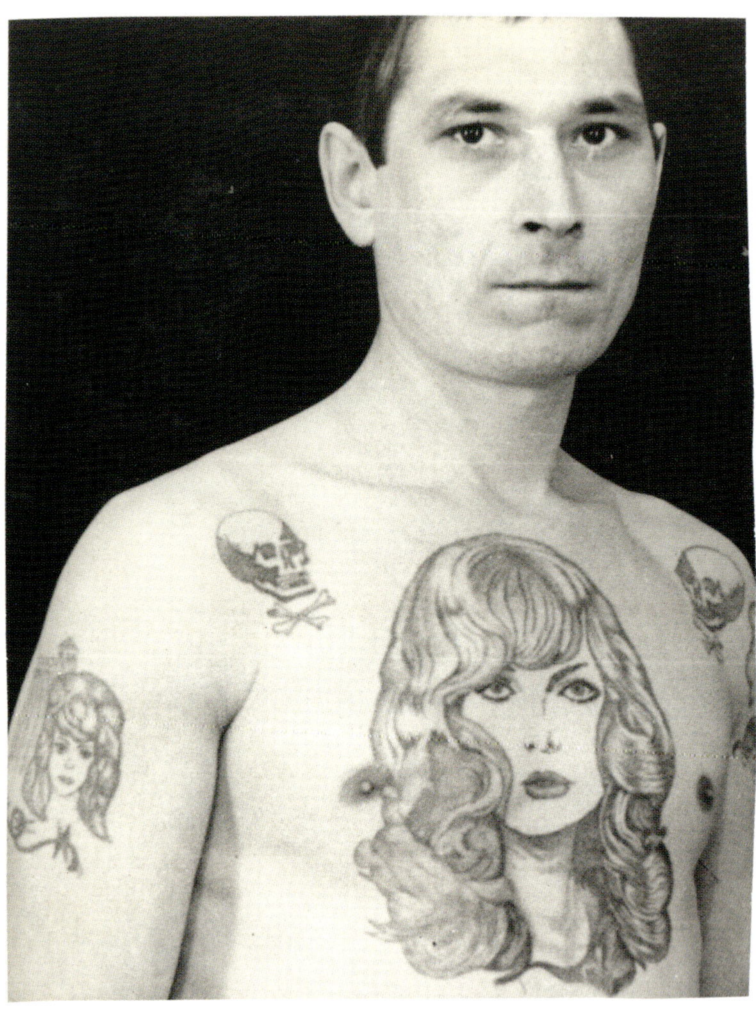

The skull and crossbones were originally tattooed as the symbol of a criminal who had received a death sentence which had then been commuted to a life term. Usually applied to the left arm, between the shoulder and elbow, they were reserved for those deemed to be 'fascists' in the eyes of the authorities: inmates who had been convicted under Article 56 for particularly dangerous crimes against the state. Today this symbol only means life imprisonment.

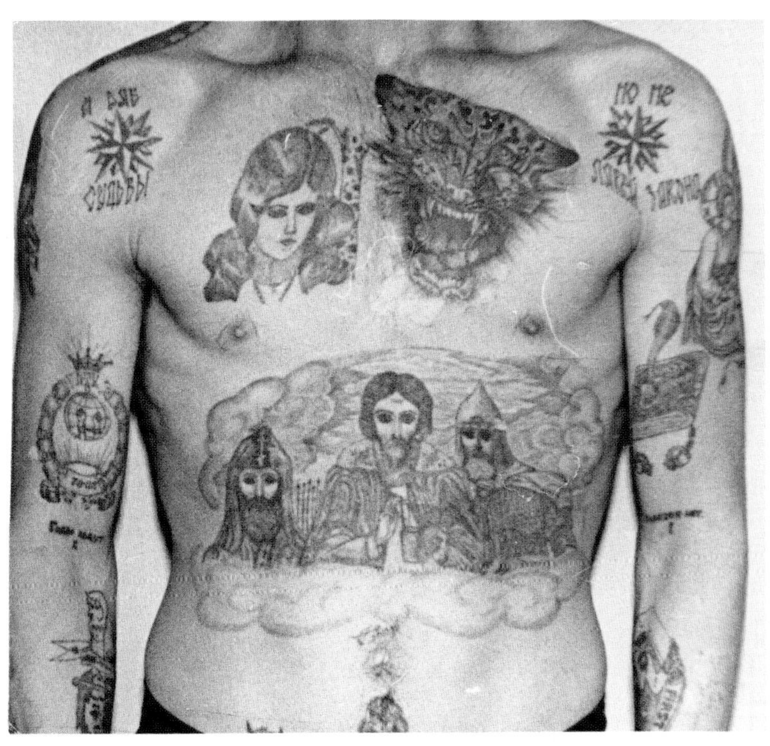

Text at the top of the chest reads **'I'm a slave to fate / but no lackey to the law'**. Text on the left arm reads **'The years go by'**. Text on the right arm reads **'There is no stagnation!'**.

An authoritative thief who is against the regime. The leopard on the chest is a 'grin' against the authorities. On the right arm a derivative Soviet coat of arms is crowned with the letters 'ITK' standing for *Ispravitelno Trudovaya Koloniya* (Correctional Labour Colony). On the left arm a snake, the traditional symbol for treachery and betrayal, sits on top of the Penal Code of the RSFSR. Three bogatyrs are tattooed on the stomach as a further anti-Soviet, aggressive statement, see also page 195.

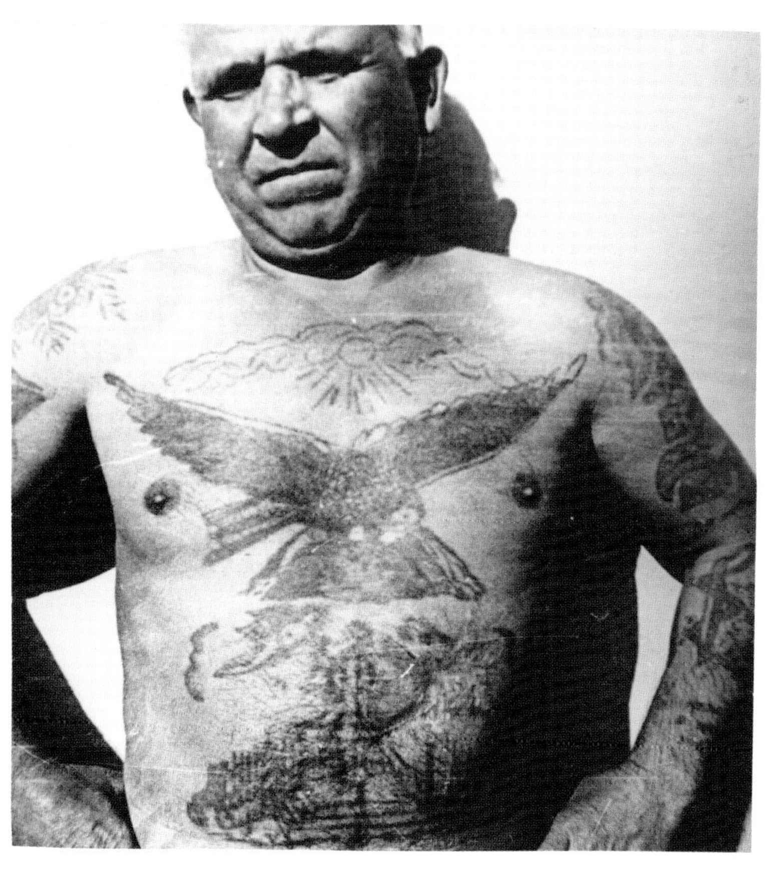

An old thief wearing the traditional thieves' tattoo of a large eagle on the chest. The longer rays coming out of the sun stand for convictions, the shorter rays between them for imprisonment by a court. The dagger entwined with a snake on the left arm is the sign of a high-ranking thief; it signifies 'Our life is a fight'.

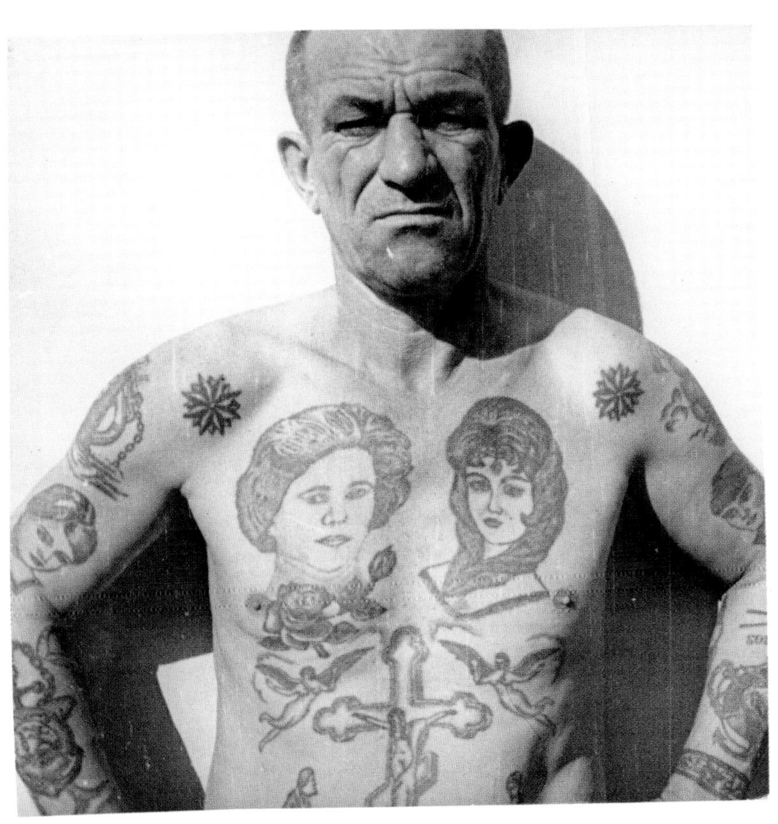

The stars on the shoulders denote an authoritative thief. The rose on the chest means he turned eighteen while in prison. 'SOS' on the right forearm is an acronym with various meanings, see pages 113, 154 and 191.

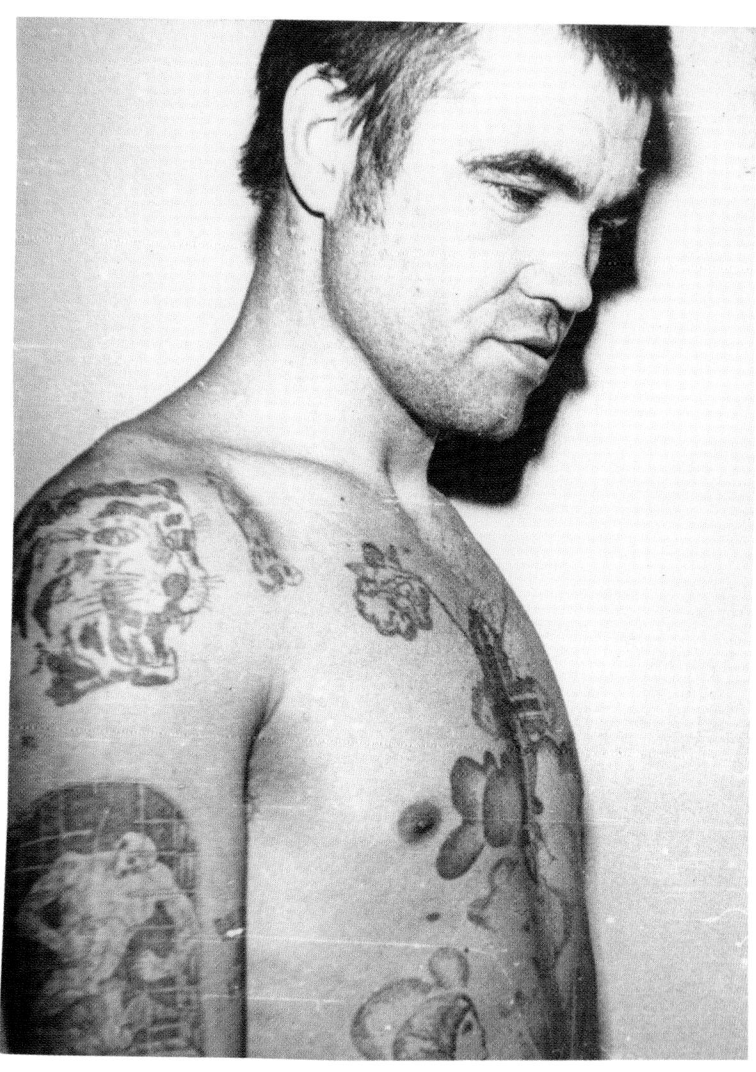

The tattoo of a tiger's head on the chest or shoulder signifies cruelty and fury. This inmate is a 'bull' thief who carries out attacks on other inmates under the orders of the *pakhan* (authoritative thief). On his left arm a woman dressed in a German uniform performs the Nazi salute while carrying a submachine gun: a display of aggression towards the administration.

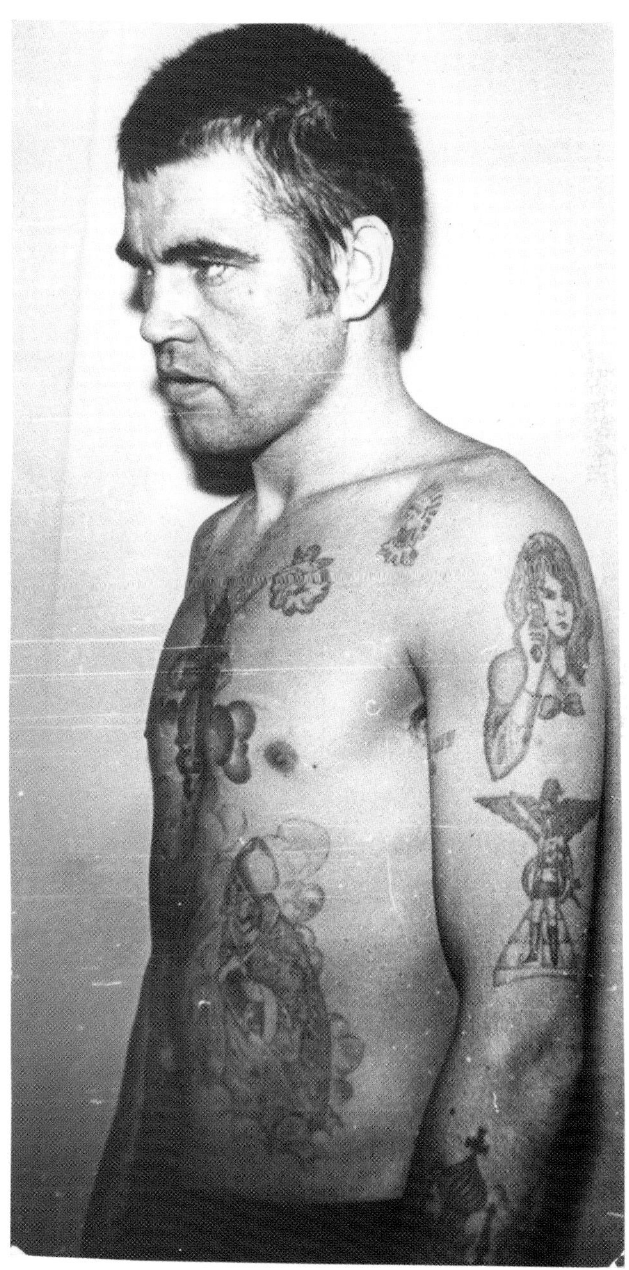

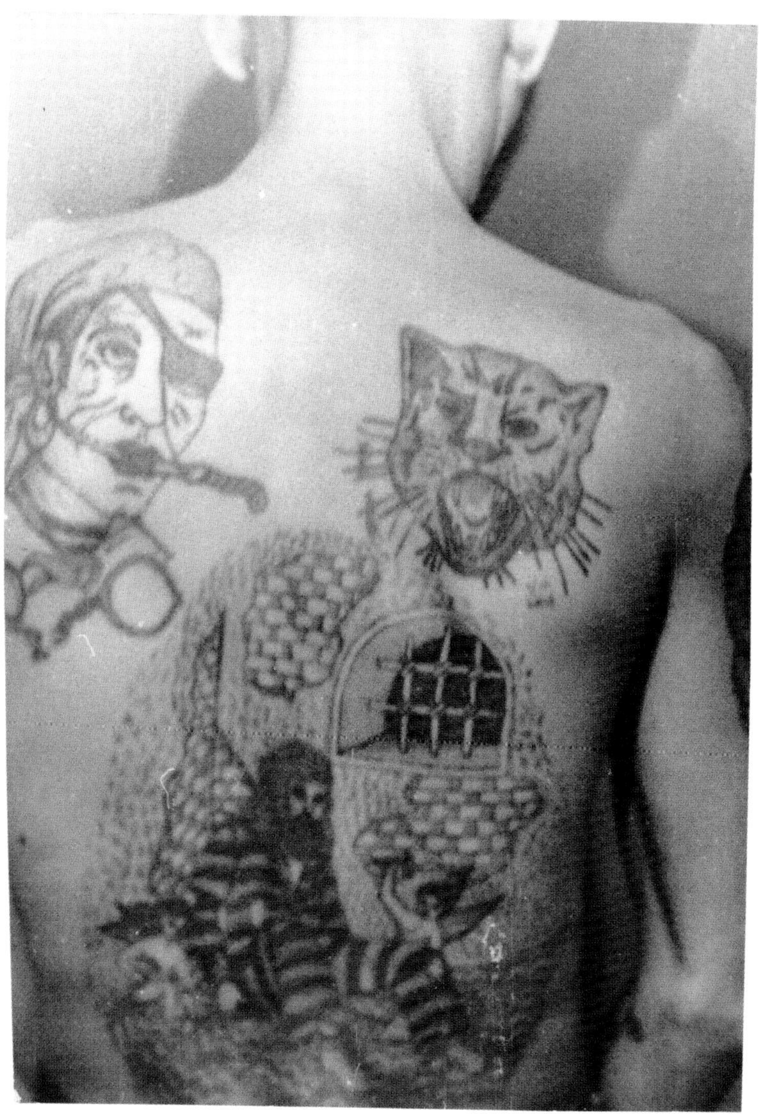

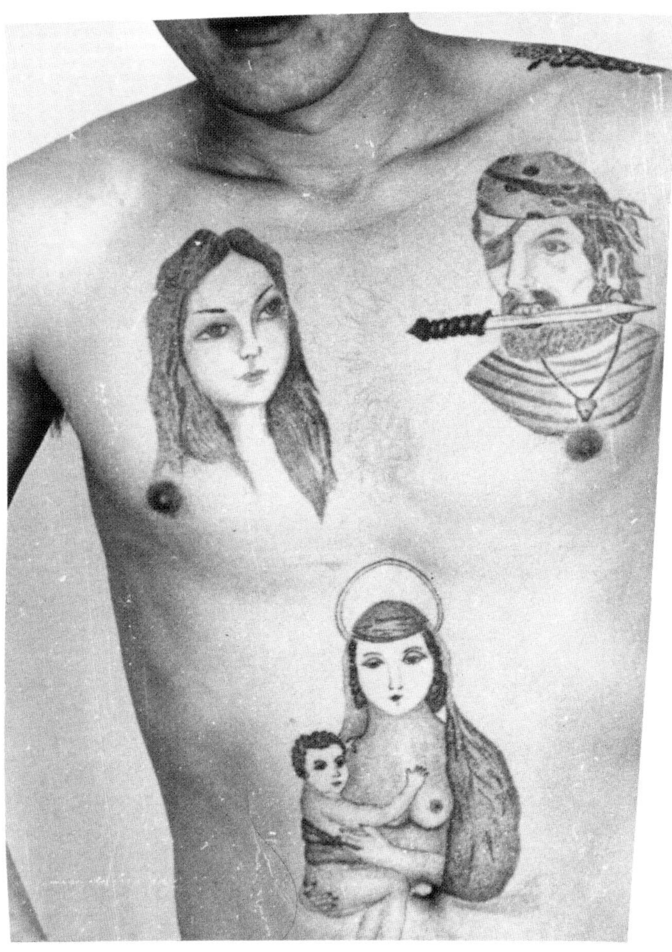

Tattooed on the chest or shoulder, a pirate with a knife in his teeth is often accompanied by the acronym '*IRA*' (a Russian female name) written on the knife, which stands for *Idu rezat aktiv* (I'm off to kill the activists). Worn by *otritsaly* (prisoners who refuse to submit to the prison rules) it denotes an inclination to brutality, sadism, and a negative attitude towards activists – prisoners who openly collaborate with prison authorities. The administrative name for activists is *Slyzhba Vnutrennevo Poryadka* or *CVP* (Internal Order Service). This has been reinterpreted by the *otritsaly* as *Suka Vishla Pogulyat* (The bitch went out for a walk) and *Suka Vishla Polovina* (The bitch got half), meaning the activist received an early release in return for siding with the authorities.

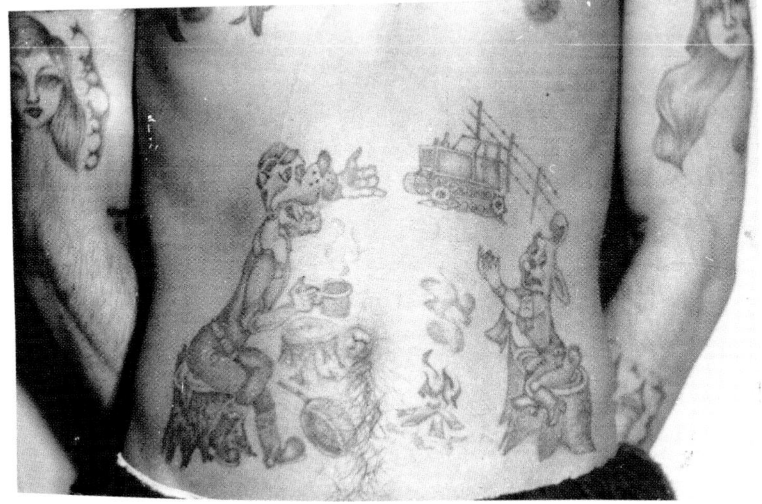

right: Text on the thigh reads **'The devil took my happiness away'**. Above this phrase is a devil carrying a patched sack (a sign of misfortune). When applied in this position on the leg, the bearer is either a 'sandpiper' or a 'hooper': a conman who attempts to pass off copper filings as gold, or copper products as gold products respectively, these swindlers are constantly afflicted by bad luck and misery. Text on the shin reads **'They're tired but they won't give in'**. The manacles on the ankles can only be tattooed on people who have served at least five years in prison (as with bracelets on the wrists).

The Wolf and Hare characters from *Nu, Pogodi! (Well, Just You Wait!* [1969–2006])* are depicted on the stomach (above) sitting around a campfire, overseeing the construction of the camp perimeter. On the top of the thigh (right) they are shown dancing together on ice skates, see also pages 75, 77 and 177. The guitar-playing dancing skeleton symbolises a courageous attitude. The bearer is not afraid of taking risks, and has a contempt of death. Originally from Mexico's 'Day of the Dead', this tattoo became popular in the USSR during the 1960s. Originally tattooed on the shoulder or chest, now its placement varies. The knife running through the cards tattooed on the shin is known as the 'Death Suit' and indicates that the bearer is a violent repeat offender, who is part of the criminal thieves' elite.

* The Wolf is the main villain of the children's cartoon series *Nu, Pogodi!* (1969-2006) in which he continually attempts to catch the Hare. The title itself (spoken by the Wolf after another plan to catch the Hare has failed) could be seen as an imprisoned thief's threat to the authorities. In the earlier Soviet-era episodes the Wolf was portrayed as a hooligan and vandal, who abuses minors, breaks the law, drinks beer and smokes continuously. This is why this anti-hero was championed by real criminals. During his pursuit of the Hare he reveals many unexpected talents (such as figure skating, gymnastics and ballet dancing). He is also a very capable guitar player and rides a powerful motorbike. The cartoon contained very little speech, but was punctuated by popular songs of the day performed by the characters. It was only during the late Soviet and post-Soviet era that the Wolf's image was sanitised, being slowly transformed into a standard cartoon character with fewer criminal characteristics.

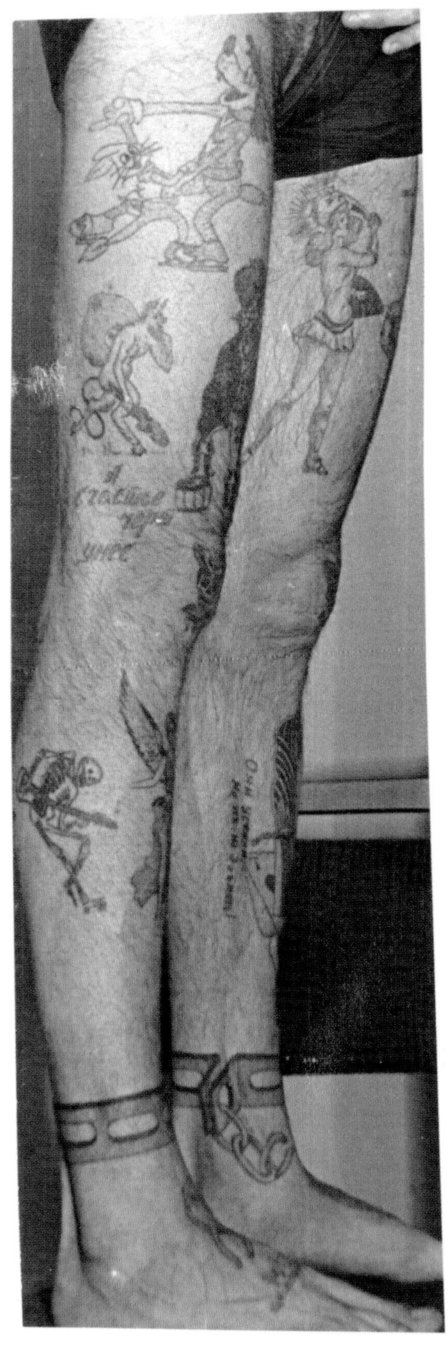

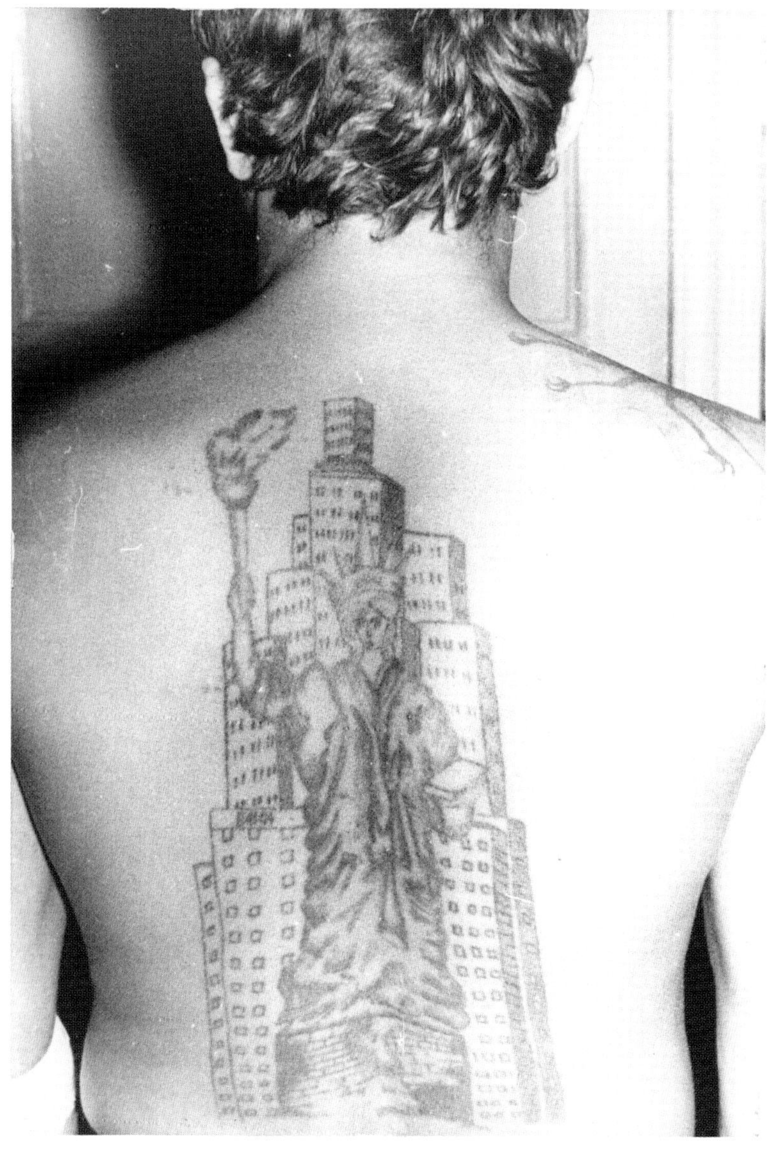

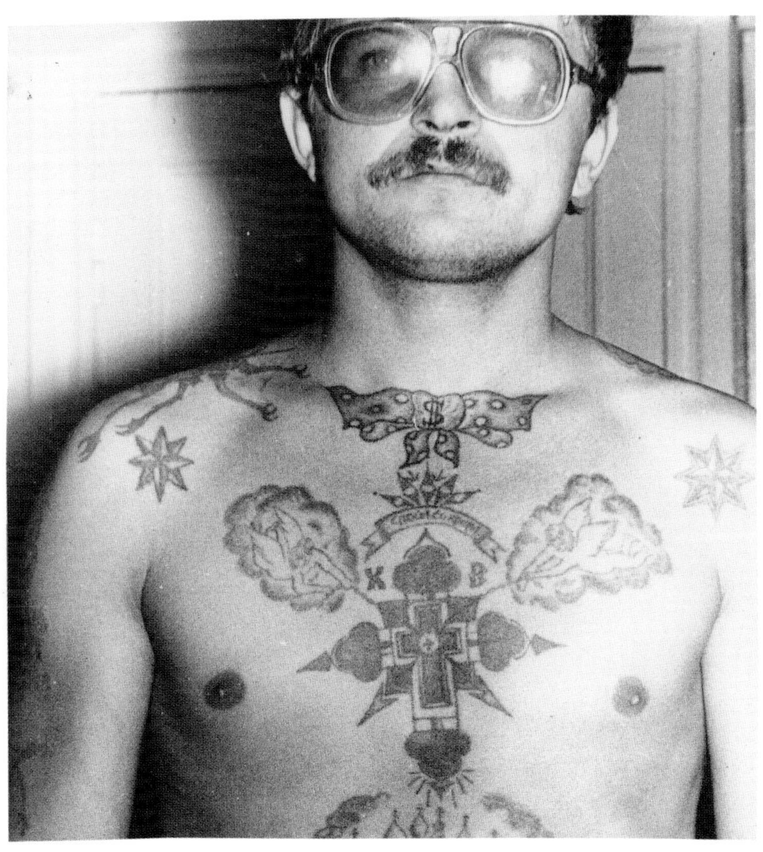

above: Text on the chest reads **'Save and protect'**. Text either side of the cross reads **'XV'** *Hristos Voskres* (Christ has Risen).

The eight-pointed stars on the clavicles denote a high-ranking thief. A bow tie* tattooed on the neck is often found in strict regime colonies. The dollar sign on the bow tie shows the bearer is either a safecracker, money launderer or has been convicted for the theft of state property.

left: The beetle tattooed on the shoulder is a symbol of good luck for a thief. The Statue of Liberty and American-style skyscrapers tattooed on the back display an anti-Soviet attitude alongside a longing for freedom.

* Originally bow ties were a dishonourable tattoo. They were forcibly applied underneath the clavicle cat tattoos of pickpockets who had broken the 'thieves' code' and sided with the authorities. Today, however, there is no stigma attached to them.

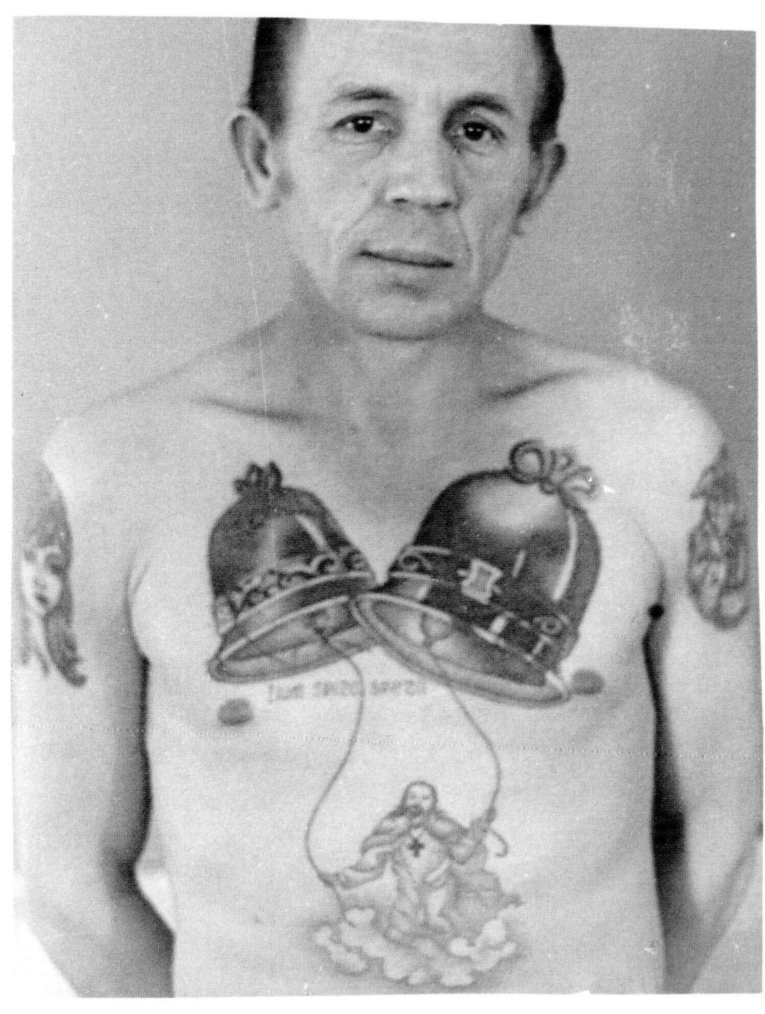

Latin text on chest reads *Dum Spiro Spero* **'While I breathe, I hope'**.

A saint ringing the bells: 'Ring the bells, father, your son is coming home'. Initially this tattoo was made to show that the bearer had a long sentence with no opportunity for an early release. Its purpose was to signify his standing within criminal society, to allow him to receive his ration before other inmates and to protect him from being raped. Today it denotes a criminal who served his time without cooperating with the administration, meaning he received no reduction in his sentence, no privileges and no early parole.

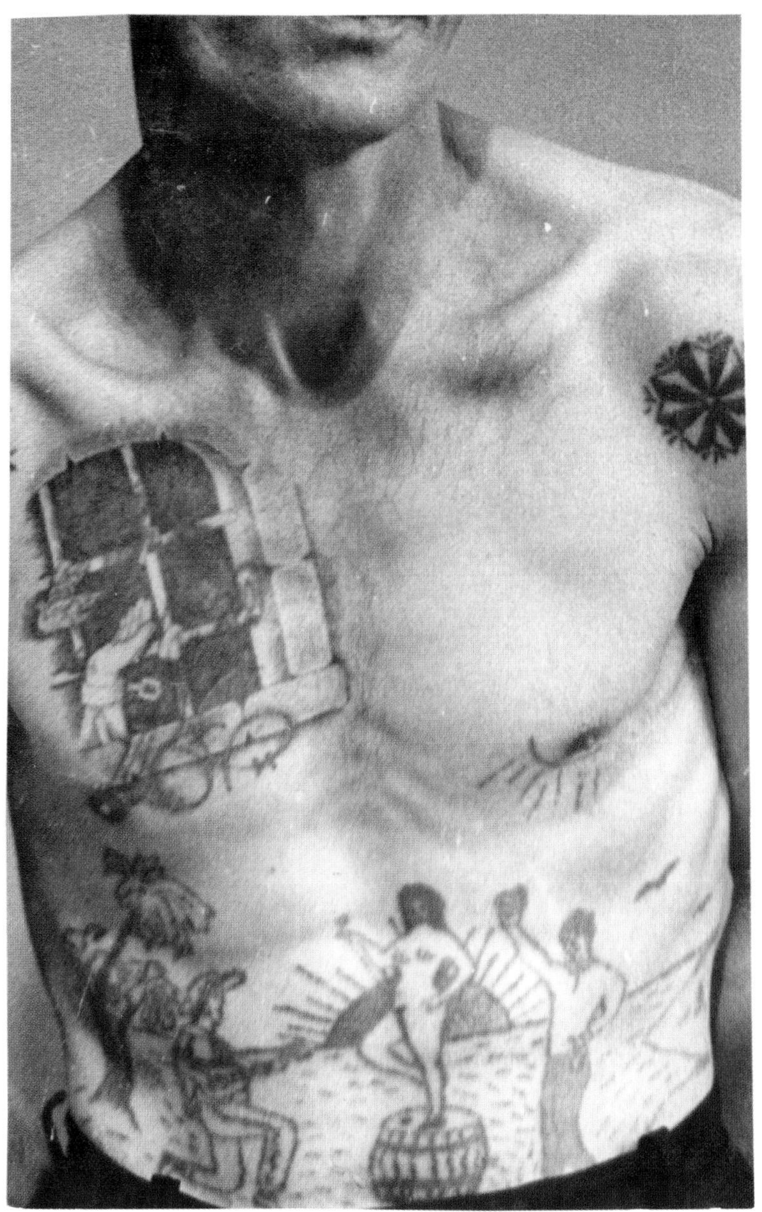

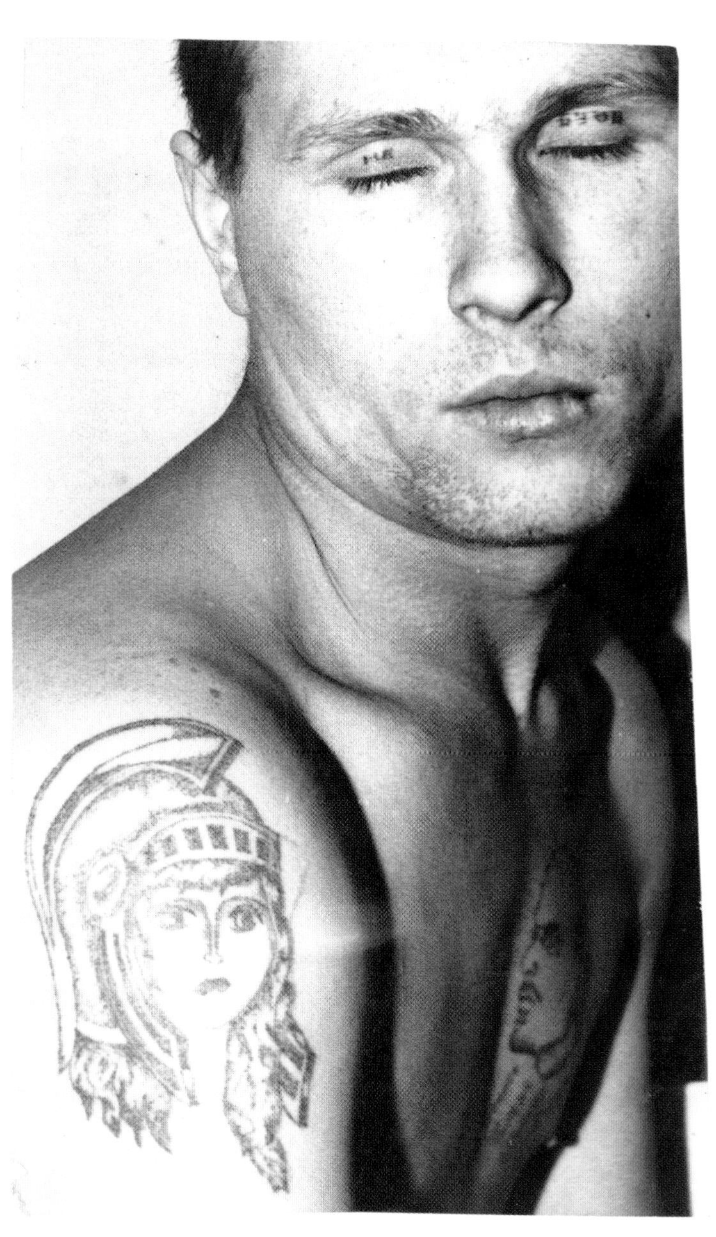

Text across the eyelids reads **'Do not / wake me'**.

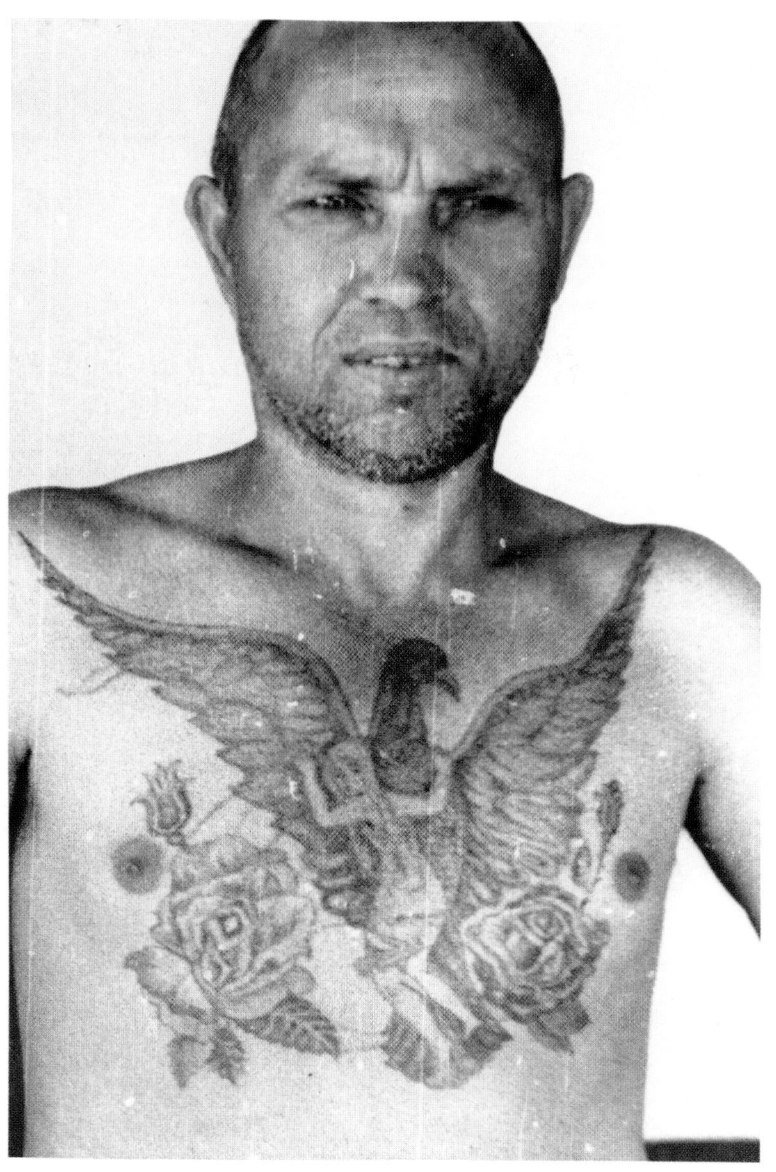

Rapists often picture themselves as eagles carrying the victim. To the criminal mind this is a symbol of forcefulness and power.

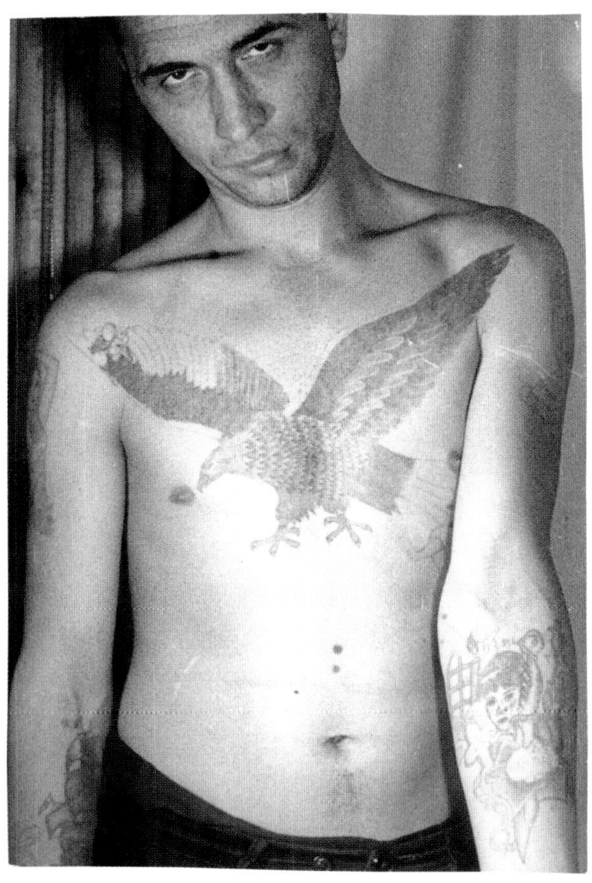

right: Text on the stomach reads **'God created three evils – women, devils, goats'**. 'Goats' are traitors in prison jargon. (To call a criminal a 'goat' is extremely offensive, resulting in a violent reaction from the insulted party.)

Here the image of a woman represents treachery: it is because of women that man is driven to crime; the devil pushes man to commit bad deeds; the 'goat' will betray you in the zone (in prison slang a 'goat' *kozel* is a stool-pigeon, a prisoner who works with the authorities). This tattoo would have been forcibly applied, either because the prisoner lost at cards or because he was found to be in league with the prison administration. This 'lowering' would have serious consequences as the prisoner would essentially become regarded as worthless by his fellow inmates, whereupon he would be raped and forced to do the dirty work.

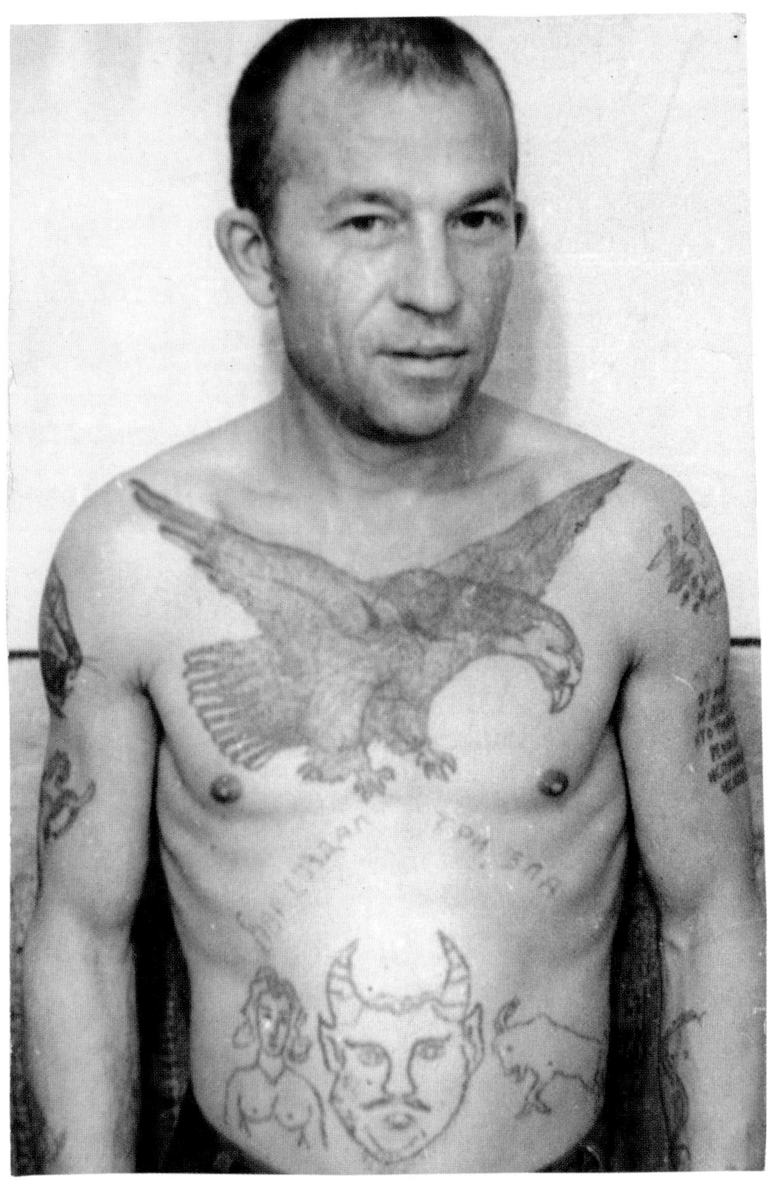

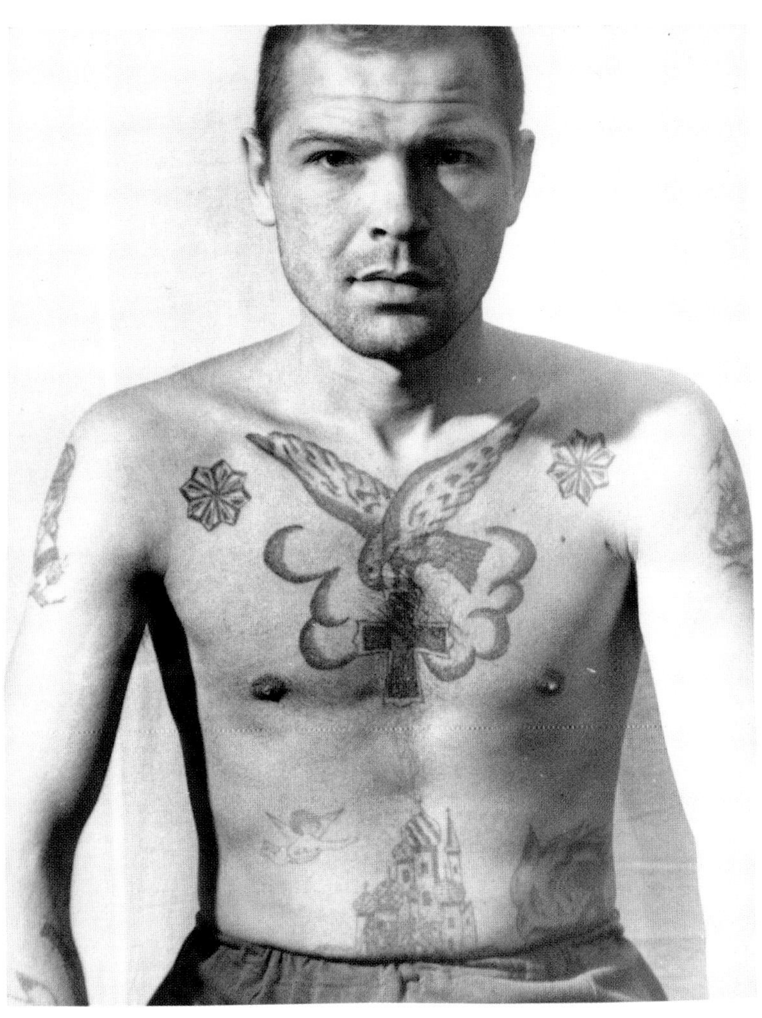

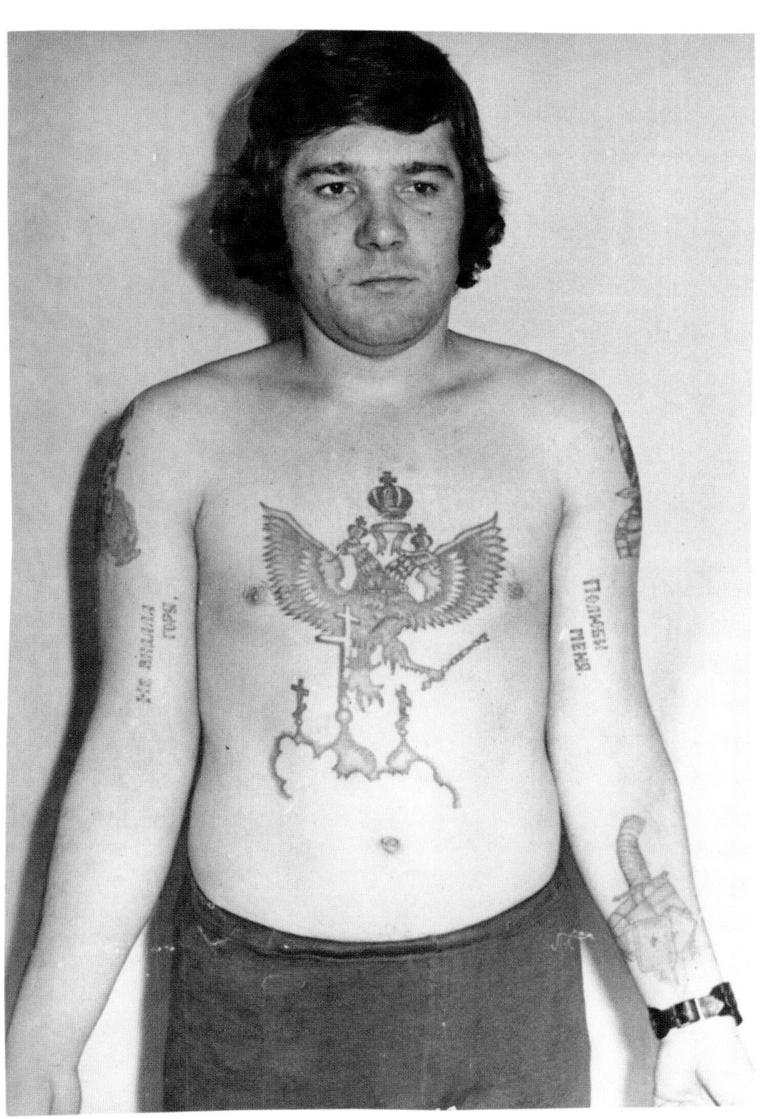

Text across the arms reads **'If you haven't seen grief / love me'**.

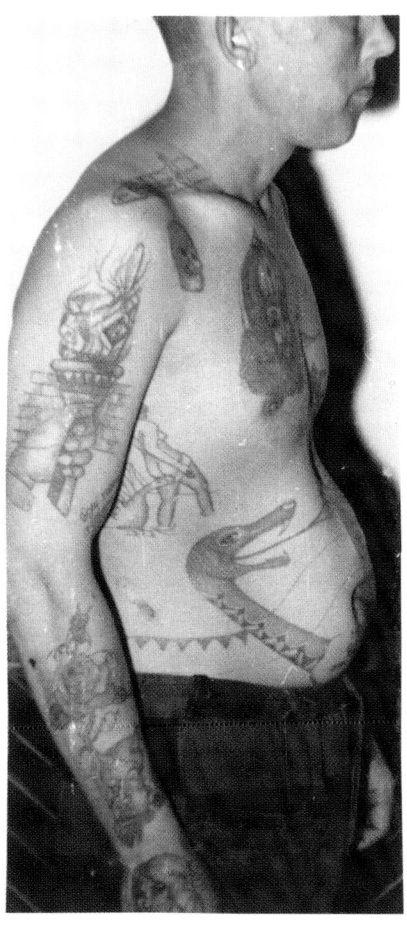

above: Text on the arm reads **'If you want to grab grief, fall in love with me'**.
right: Text on the arm reads **'Prison has taught me to laugh through my tears'**.

The skulls on the shoulders show that this inmate is a murderer. The knife tattooed across the shoulders and into the neck means that he is for 'hire' to commit further murders. The torch on the arm (above) signifies an inmate who was imprisoned through recklessness and the desire for freedom. The flames cover up an earlier tattoo. The swan pulling down the woman's underwear, the mermaid on the right arm and the fishing hook 'catching' the woman's dress are all tattoos of a hooligan rapist, see also pages 99 and 131. The snake wrapped around the stomach is a sign of addiction.

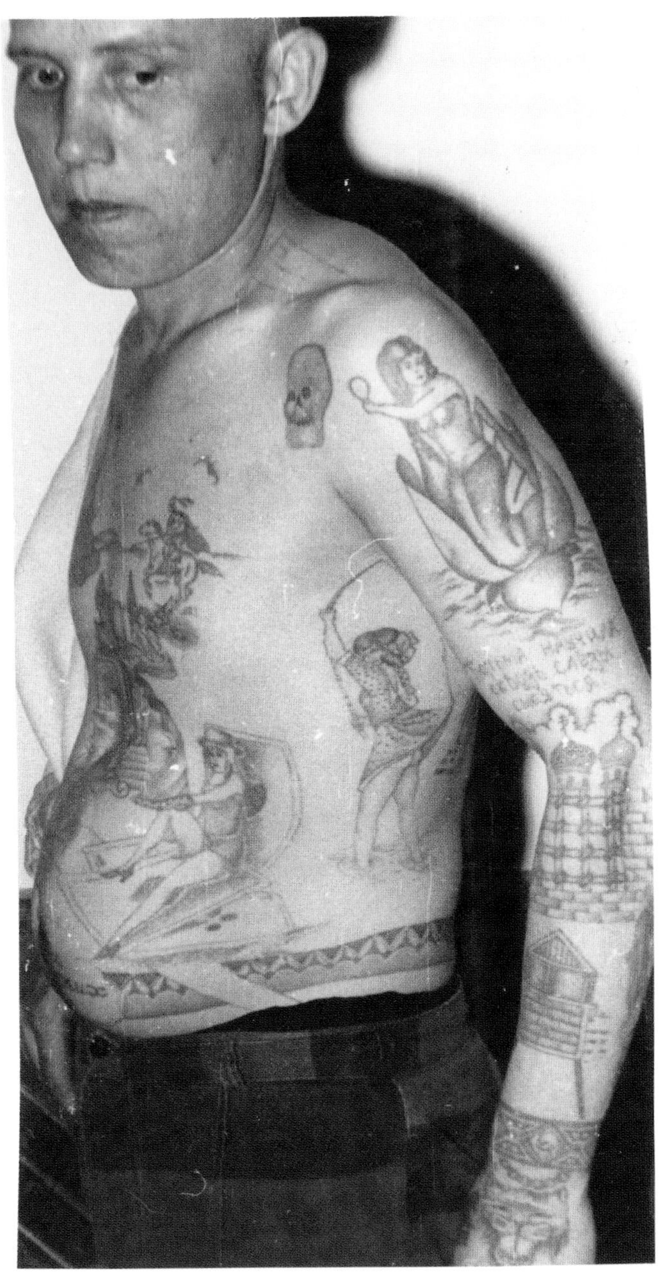

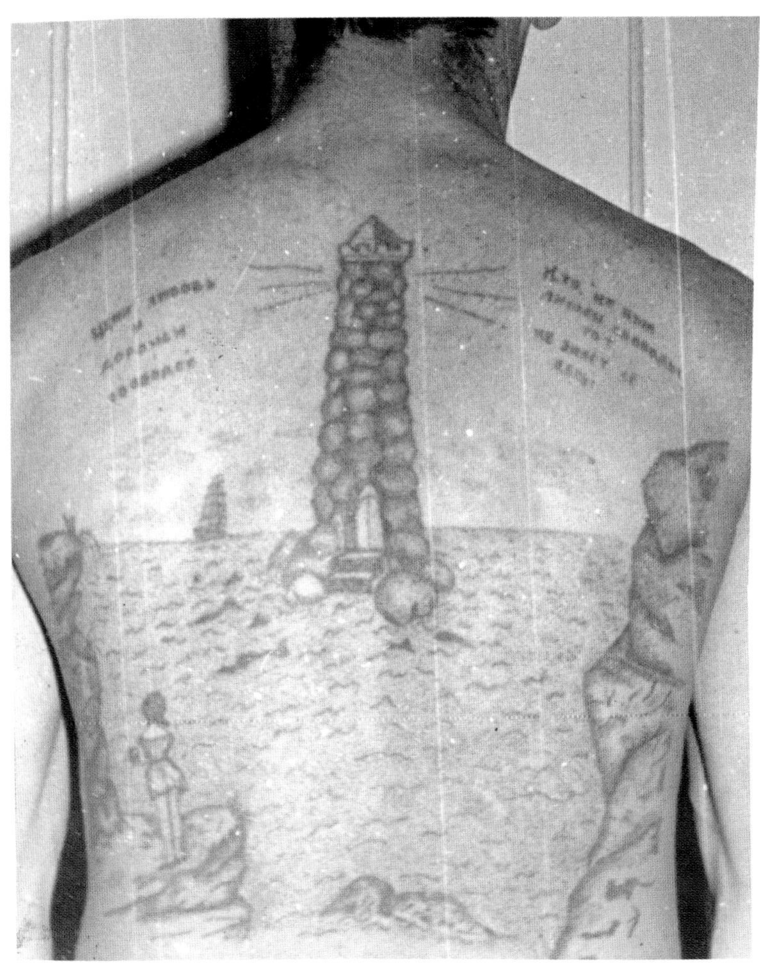

above: Text on the back reads **'Protect love and cherish freedom'** and **'Those who have never been deprived of freedom do not know its value'**.

right: This type of tattoo is a display of longing for a wife, girlfriend or *biksa*, see footnote on page 134.

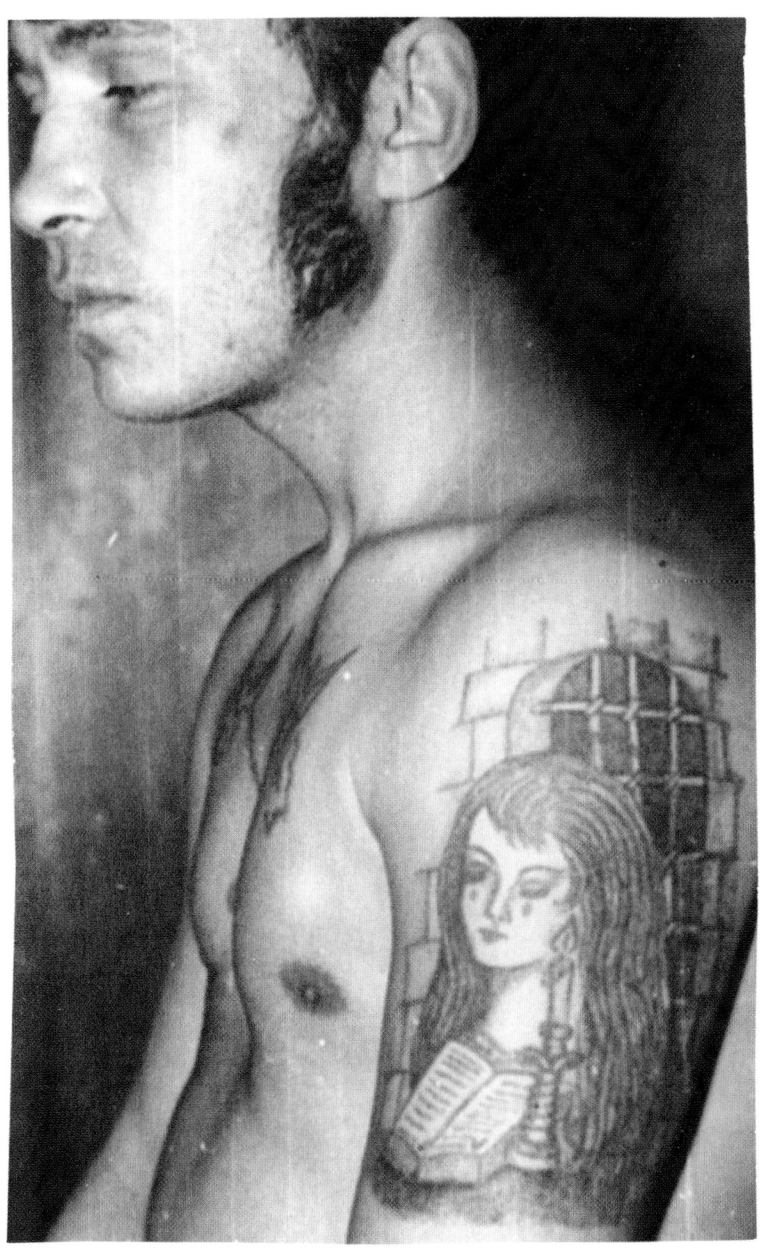

The main motivating factors for tattooing and the selection of designs are: the 'unwritten code' of accepting inmates into the environment; self-assertion in a specific group; vanity; bravado; eagerness to demonstrate endurance of pain; predilection for suffering or uniqueness and superiority over others; imitation of more experienced criminals with tattoos; memory of the time spent in prison; expression of protest against laws and law-enforcement services; boredom and idleness with some narcissistic aspects; as well as old customs and traditions of tattooing.

Tattoos like the crude drawing of a face on this man's stomach are generally made when the bearer has lost at cards and is unable to pay his debt. Card games are taken very seriously by thieves, and knowledge of the language and symbols of cards in the criminal context is extremely important. Clubs and spades (the black suits) are the most noble signs for criminals. The phrase *derzhat mast* (to hold the suit) means to have power over a community of thieves, to maintain order and the observance of the thieves' law. A *shesterka* (literally a 'sixer') refers to the lowest card in the Russian thirty-six card deck. This is the name for an underling who runs errands for the high-ranking thieves, see also pages 21 and 145. By contrast the red suits are the symbols of thieves who have been 'sunk' or 'lowered'. They may be punished by having diamond or heart knave card symbols cut into their buttocks with a razor, making them untouchables. A crown containing the red card suits tattooed on to the back of an inmate is the sign of the 'King of all Suits'; it denotes a passive homosexual who will engage in all forms of sodomy. A common card game played by the *otritsaly* (prisoners who refuse to submit to the prison rules) is known as *Igra na sakharok ili pederasta* (playing for a sugar-cube or your virtue). These cunning and sadistic prisoners lure inexperienced inmates into a game of cards, where the price of losing can be the victim's manhood.

overleaf: Text in the halo reads **'Love God'**. The single eight-pointed star on the right shoulder is the sign of a criminal semi-authority.

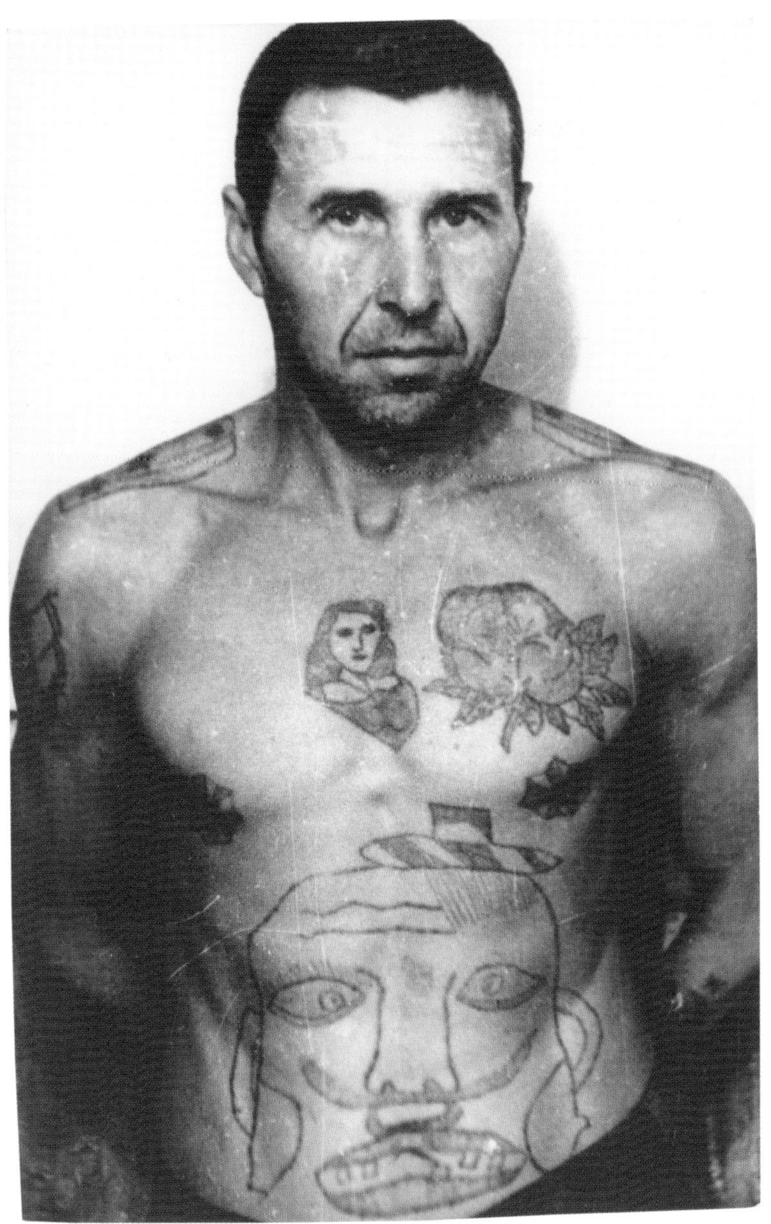

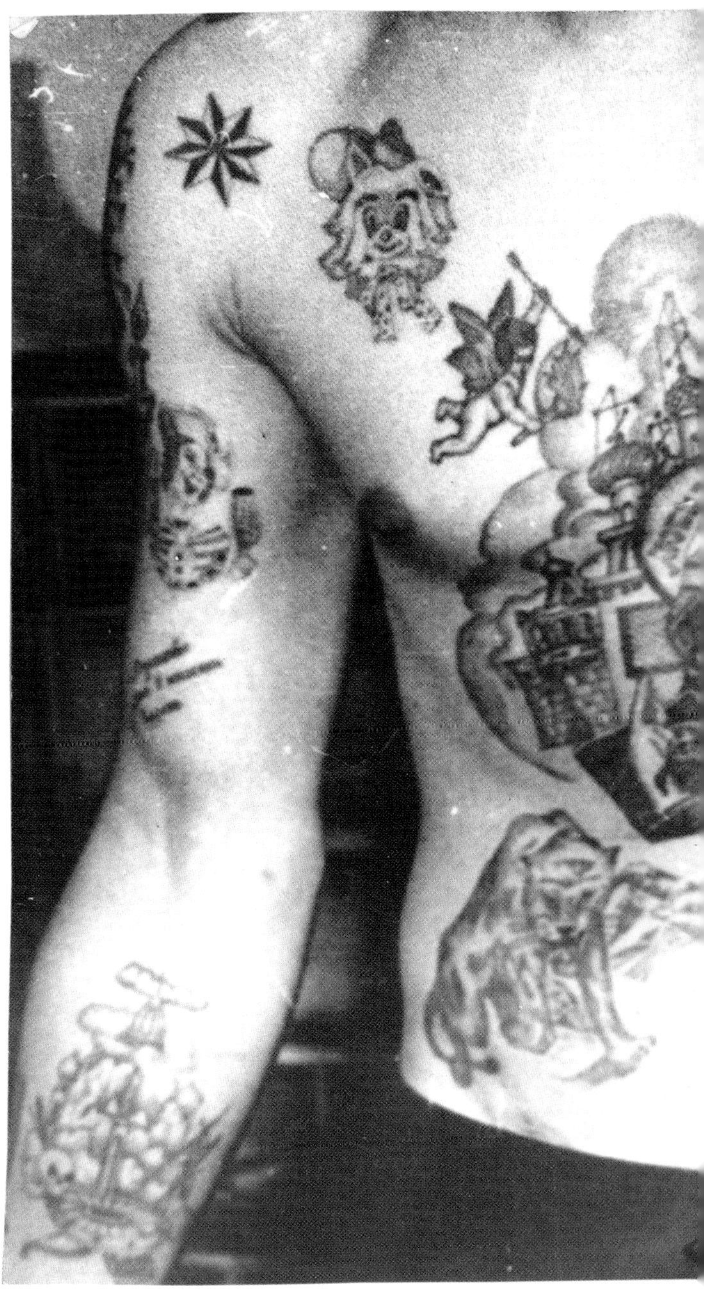

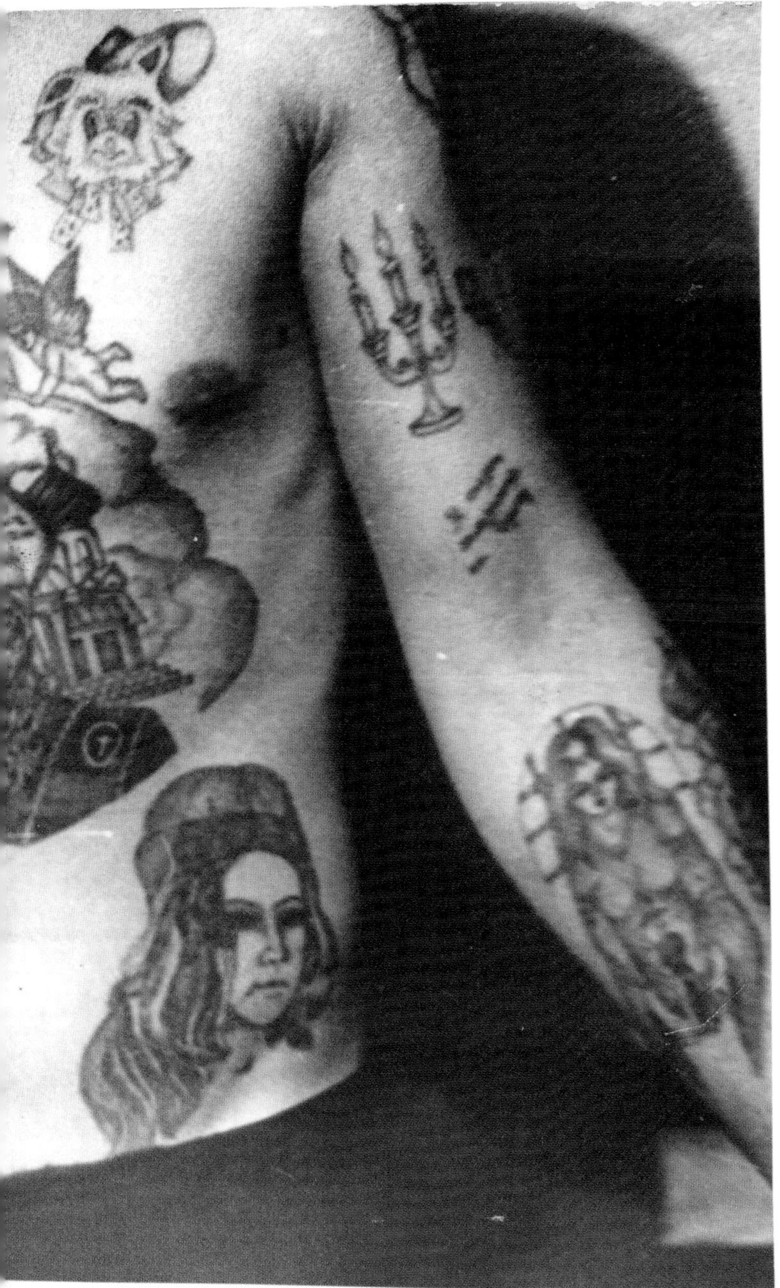

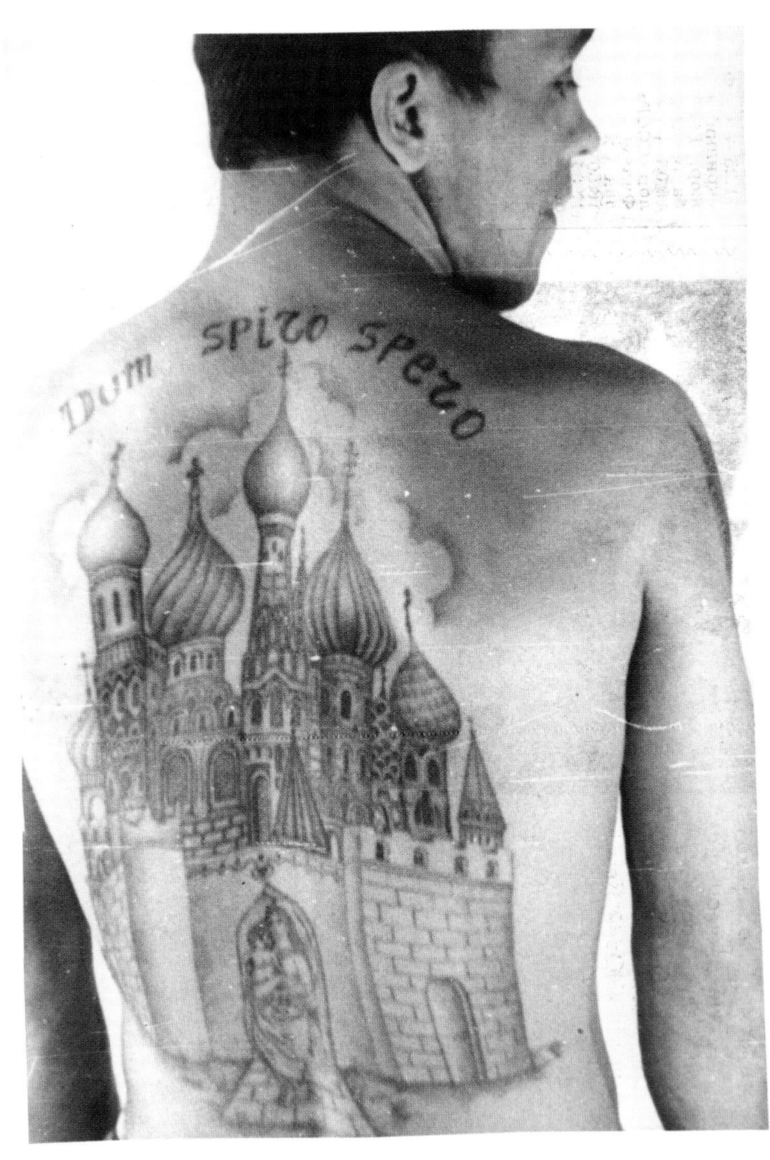

Latin text reads *Dum Spiro Spero* **'While I breathe, I hope'**.

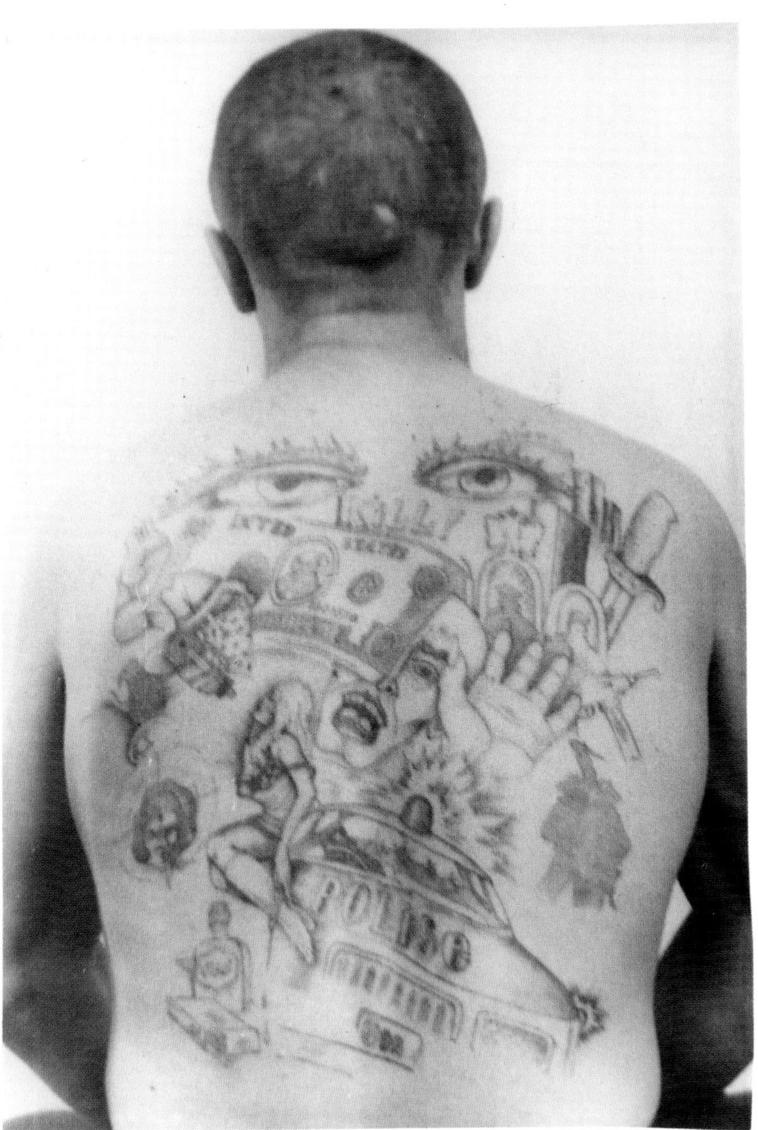

Here the elements of the 'This is what destroys us' tattoo (girls, money, drink, cigarettes) have been combined with themes of America and violence (a masked gunman, a dagger, a submachine gun) to form a disturbing composition. The eyes at the top mean 'I'm watching over you'. Altogether the embodiment of criminal aggression.

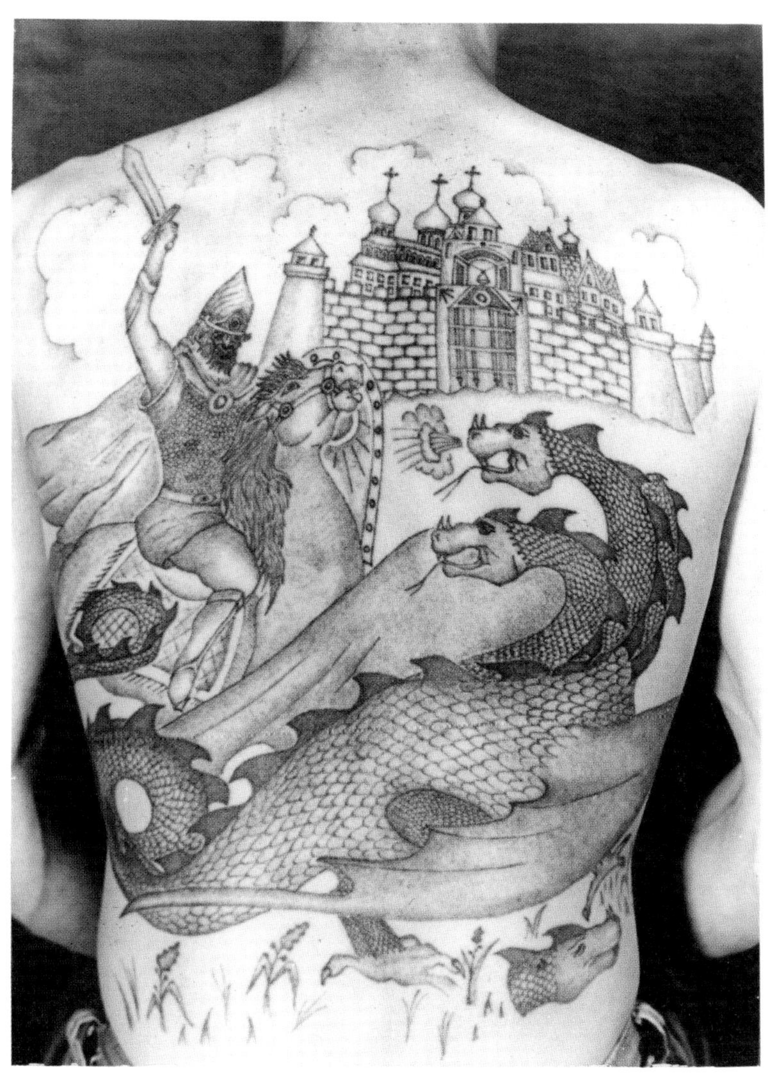

Saint George the Dragon Slayer is an early 16th century Russian icon. He is a symbol of courage and valour and the triumph of good over evil.

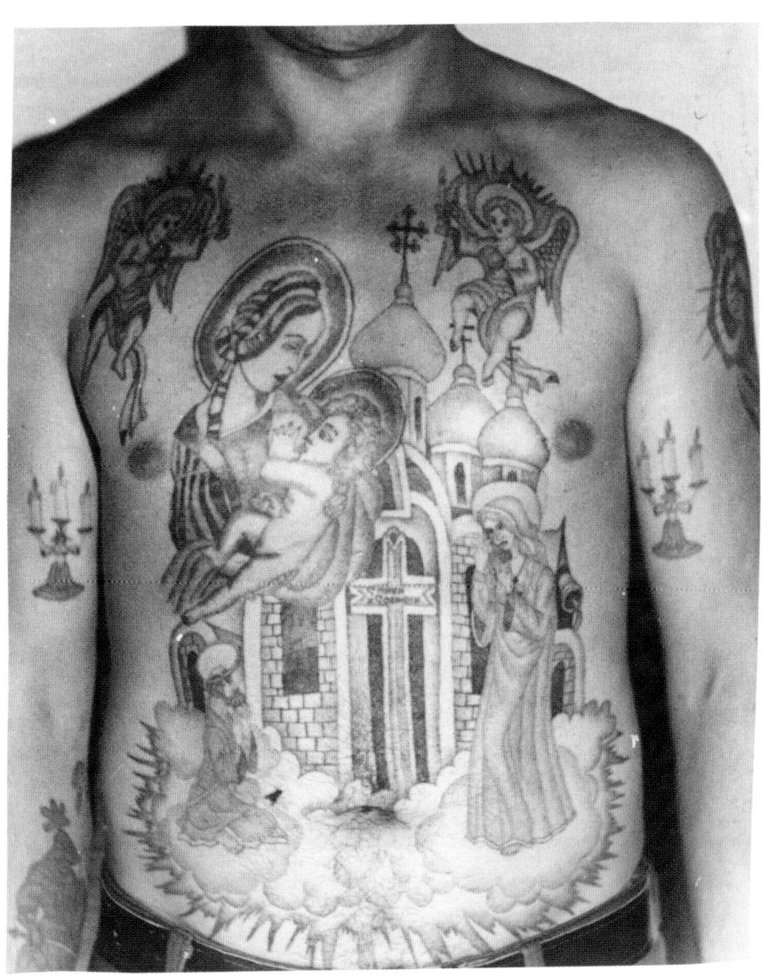

The candles on the arms mean 'My destiny is the light of one candle. I live until my candle burns out'. This common criminal motif dates from pre-Revolutionary times. This tattoo is applied to various parts of the body, but never under the collarbone. It is believed (by those infected with the romance of thieves) to work as a kind of talisman.

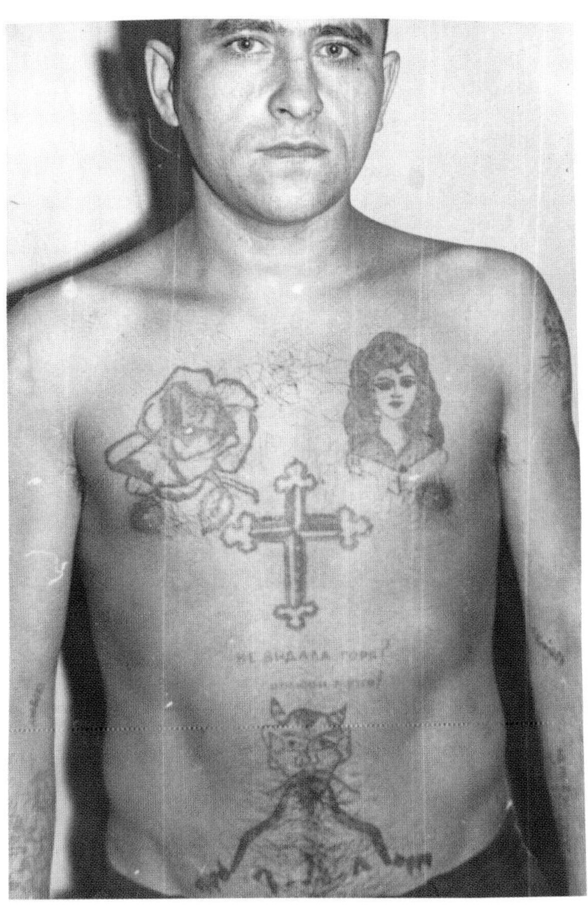

above: Text on the stomach reads **'If you haven't seen grief, love me'**. Text in left and right arm joints reads **'Love'**.

right: Text across the chest reads **'Pray mother and your son will return'**. Text on the cross reads **'Save and Protect'**. Text on the arm reads **'The more I get to know people, the more I like dogs'**.

A dagger through the neck shows that a criminal has committed murder in prison and is available to hire for further killing. The drops of blood can signify the number of murders committed. The cross tattooed on the chest is a sign of thieves. It is also a symbol of submission, captivity and slavery. In some cases the cross may be supplemented by the text 'This is the cross I have to bear, the prison has taken all my happiness away'.

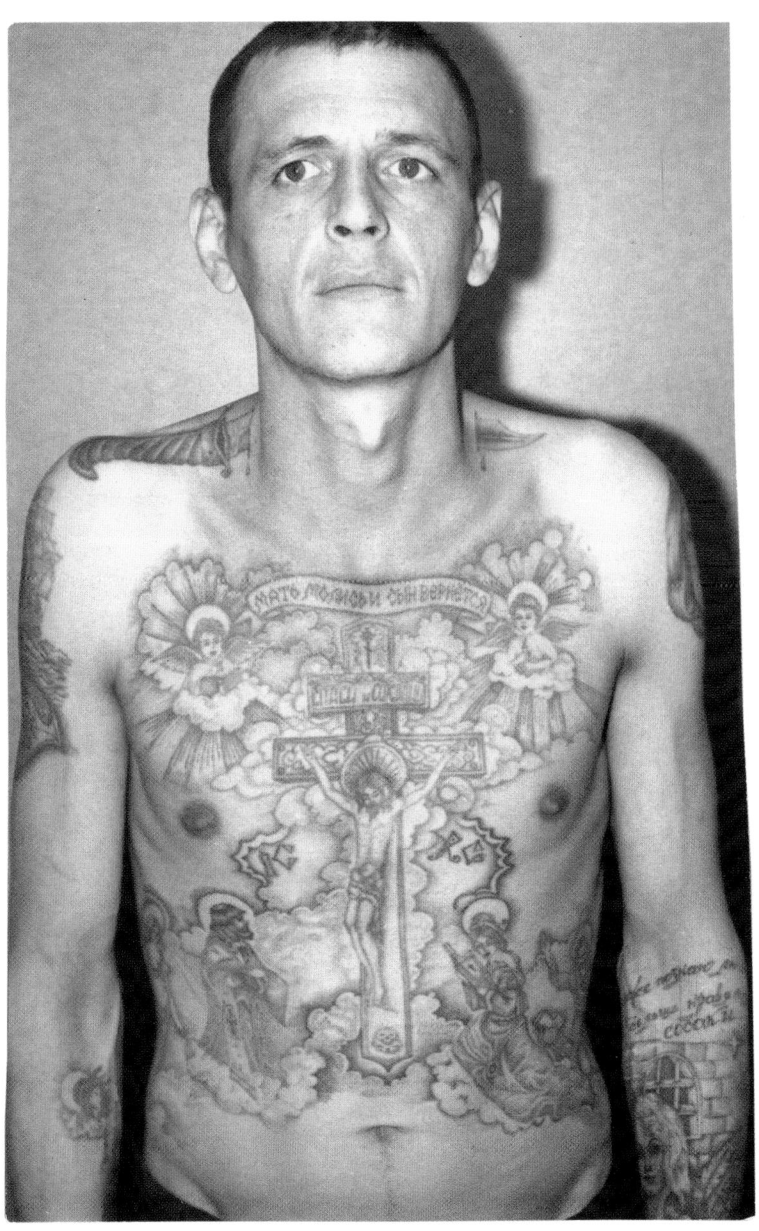

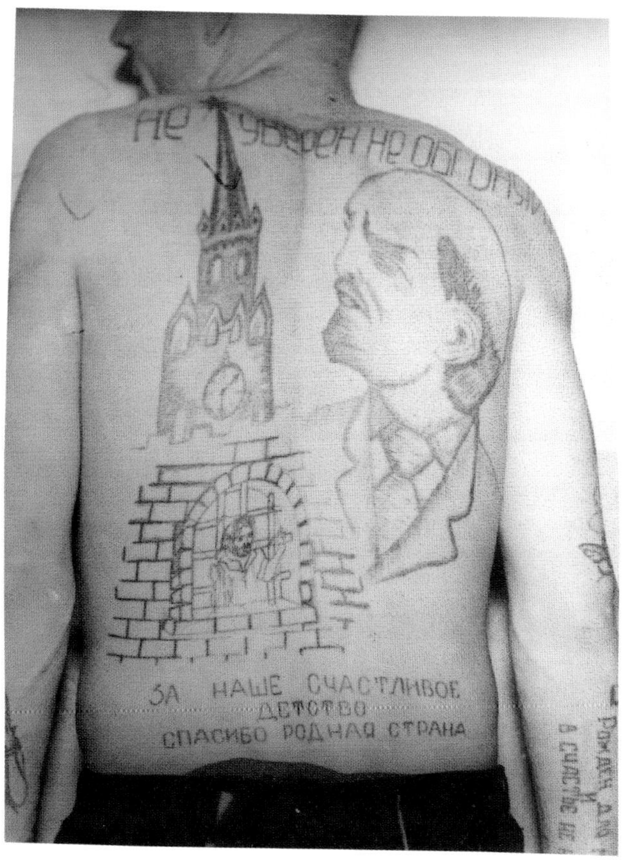

above: Text across the shoulders reads **'If you are not certain, do not over take me'**. Text above the waist reads **'Thank you Motherland for our happy childhood'**. Text on the arm reads **'I was born to be tortured, I don't need happiness'**.

right: On the index finger is a variant of an *otritsala* ring, denoting someone who is hostile to law-enforcement and the regime. They cannot be re-educated. Middle finger 'Freedom for the youth' or 'I've done time and I will steal again'. Third finger 'Ruined youth', the bearer was convicted as a juvenile. The five dots on the wrist are a common sign of someone familiar with the prison regime. They signify 'Four watchtowers and me' or 'I've been through the zone', an inmate who has served a sentence in a correctional labour or penal colony.

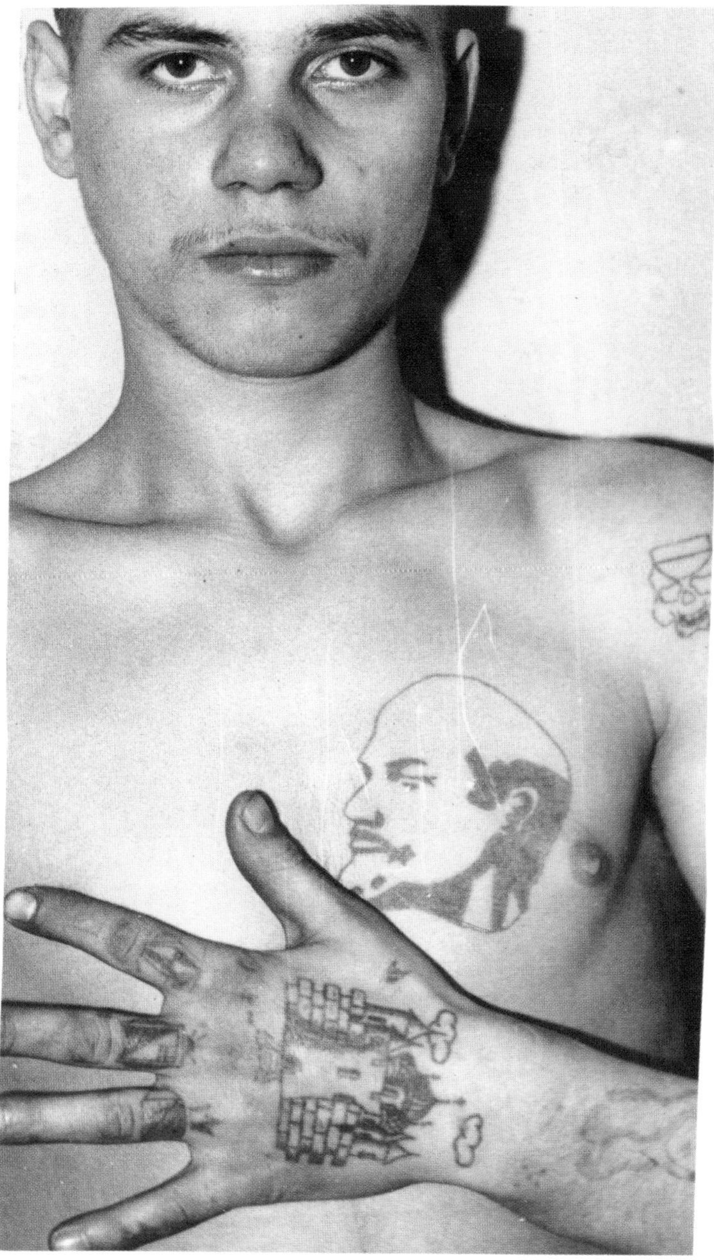

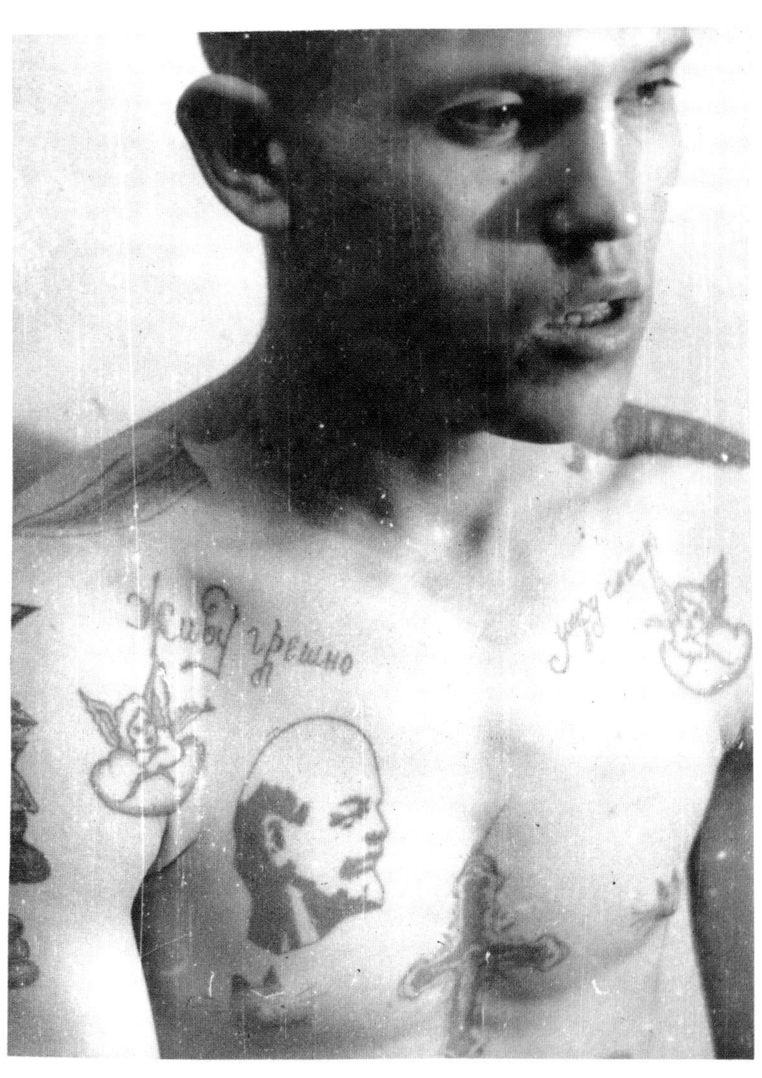

Text on the chest reads **'I live in sin / I die laughing'**.

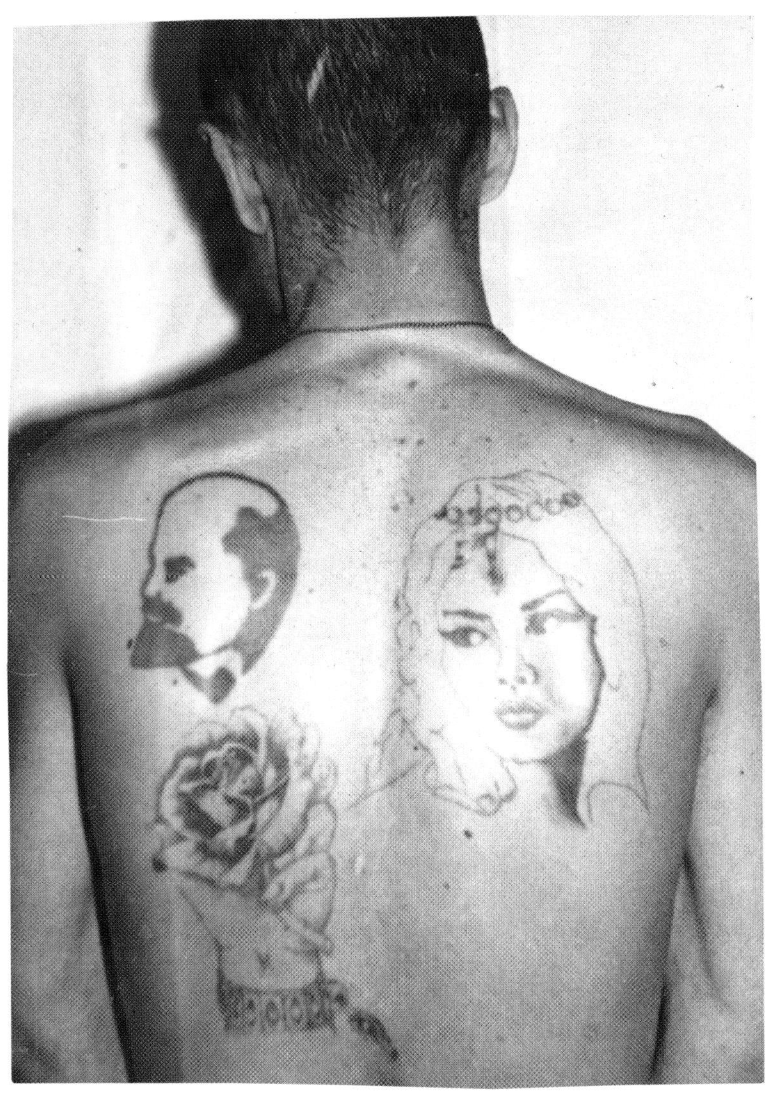

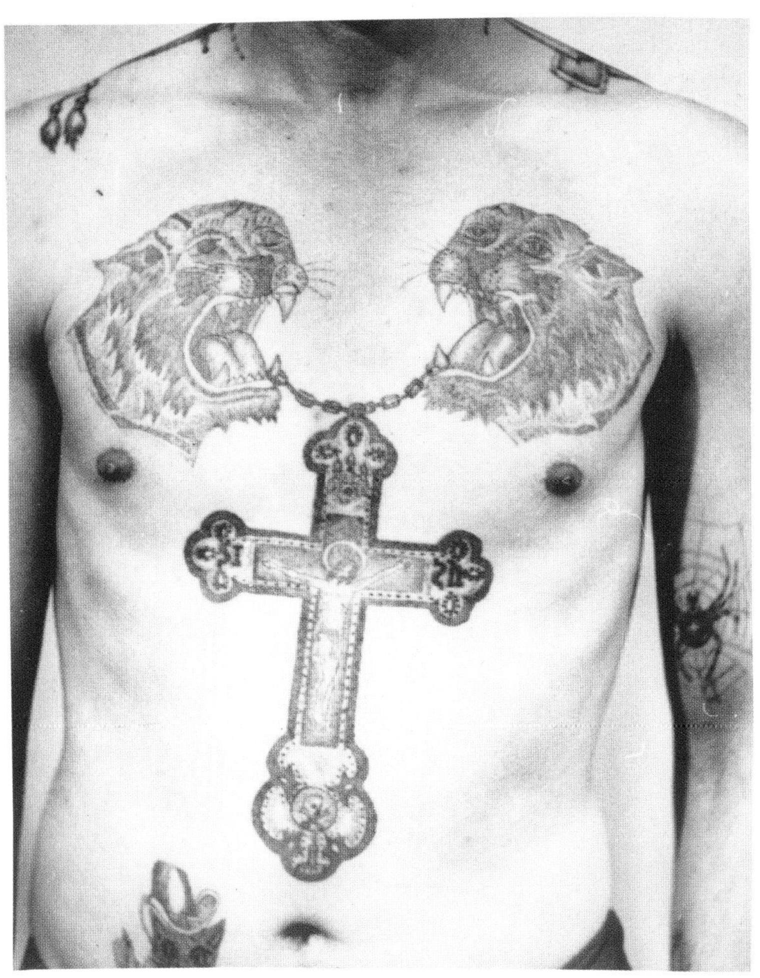

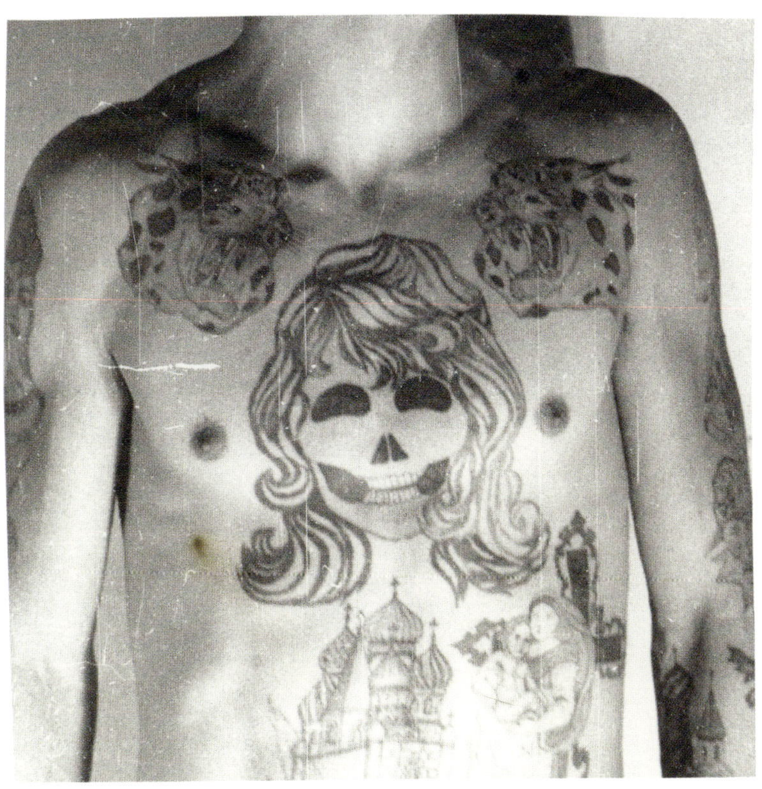

On the chest a skull replaces the woman's face. Such a negative image generally shows that a crime was spurred on by a woman – a girlfriend, wife or mother-in-law. 'Look for the woman [and you will find the cause of the trouble]', the criminals say.

Generally women are not respected by the 'thief-in-law', and any man who betrays his male friends because of a woman is ostracised. The original 'thieves' code' stated that a thief was allowed any number of women, but not to be married or have children. Thieves do not share the same values, or even the same families, as ordinary citizens. A *vor* doesn't have a real 'family' in the traditional sense, he must renounce them for his thieves' family, where his *brat* (brother) is not his real brother, but a fellow thief, and his mother is a *vorovskaya mama* – a thieves' mother (a 'position' in the thieves' world of a woman who upholds the thieves' laws and assists them in their crimes). In this way a 'thieves' family' is a group of thieves who are only related in their pursuit of the thieves' way of life.

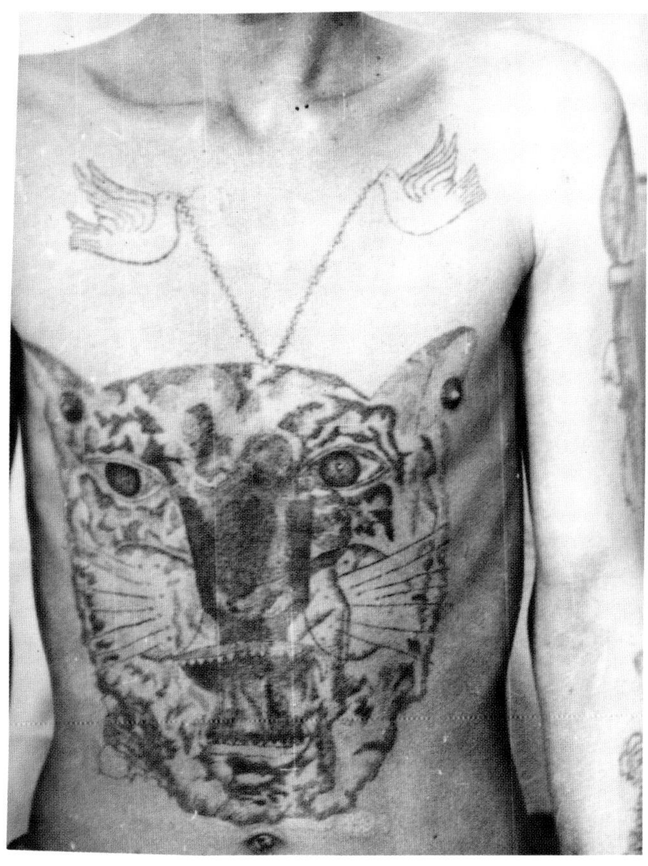

above: A large tiger's head has been used to cover up another tattoo.

The image of a leopard's head with open mouth is applied to the chest or back of criminals known variously as 'lunatics', 'grouse', 'racehorses', 'pig-face outsiders'. They are single robbers who willingly share their prey with friends. In the process of committing their crimes they will resort to threats of physical violence, however these are never carried out. People who wear such tattoos are usually tall and physically strong with a terrifying, threatening appearance.

There is a very negative attitude among inmates in the colonies to those who might receive a parcel and proceed to eat everything themselves, without consideration for their fellows. Many prisoners have even been be killed for not sharing.

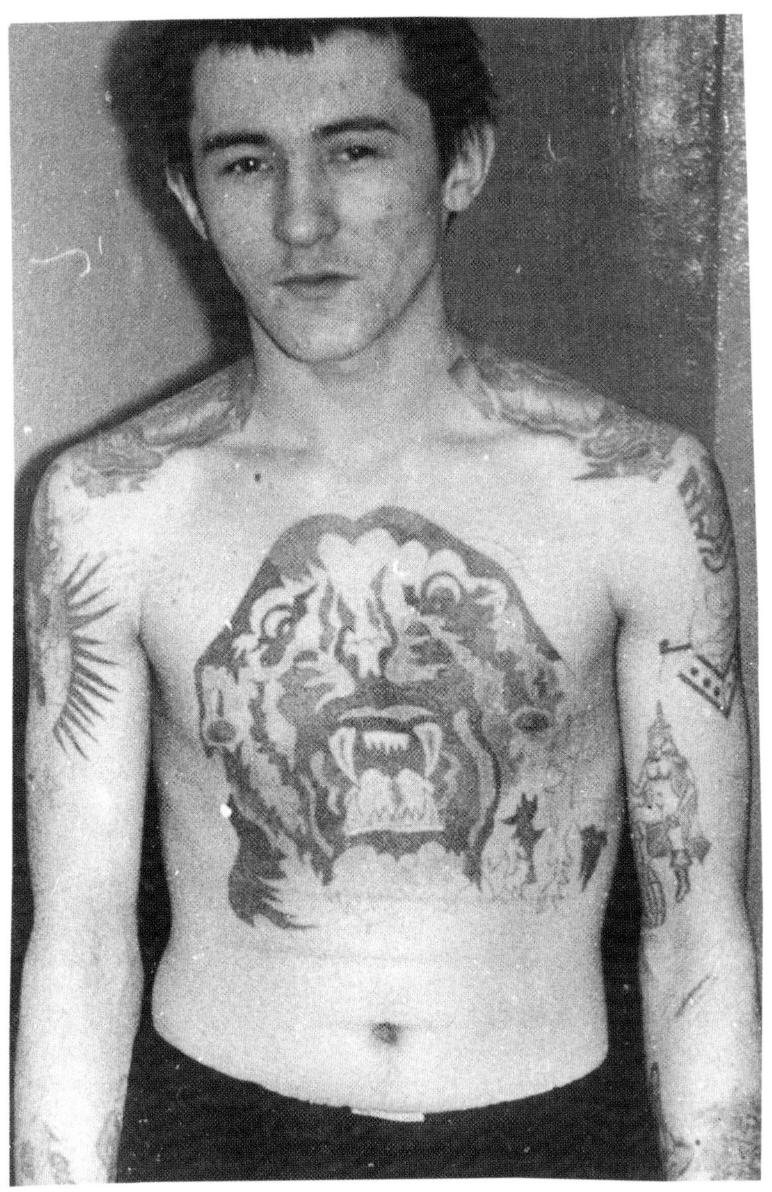

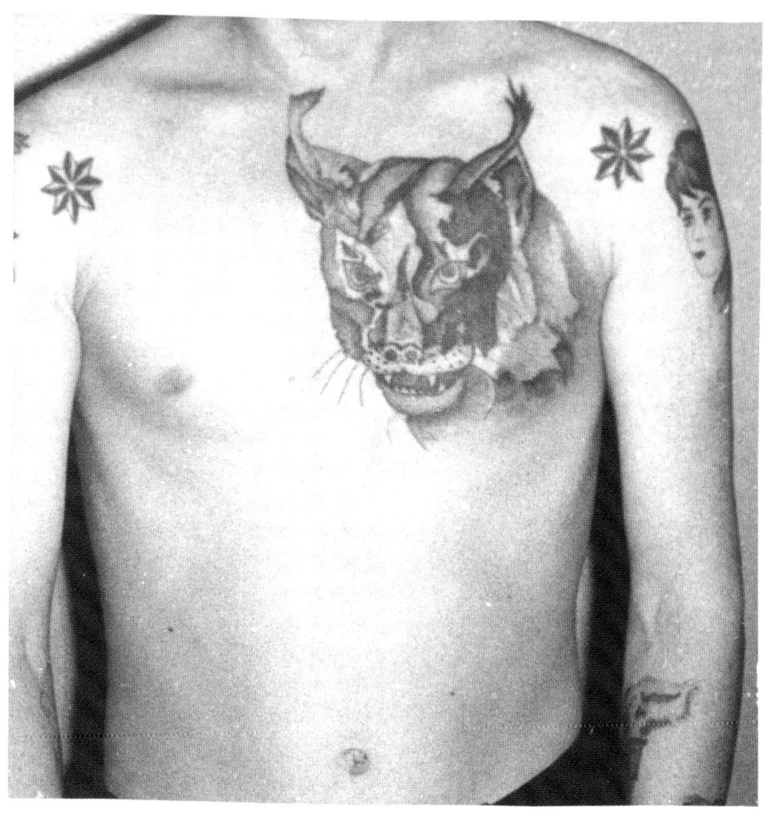

Heads of carnivorous animals (wolves, lynxes, tigers, lions, panthers) may also symbolise a specific death threat against somebody whom the bearer perceives to have wronged them.

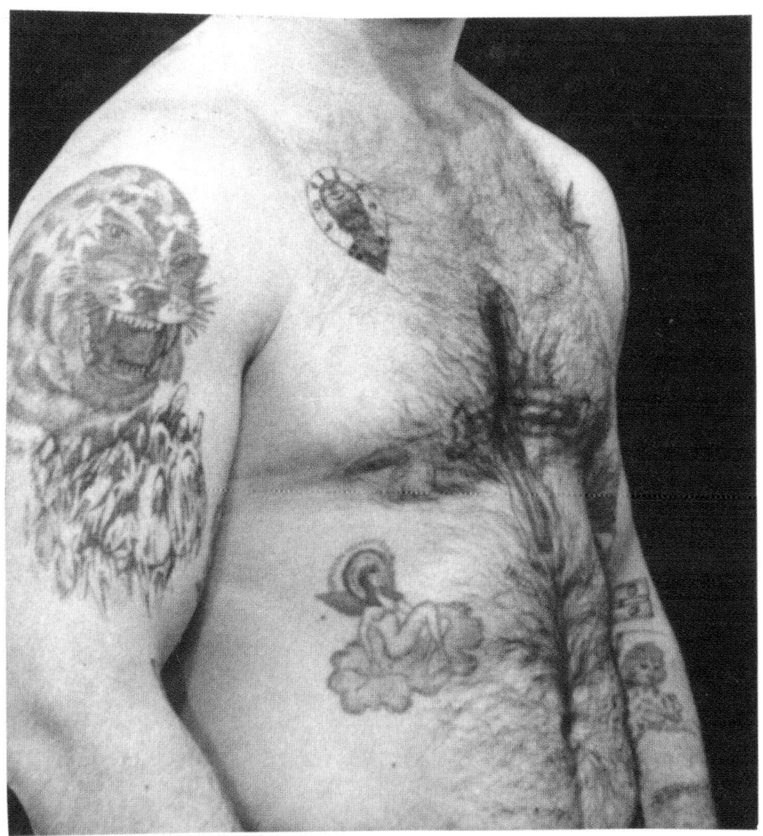

When the image of a tiger's head is applied to the upper part of the shoulder or the forearm it denotes that the bearer has been convicted of hooliganism with the use of firearms or knives (or similar weapons). In thieves' jargon these inmates are known as 'shags', 'chops' or 'Decemberists'* (if the convict had subsequently been sentenced to death). The tattoo conveys a readiness to resort to violence against anyone who encroaches on their rights or dignity, and an ability to fend for themselves.

* After the Russian uprising of 1825 when a group of 3,000 soldiers marched against the newly appointed Tsar Nicholas I, who dealt with them swiftly and brutally.

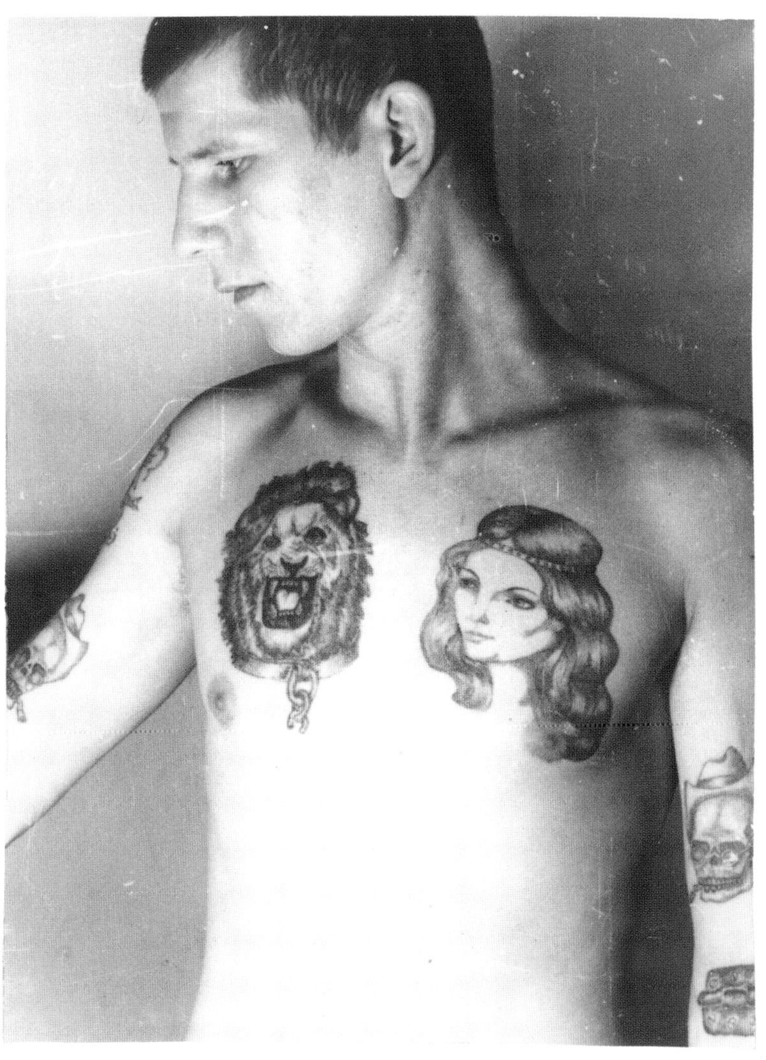

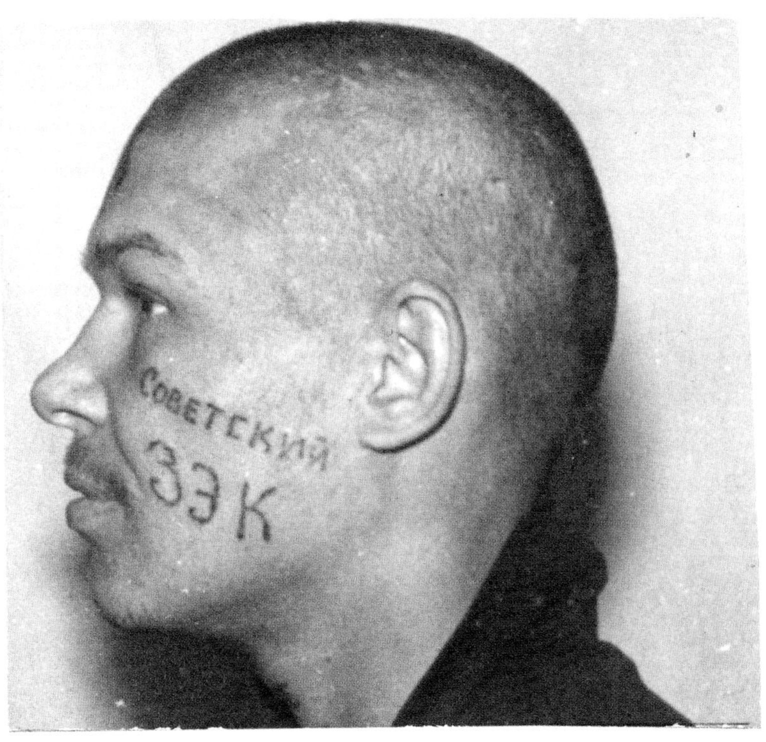

above: Text on the face reads **'Soviet prisoner'**. This is likely to be a forcibly applied tattoo, rather than a sign of protest.

According to research from the Ministry of Internal Affairs, ninety-six per cent of inmates with tattoos had them made by their own will as a mark of their 'achievements'. Only four per cent had tattoos forcibly applied. Those are the 'lowered', who may have lost at gambling. Losers have a choice – to become executors of death sentences given by inmates themselves, to be lowered, or to get a swastika or the word 'RAB' (slave) tattooed on the face. Card games are of vital importance to the thief. They are a way of asserting power and displaying bravado within the prison. A favourite pastime is for a thief to gamble with the belongings of other inmates; the amusement comes when he loses and has to demand the item to pay his debt.

Text on the bells reads **'Gentlemen Communist-Satanists, damn you for my hungry childhood!'** Text on the plinth in front of the headquarters of the Council of Ministers of the Soviet Union (the state body that ran the country) reads **'UK RSFSR'** (the Penal Code of the Russian Soviet Federative Socialist Republic), the predator cats (panther, lion, leopard) on the monument are a 'grin', a statement against the authorities and their laws. Text on the hand reads **'It's dangerous to spoil the criminal's mood'**. Tattooed ring on third finger of bearer's right hand 'I served my time in full', the prisoner served his complete sentence with no remission for working with the system. This tattoo can be applied to cover 'lowering' tattoos, once the inmate has left the zone. Index finger of left hand 'I took the thieves' path', the bearer was convicted of theft. Middle finger 'I took the road through the zone as a juvenile', the first time the bearer went through the VTK was in the general regime. Third finger 'I spent half of my life in prison', a variation of 'I do not shake hands with cops', the bearer is a recidivist likely to be re-arrested.

Church bells without a chain mean the wearer has served an entire custodial sentence, literally 'from bell to bell', or 'waiting for the bell to ring' (to be free). A window with bars means that the inmate has been locked in a special correctional school in the penal colony.

overleaf left: The manacle means a sentence of five years or more. The sailing ship between thumb and forefinger means the bearer is prone to escape (this has been made in an attempt to cover an earlier 'rising sun' tattoo, typical of a pickpocket, see also page 191). The ring on the index finger 'Convicted under Article 191 of the Criminal Code' (malicious hooliganism and an attempt on the life of an officer of the militia [police] in connection with the exercise of their duties to maintain public order). Middle finger 'beetle', a pickpocket's talisman, means 'I wish you success with your stealing'. Little finger 'I was a juvenile thief in a VTK [Educational Labour Colony]' (this tattoo may cover a 'convicted of rape' ring tattoo). Between the knuckles and fingernails card suits (tattooed over to make them unreadable) denotes a card cheat. The order *Kresti* (clubs), *Vini* (spades), *Bubny* (diamonds), *Chervy* (hearts) stands for *Kogda Vyidu Budu Chelovekom* ('I'll be a man when I get out', see also page 23). Thieves who have been 'lowered' may have their hand tattoos changed or even completely covered over by order of the *pakhan* (thief-in-law). This blacking out obliterates their previous criminal history, erasing any symbols of status in the zone.

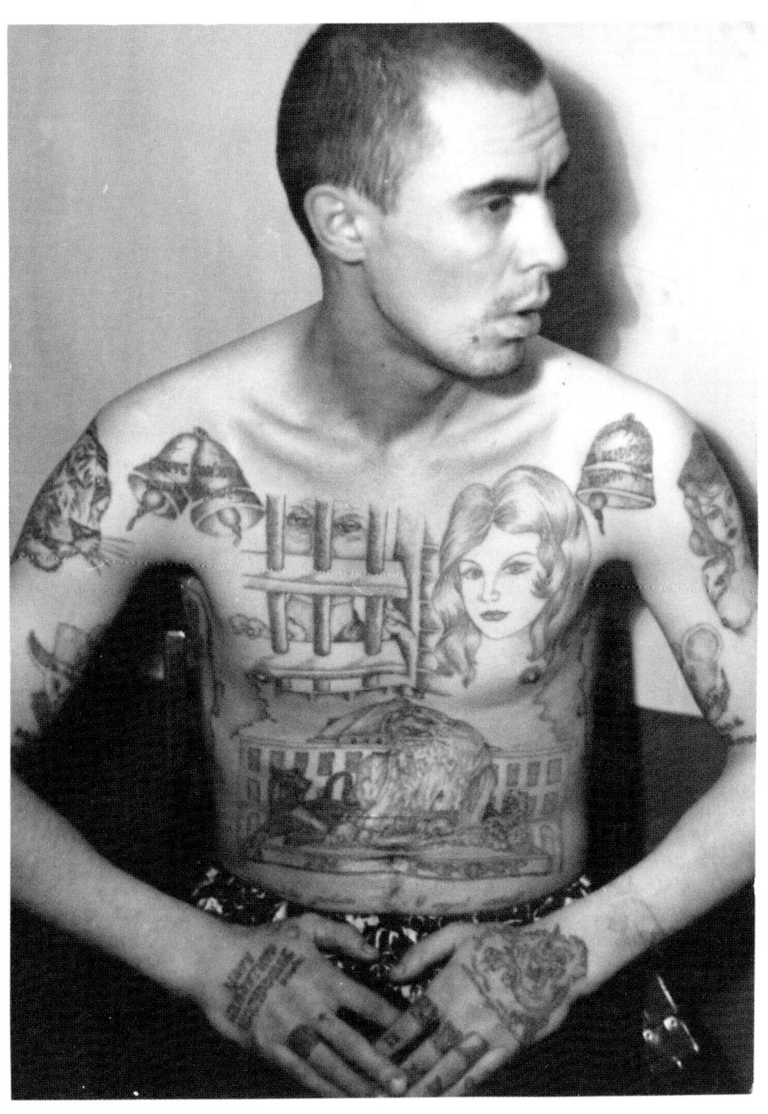

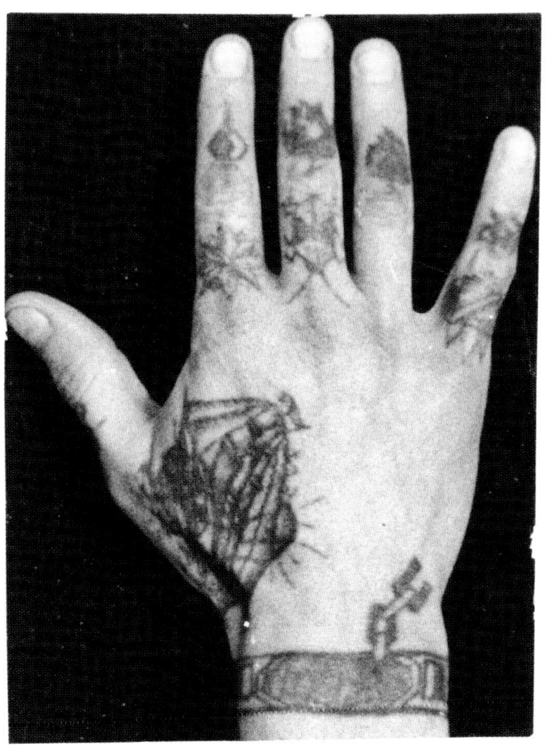

right: Text on the wrist reads **'Vora Casa'**, a combination of Russian and Latin meaning 'The house of a thief' (a reference to the cell window below). A white dove against a background of bars in a cell window means that the bearer spent his childhood in places of detention. Latin text on the back of the hand reads *Christus nos liberavit* meaning **'Christ has freed us'**.* The ring on the index finger means 'Broken hearted in the colony', the bearer was either cheated on by a woman or she broke off correspondence between them while he was in the zone. On the middle finger a 'chess ring' of four squares: the bearer was convicted under Article 144 of the Criminal Code (theft of personal property). Third finger the 'Dark Life' or 'A Life in Prison': a symbol of the continuation of a life of crime. Could also be 'I served my time to the bell': the bearer served his prison term completely with no remission for work or good behaviour (he did not compromise with the prison regime to make the 'sitting' of his sentence easier). Little finger 'At home among thieves' shows the status and outlook of the inmate.

* Used as a chapter title in the book *Les Misérables* by Victor Hugo.

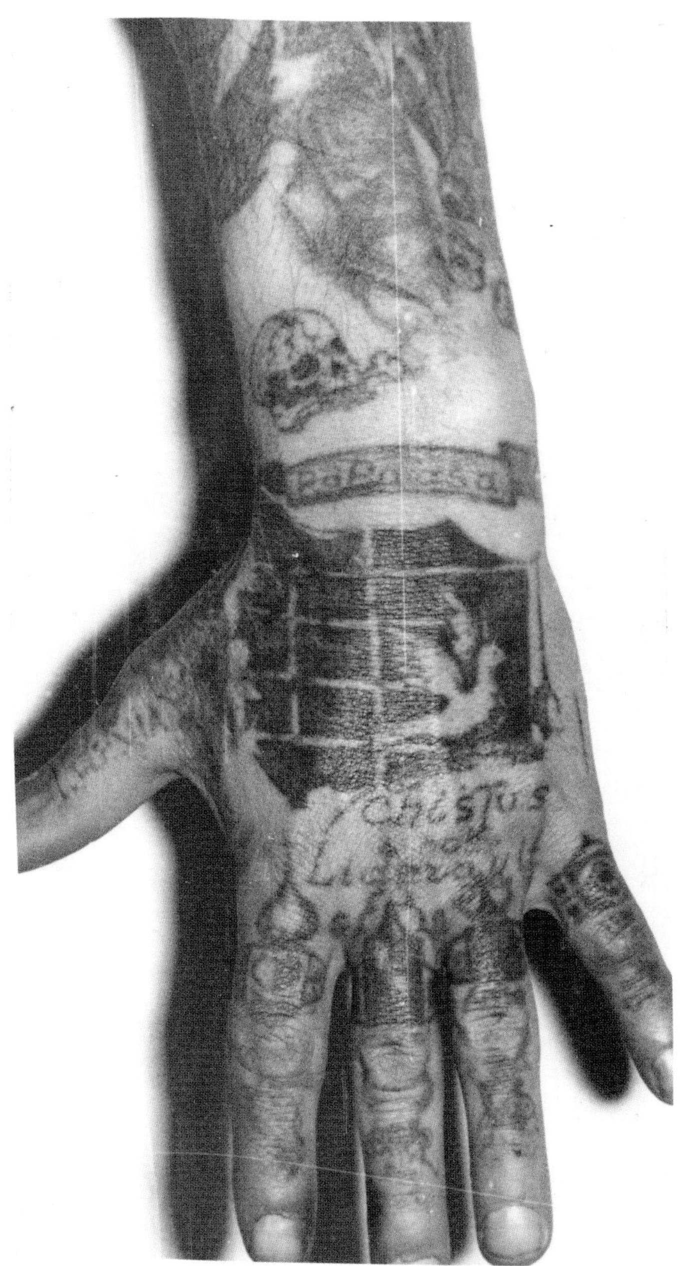

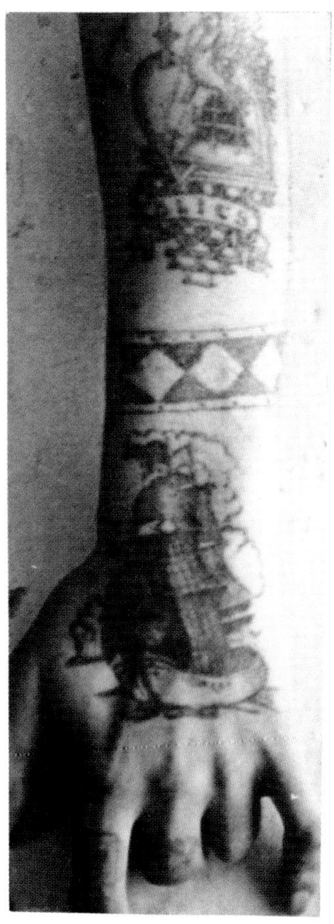

above: The loss of a thief's fingers might be caused by any number of reasons. The 'thieves' code' forbids them to work in the zone, so it is unlikely that this criminal lost his fingers in the sawmill. Self-mutilation is widespread: inmates might cut off parts of their bodies as statements against the regime, or to gain entry into the hospital as respite from the monotony of the zone. Others do it simply because they are depressed. In this photograph, however, it is likely that these fingers were lost as payment for a bet. If a *vor* loses at cards and his debt cannot be paid then recompence can often be cruel and violent. A thief might lose a 'twig' (finger), or a 'dumpling' (ear), or even a 'headlamp' (eye). This 'payment' would be made in front of the other prisoners as witnesses, and the wounds then powdered with hot ashes from the barrack stove. Such wounds would be a source of pride, evidence of the *vor*'s bravery, and that he is truly living the life of a thief.

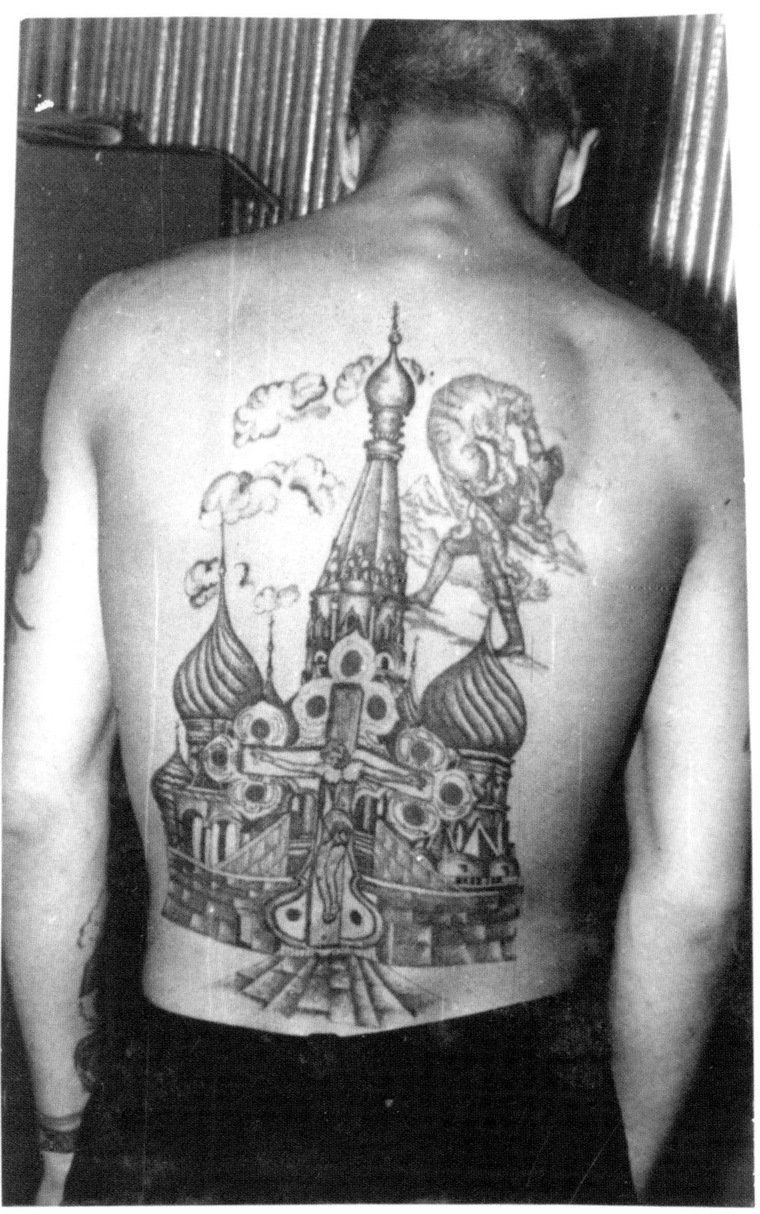

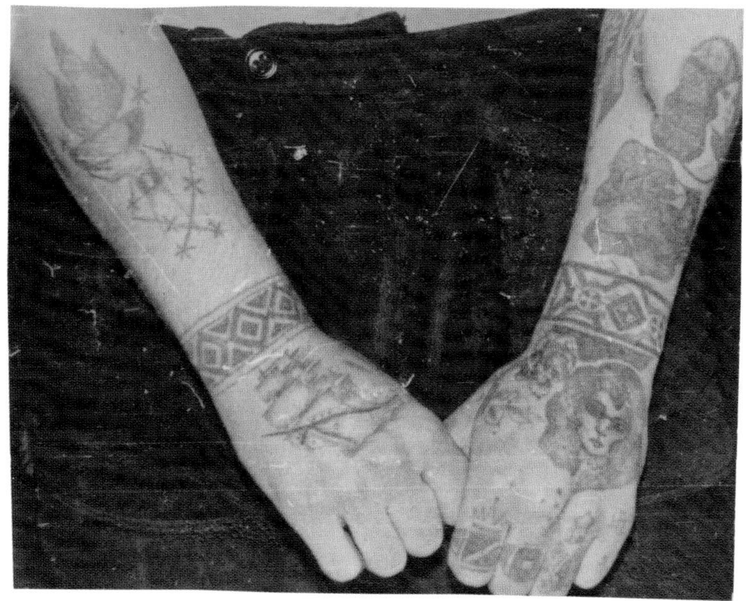

above: The burning torch behind barbed wire indicates a long sentence in a Corrective Labour Colony; the number of barbs on the wire indicates the number of years (in this case eight). Bracelets on both wrists indicate a sentence of at least ten years. A sailing ship with white sails means the bearer does not engage in normal work and is a travelling thief who is prone to escape. The ring on the index finger denotes a 'corner', the bearer was convicted for the first time when he was a juvenile. The black rectangle indicates the intention to continue to engage in criminal activity. Middle finger: unknown variation. Third finger 'Anti-social', an '*Otritsala*' or inveterate transgressor of the prison regime who refuses to work. Little finger 'swastika', an 'anarchist' convict who rejects the camp and prison laws. These arrogant inmates are often not tolerated by either the prison regime or the thieves-in-law.

As more people in the outside world are being tattooed, fewer people inside prison are. Today a person can get any tattoo of 'achievements' in a tattoo studio and buy such 'achievements' at a meeting of *blatniie* in a restaurant. They often buy the 'Thief-by-law' title; they used to spend years earning respect, and now they can pay for it. The wave of interest in prison tattoos has descended dramatically in Russia. During the Soviet Union sentences were always served far from the place of residence. Back then, nobody paid such attention to nationality, place of birth or religion. Now there are more 'patriots'. Muslims, for example, or people from the Caucasus in particular tend to distinguish themselves with their tattoos. They like to form groups of fellow countrymen.

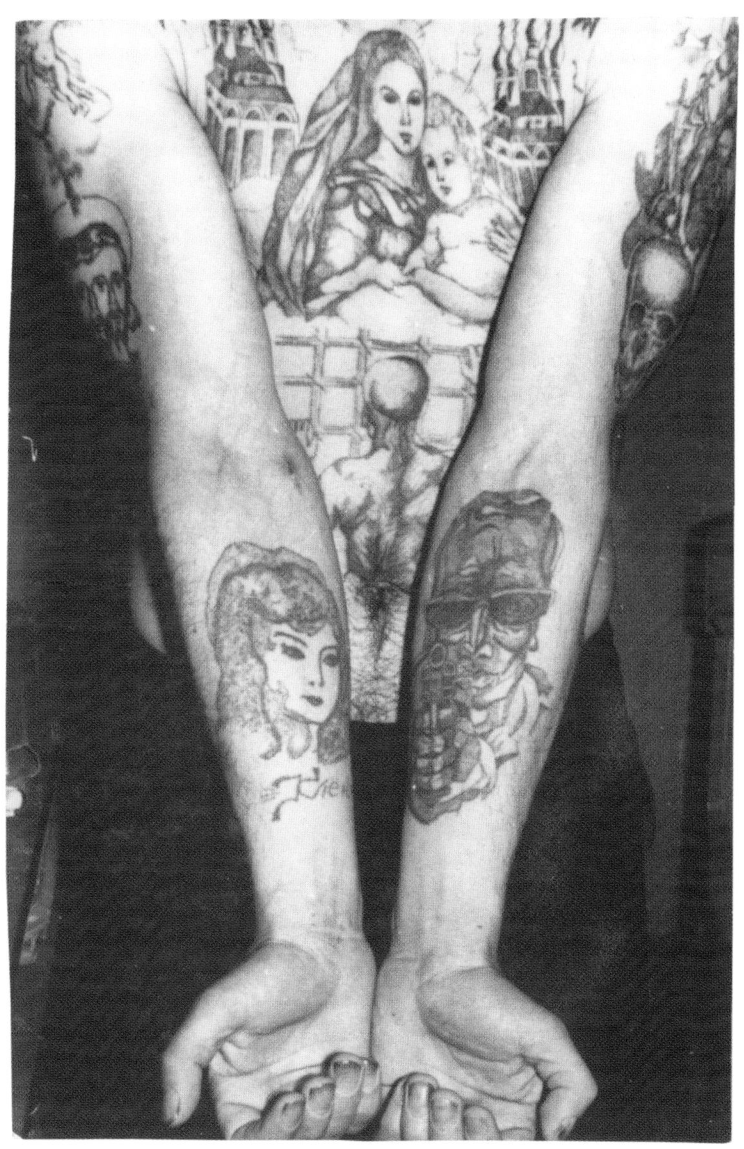

Under the woman's face is the acronym **'KLEN'** that means both *Klyanus Lyubit Eyo Navek* **'I swear to love her forever'**, and *Kazhdogo Legavogo Ebi Nozhom* **'Fuck every policeman with a knife'**.

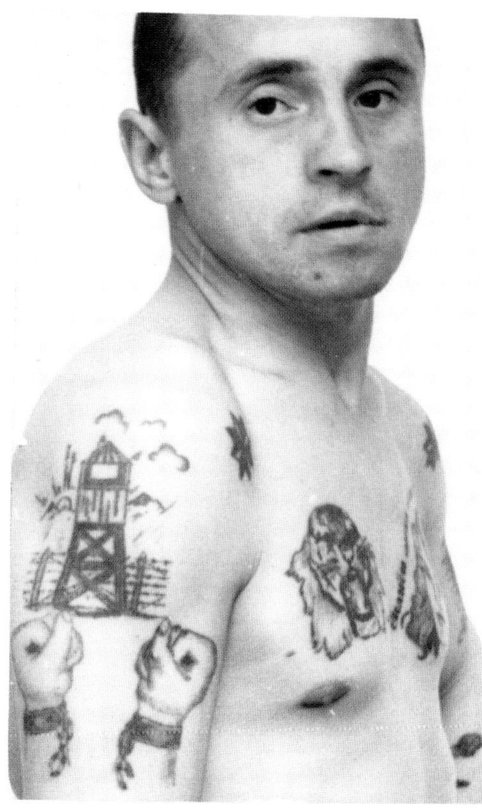

Watchtowers and barbed wire are a common theme of convicts' tattoos. Inevitably they are accompanied by stories of harsh cruelty and injustice meted out by the regime.

right: The dove carrying a sword and shield hovers over an image of an inmate attempting to escape the camp. This motif signifies the struggle against evil, violence and injustice.

'There were times when the escort guards [the warders charged with marching the inmates to their places of work and guarding them there] were like animals. If they spotted a new prisoner who didn't know the ropes, they might send him to fetch something from outside the working area, which was marked off with signal flags. On reaching the marked-off area, the prisoner would be shot for attempting to escape. The guard who fired the shot would be rewarded with two weeks' leave.'
Inmate, Logging Camp, Arkhangelsk Region, 1979.
Avraham Shifrin, *Prisons and Concentration Camps of the Soviet Union* (1980)

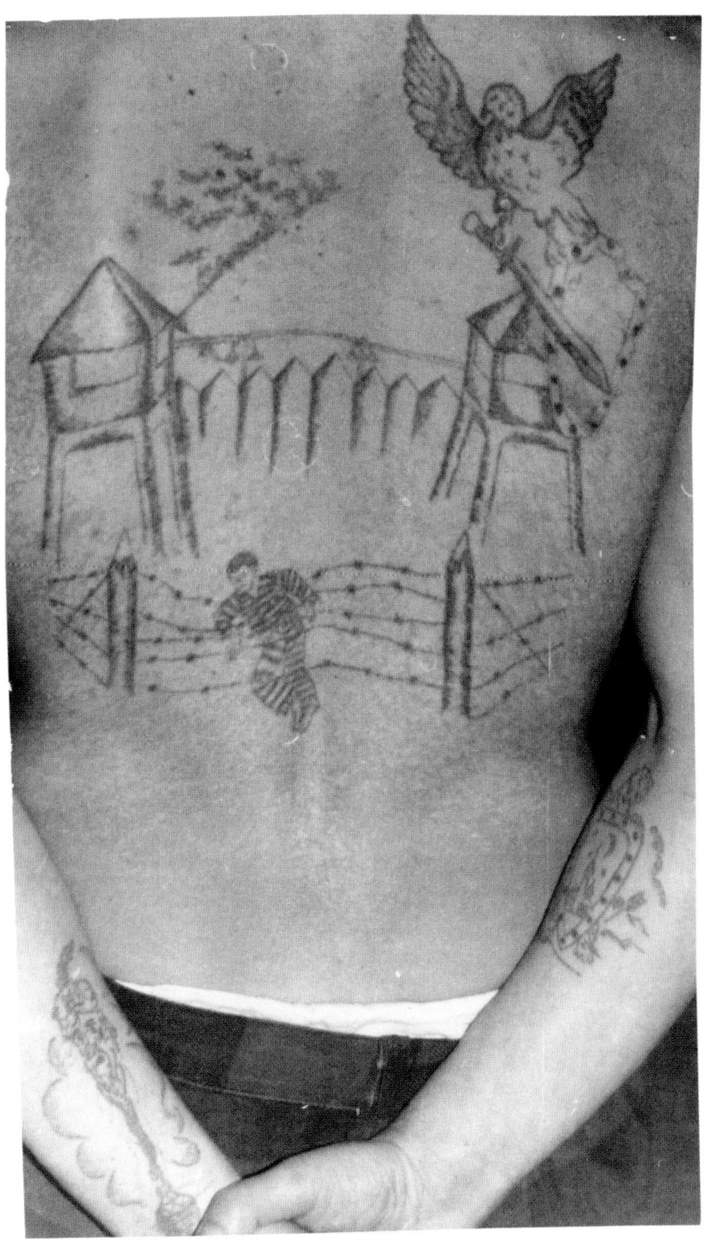

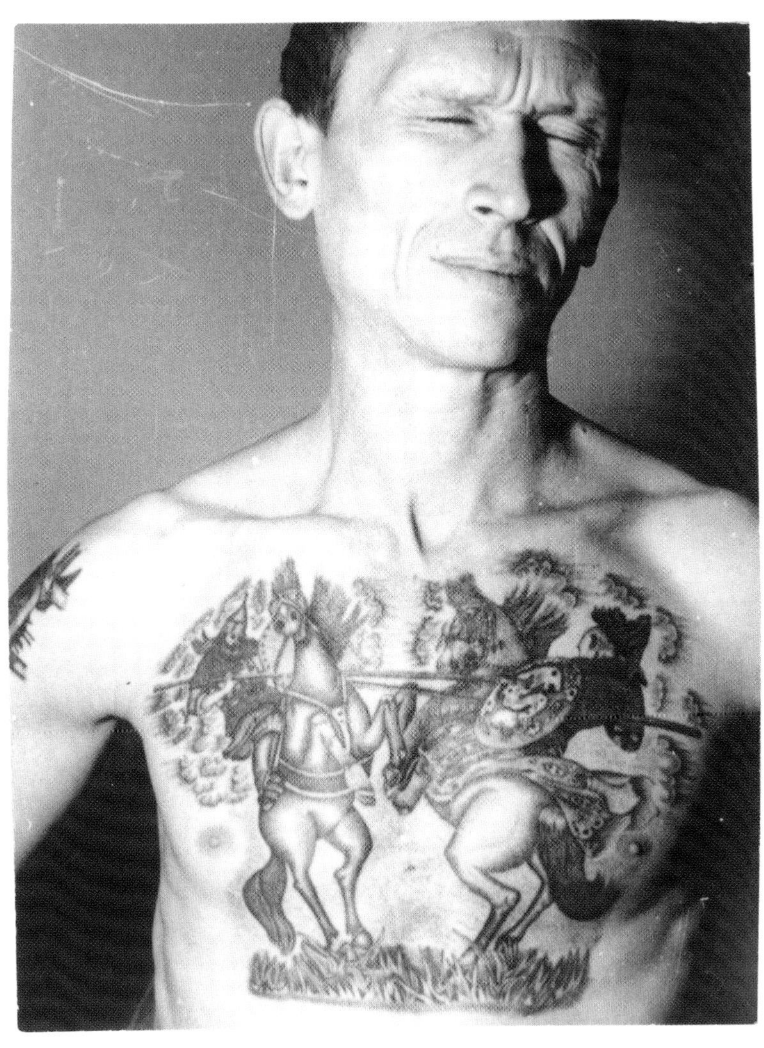

right: This tattoo is a variation on the myth of Prometheus, who, after tricking Zeus, was chained to a rock in eternal punishment. The sailing ship with white sails means the bearer does not engage in normal work; that he is a travelling thief who is prone to escape.

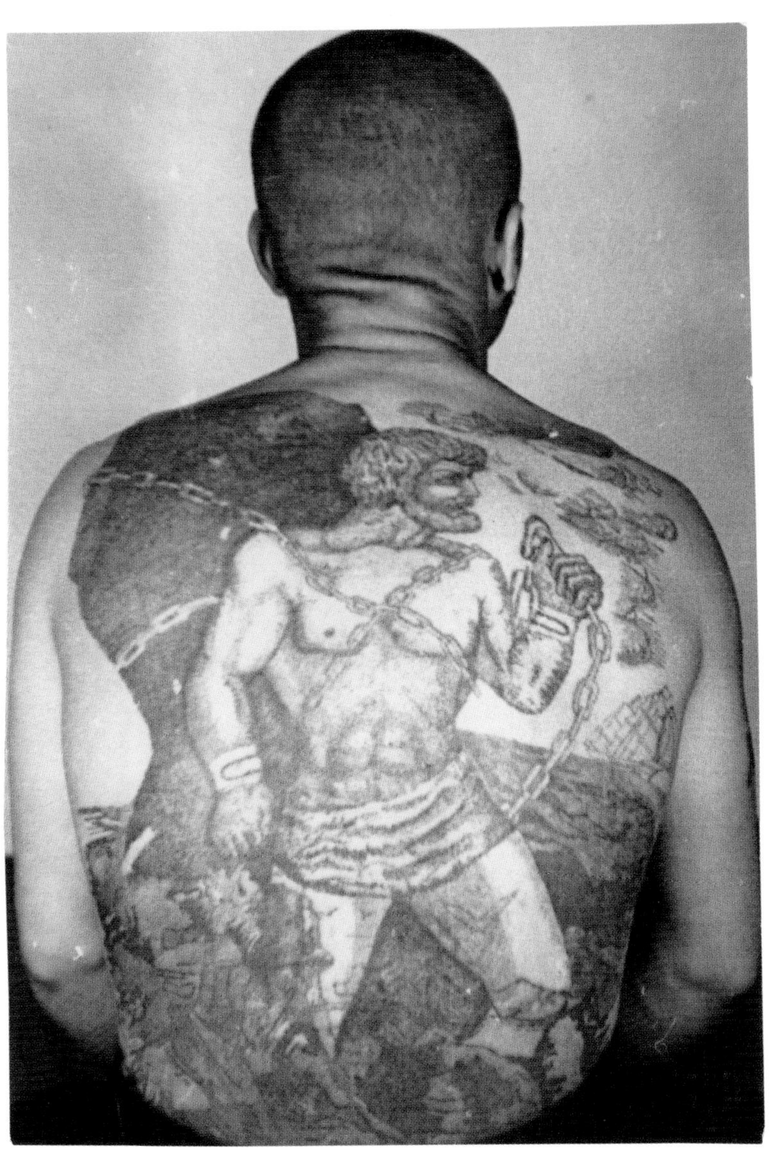

First published in 2014
Reprinted in 2016

FUEL Design & Publishing
33 Fournier Street
London E1 6QE

fuel-design.com

Photographs and text © Arkady Bronnikov / FUEL

The publishers would especially like to thank the following people
for generously giving their time and expertise:
Julia Goumen, Margarita Baskakova, Alix Lambert

ISBN: 978-0-9568962-9-2

Scans by Happy Retouching

Printed in China